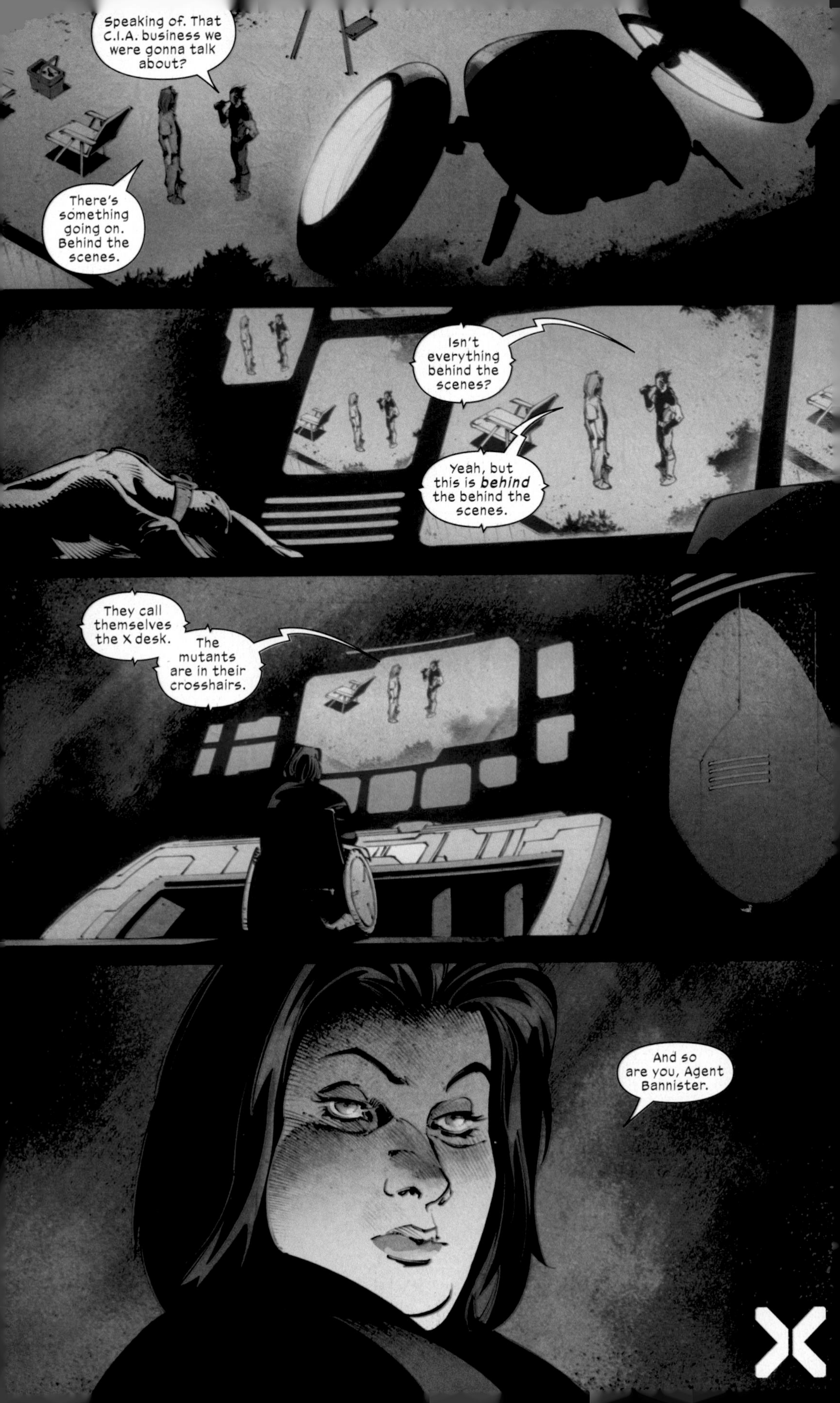
Speaking of. That C.I.A. business we were gonna talk about?
There's something going on. Behind the scenes.
Isn't everything behind the scenes?
Yeah, but this is *behind* the behind the scenes.
They call themselves the X desk.
The mutants are in their crosshairs.
And so are you, Agent Bannister.

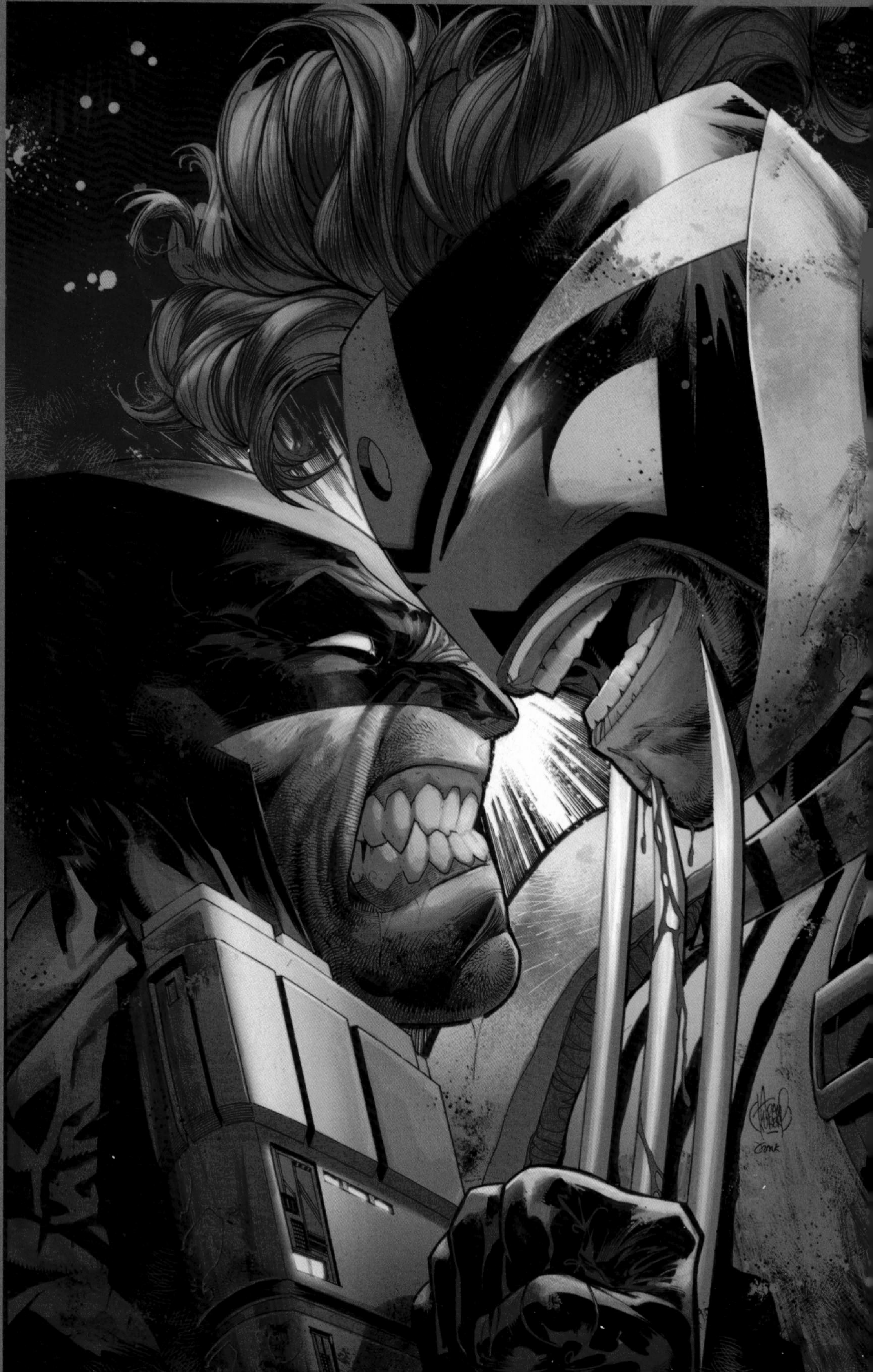

Prologue: War Stories
and
The Past Ain't Dead

[00_best_]
[00_there]

THE TIES THAT BIND

Krakoa has survived the tournament of swords, but danger still looms. Russian super-soldiers have attacked the mutant nation. Dracula and his vampires still lurk in the shadows. Can you trust the safety of the island, your neighbors... yourself?

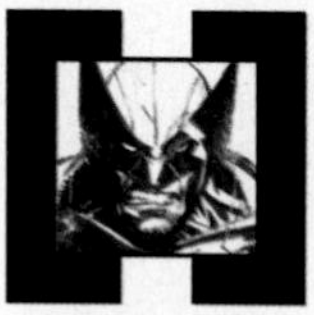
Wolverine

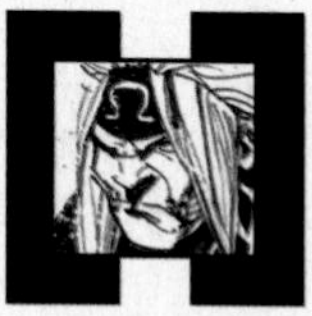
Omega Red

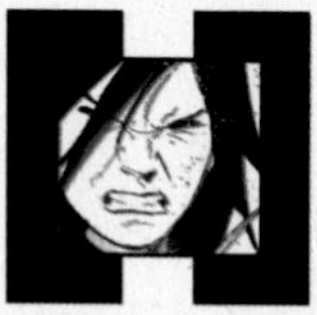
Scout

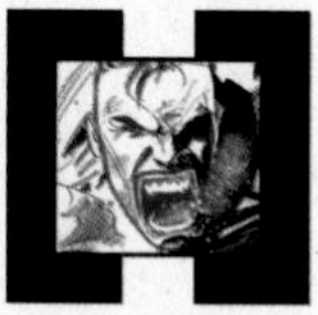
Daken

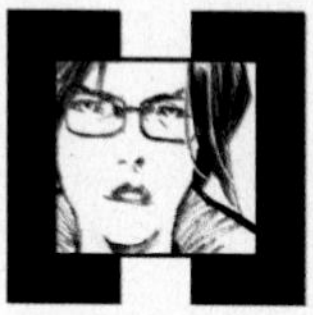
Sage

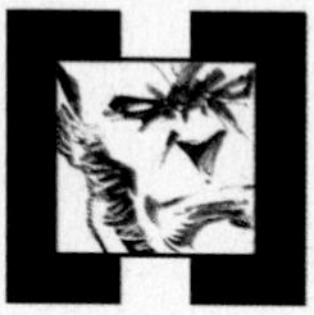
Beast

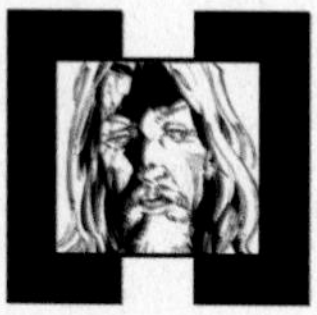
Jeff Bannister

*Chapters 6-7 can be found in X OF SWORDS.

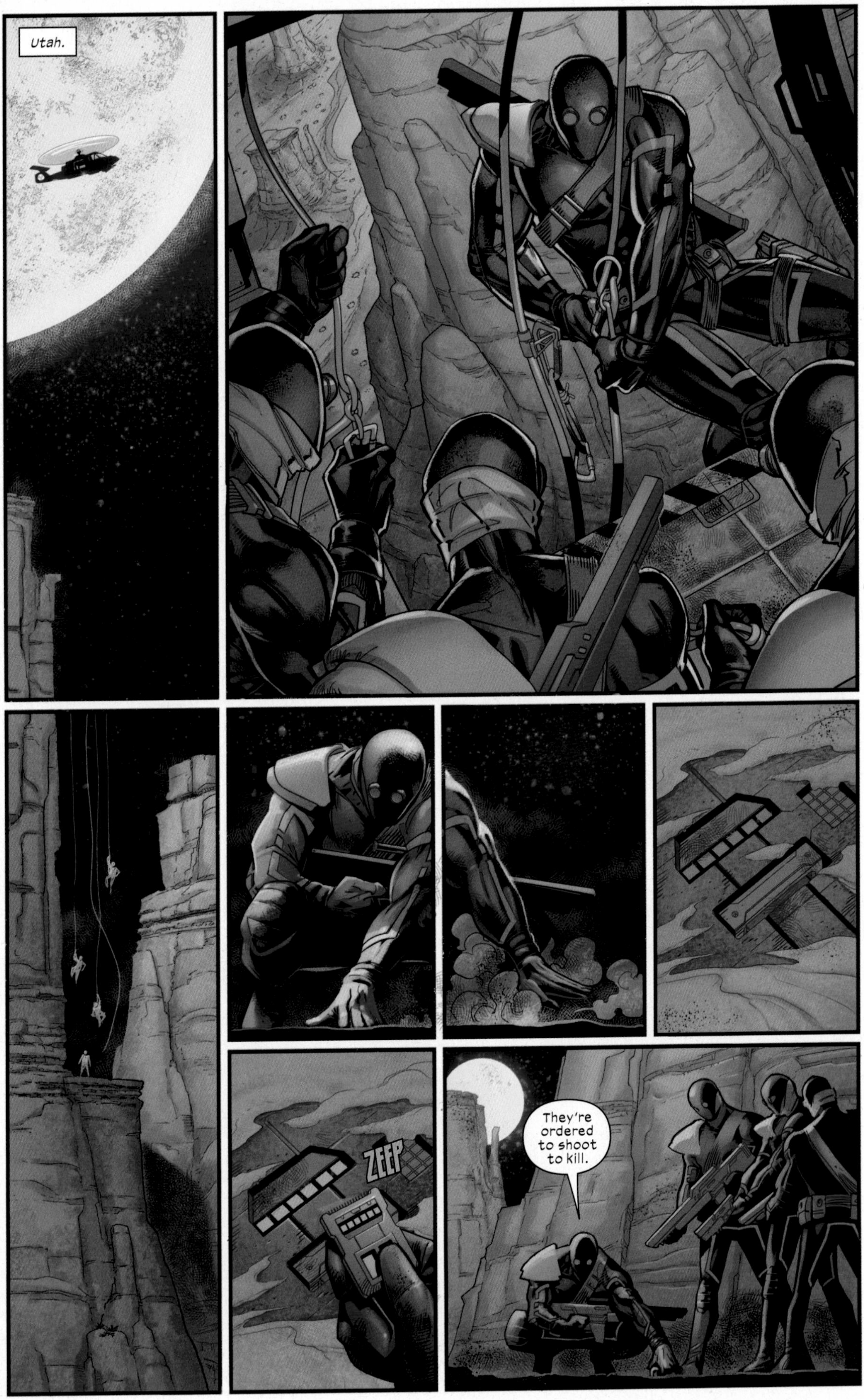
Utah.
ZEEP
They're ordered to shoot to kill.

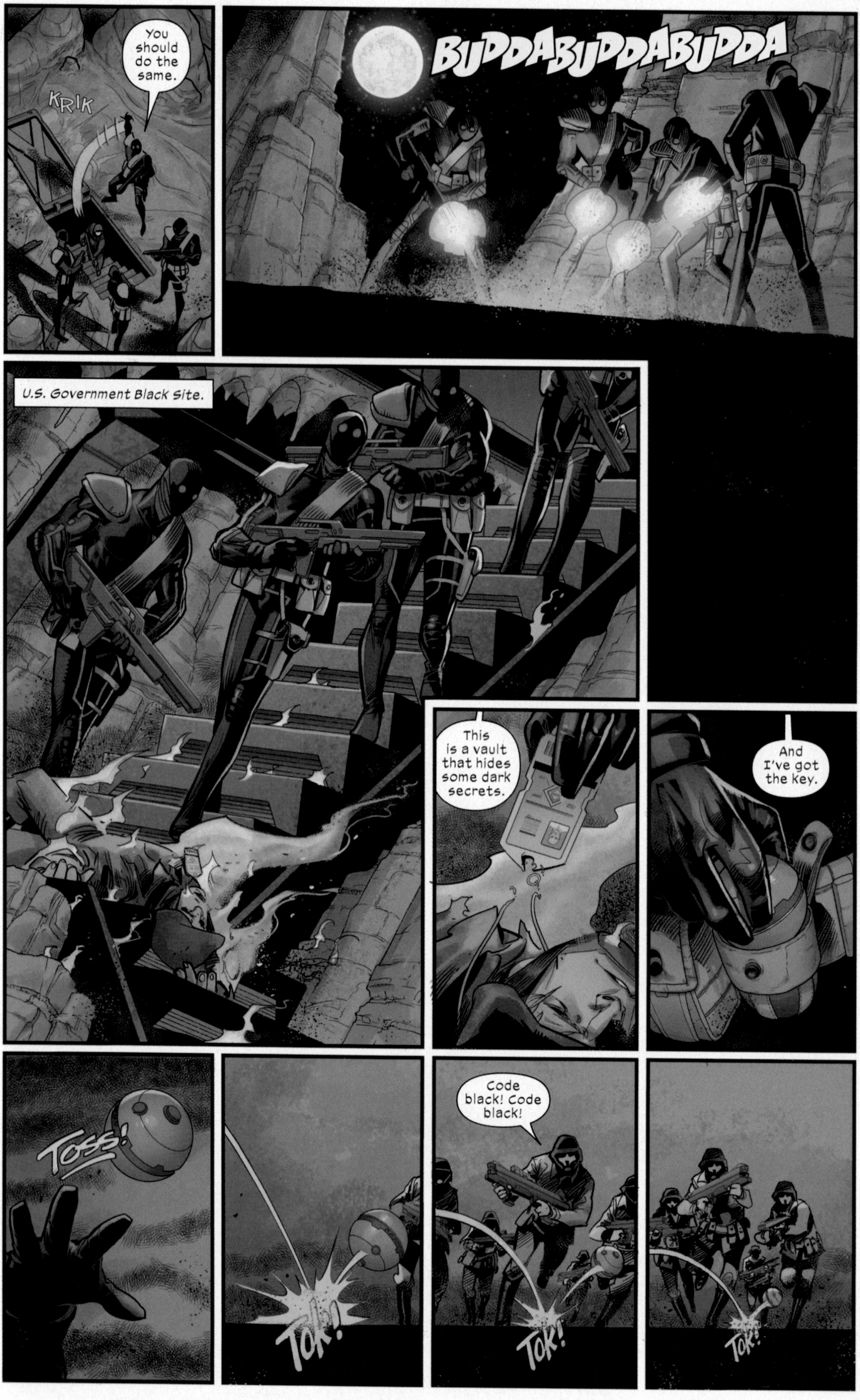

You should do the same.
KRIK
BUDDABUDDABUDDA
U.S. Government Black Site.
This is a vault that hides some dark secrets.
And I've got the key.
TOSS!
TOK!
Code black! Code black!
TOK!
TOK!

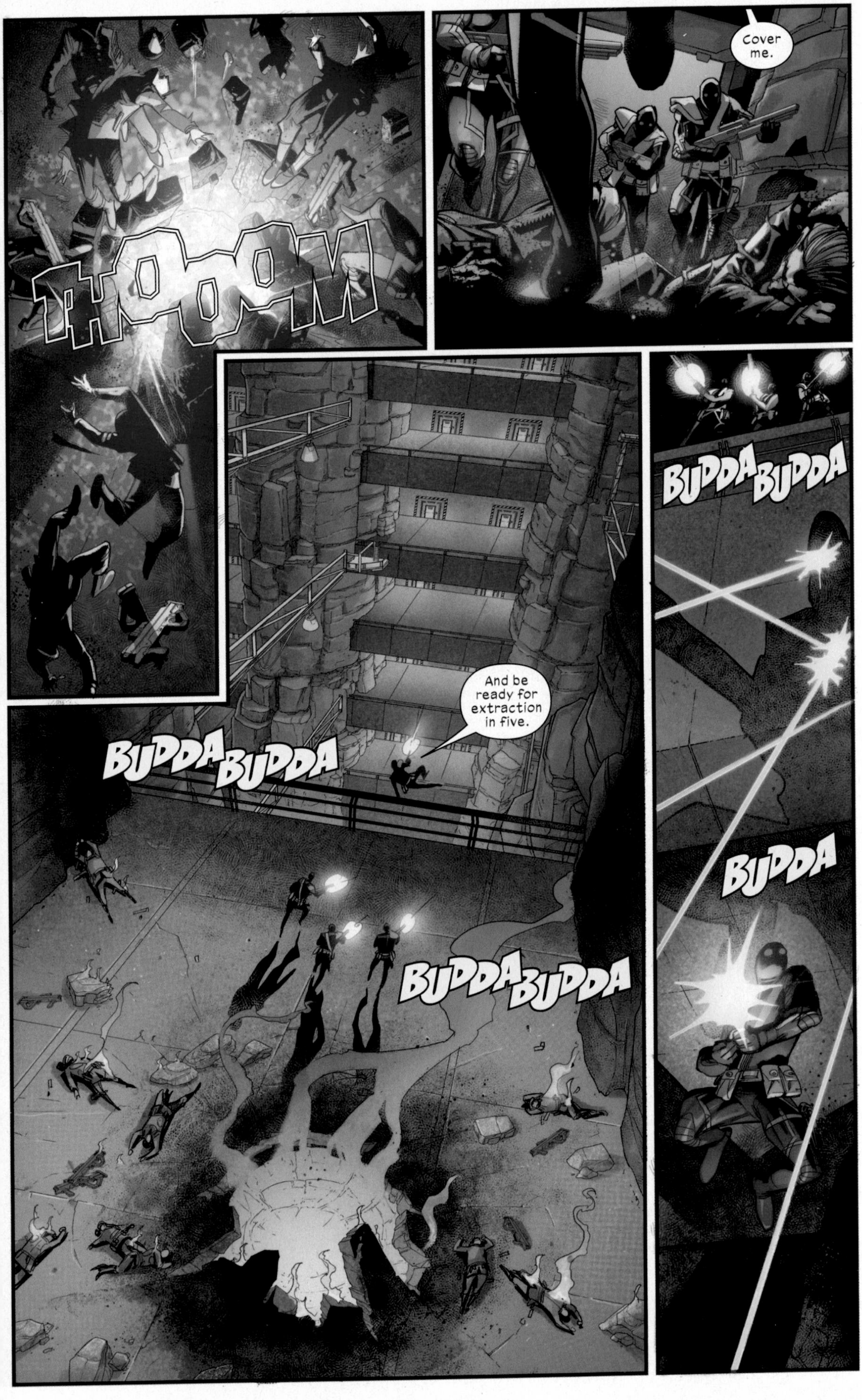
THOOOM
Cover me.
BUDDA BUDDA
And be ready for extraction in five.
BUDDA BUDDA
BUDDA
BUDDA BUDDA

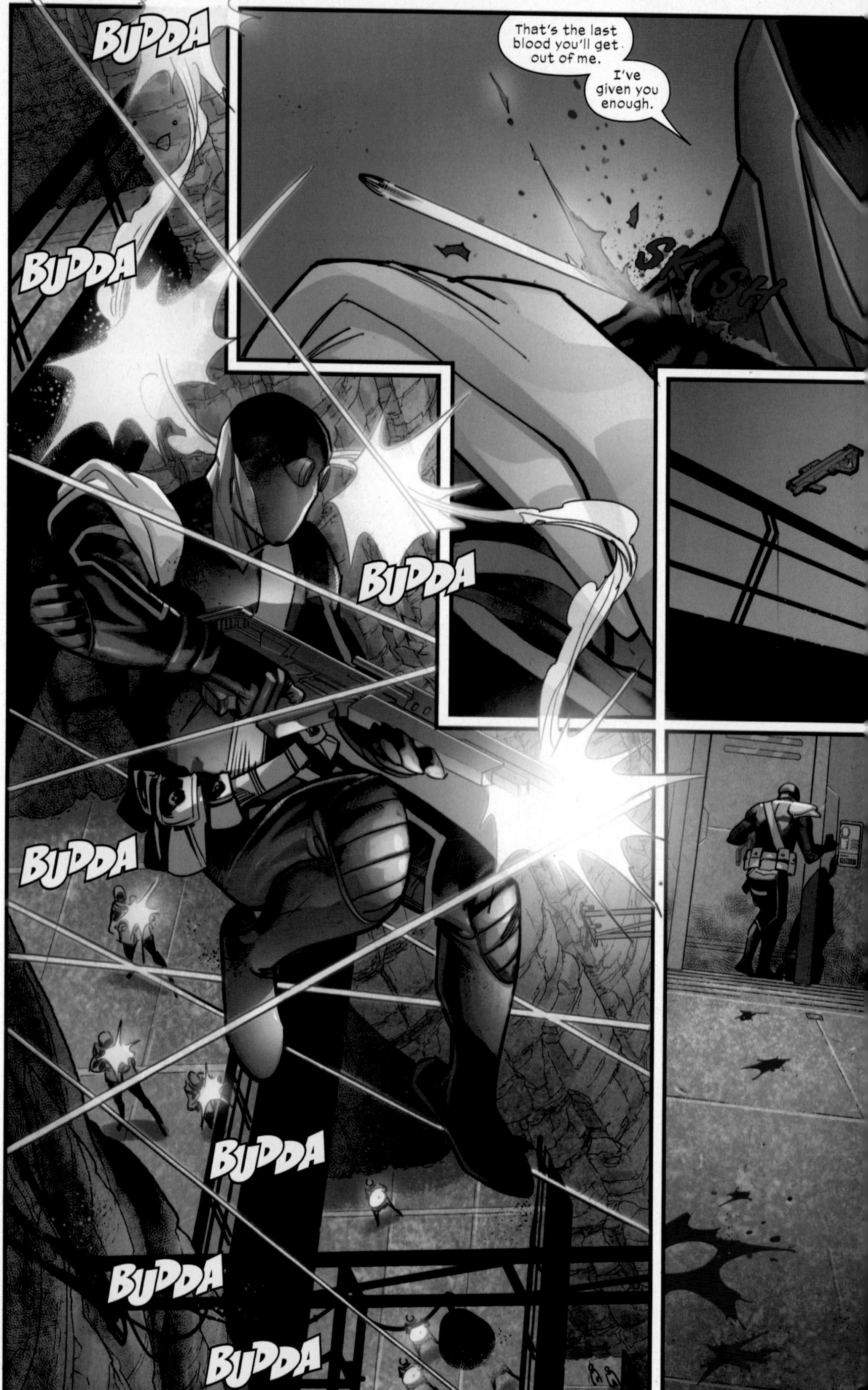
BUDDA
BUDDA
That's the last blood you'll get out of me.
I've given you enough.
SKISH
BUDDA
BUDDA
BUDDA
BUDDA
BUDDA

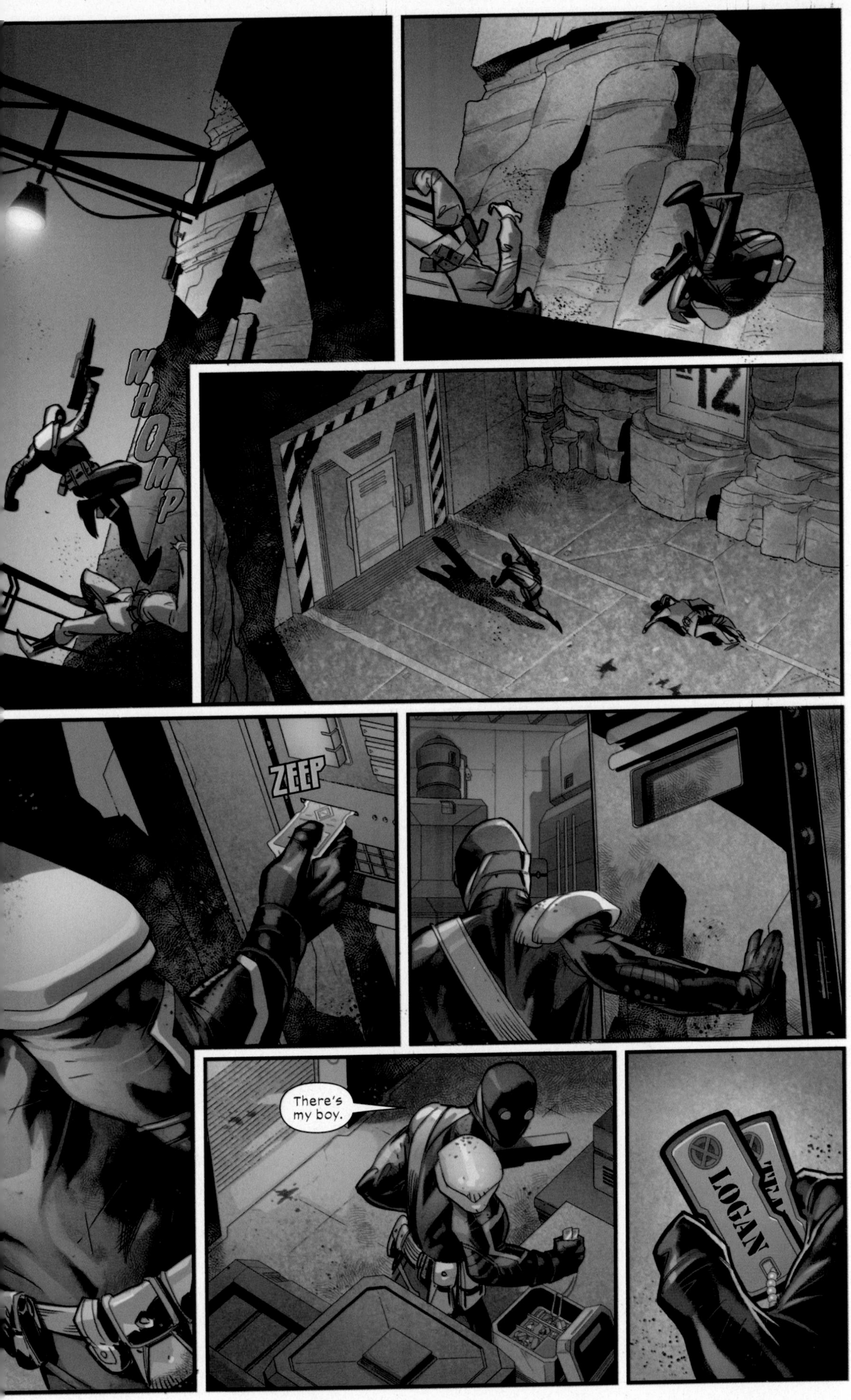
WHOMP
12
ZEEP
There's my boy.
LOGAN

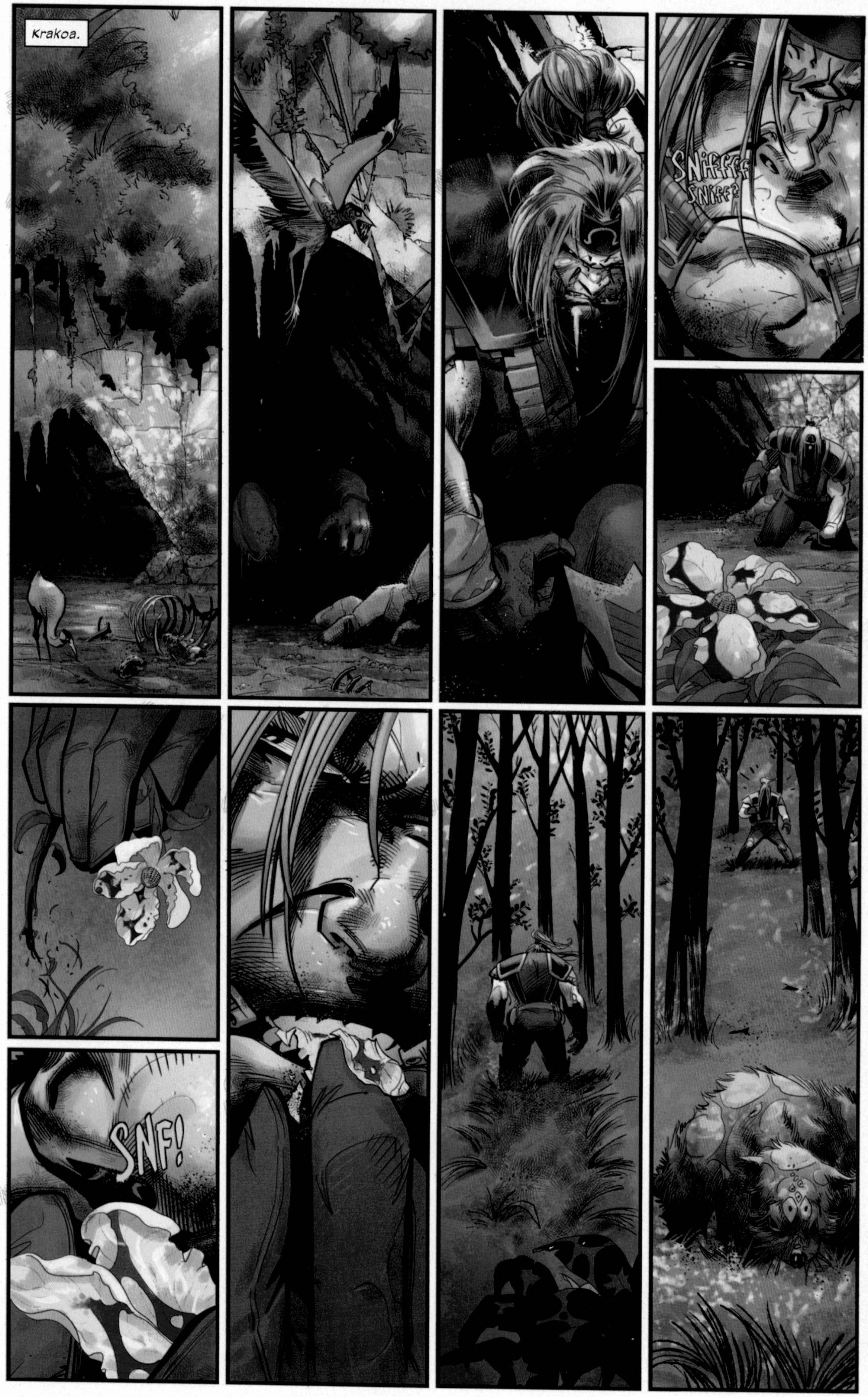
Krakoa.
SNIFFFF
SNIFFF
SNF!

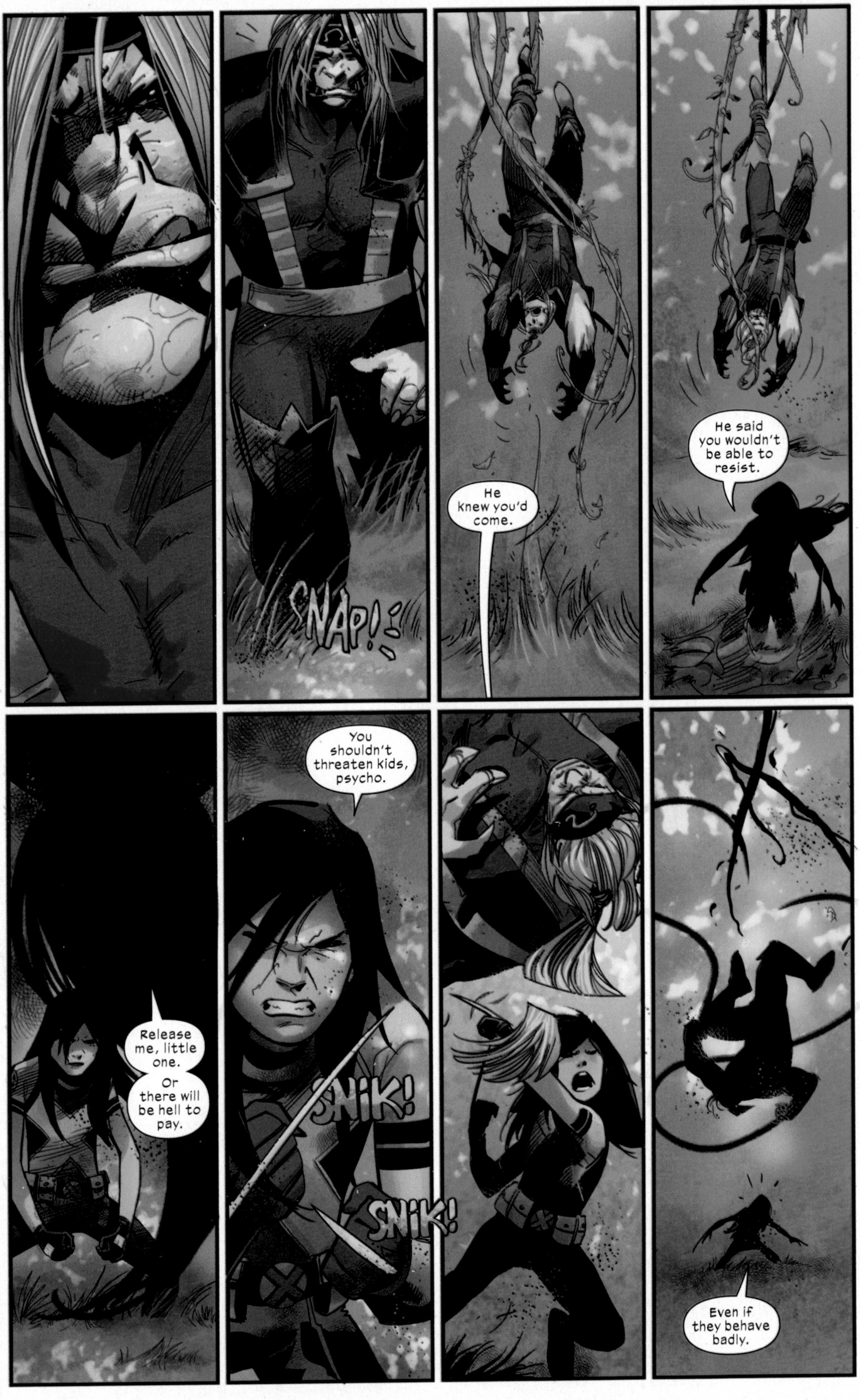
SNAP!
He knew you'd come.
He said you wouldn't be able to resist.
Release me, little one.
Or there will be hell to pay.
You shouldn't threaten kids, psycho.
SNIK!
SNIK!
Even if they behave badly.

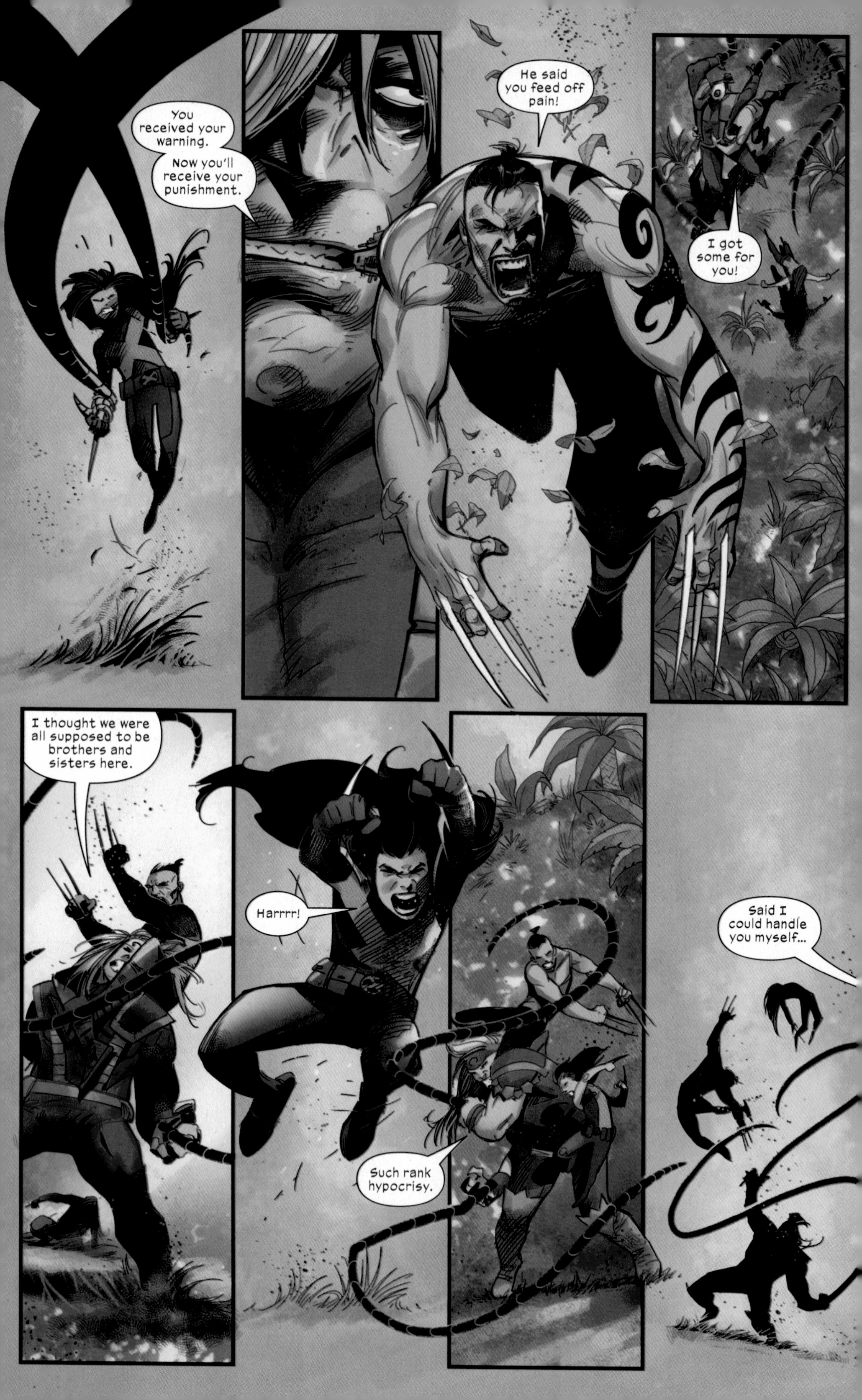
You received your warning.
Now you'll receive your punishment.
He said you feed off pain!
I got some for you!
I thought we were all supposed to be brothers and sisters here.
Harrrr!
Such rank hypocrisy.
Said I could handle you myself...

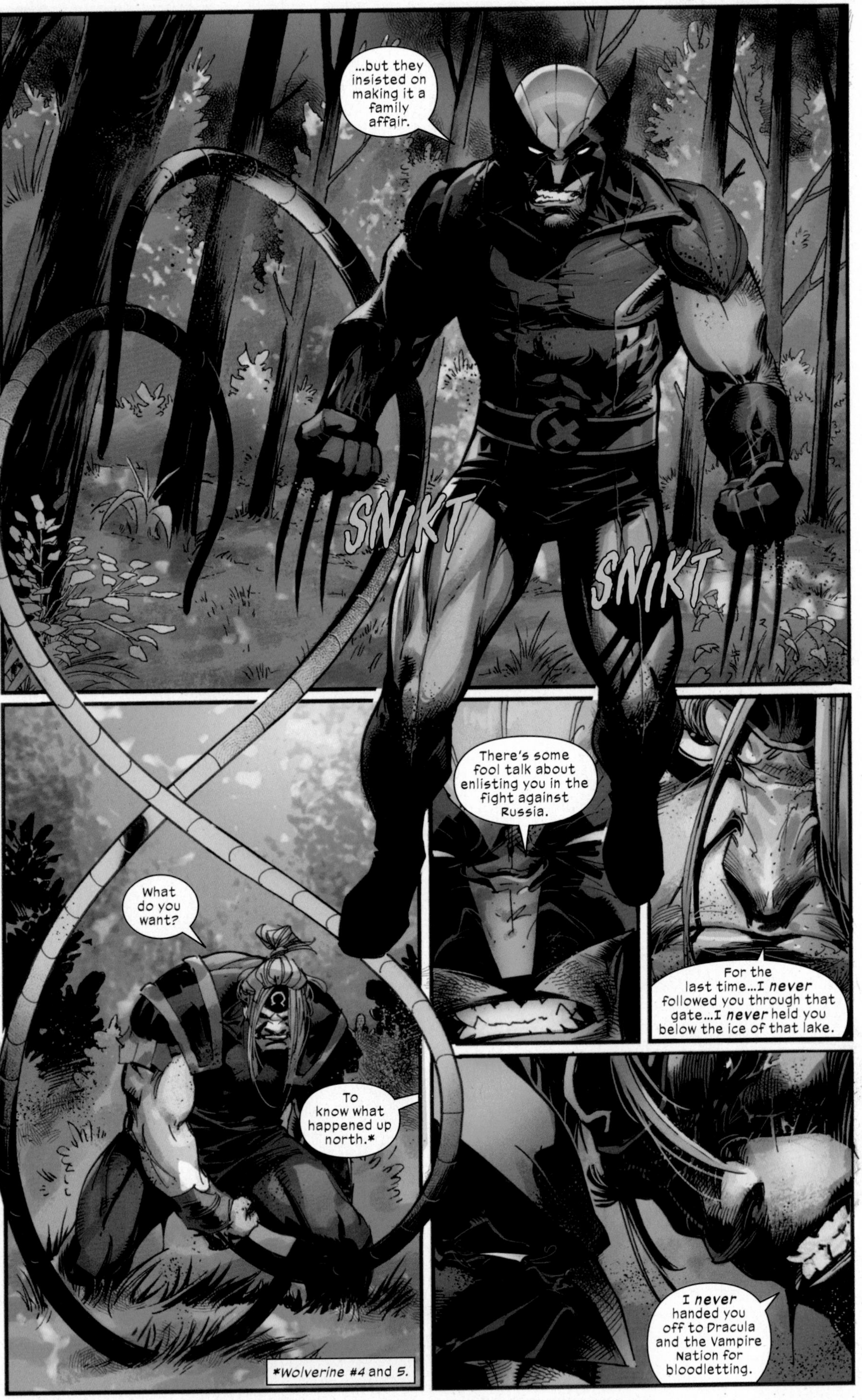
...but they insisted on making it a family affair.
SNIKT
SNIKT
What do you want?
To know what happened up north.*
*Wolverine #4 and 5.
There's some fool talk about enlisting you in the fight against Russia.
For the last time...I never followed you through that gate...I never held you below the ice of that lake.
I never handed you off to Dracula and the Vampire Nation for bloodletting.

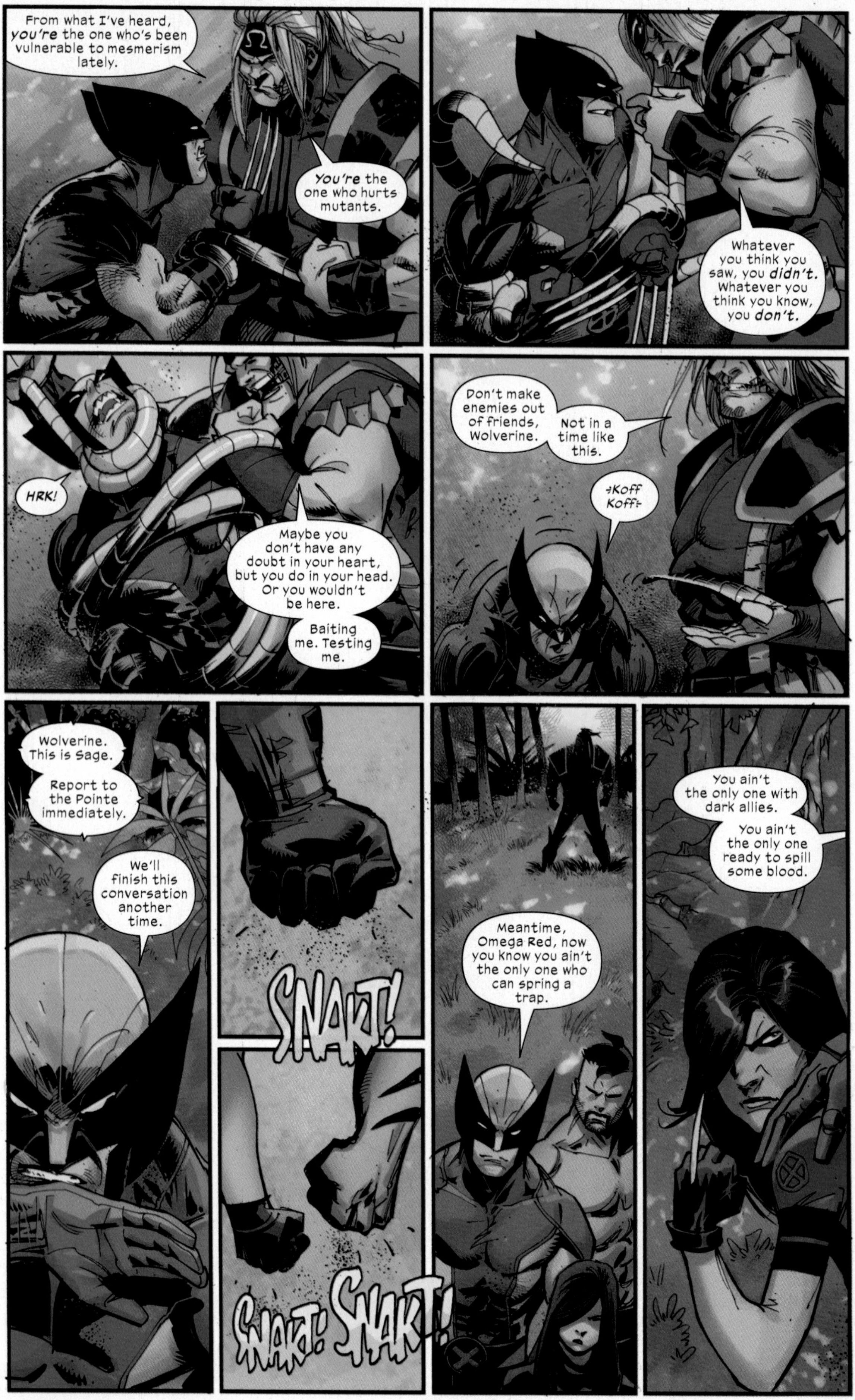
From what I've heard, *you're* the one who's been vulnerable to mesmerism lately.
You're the one who hurts mutants.
Whatever you think you saw, you ***didn't.*** Whatever you think you know, you ***don't.***
HRK!
Maybe you don't have any doubt in your heart, but you do in your head. Or you wouldn't be here.
Baiting me. Testing me.
Don't make enemies out of friends, Wolverine.
Not in a time like this.
Koff Koff
Wolverine. This is Sage.
Report to the Pointe immediately.
We'll finish this conversation another time.
SNAKT!
SNAKT! SNAKT!
Meantime, Omega Red, now you know you ain't the only one who can spring a trap.
You ain't the only one with dark allies.
You ain't the only one ready to spill some blood.

THE SINGING STONES

Developer: Forge

Supervisor: Beast

Purpose: Krakoan biotech capable of absorbing sound for storage and replay.

Recording Samples:

Vase placed in the office of [redacted], the senator from [redacted] up for re-election.

"Oh, yes. That's right. Right there. That's good. Mmmm. We should do this more often. We really, really, really should. You know...I've got to fly out to DC this weekend, and my wife decided to stay home with the kids. What if you came along? On a separate flight, of course. Maybe I'd put you up in a suite in a four-star hotel? I'd arrange everything. We could order room service and get the sheets dirty. Yummy yummy boo boo."

Paving stones of patio at home of CEO of [redacted], premier online retailer.

"Look, if they try to tax us, we threaten to bail. Pull our headquarters out and set up shop in Thailand or Brazil or the Canary Islands. They won't call the bluff, but even if they do, I've been recording conversations, okay? Those phones we make? Those speakers in everybody's houses? People know we're always listening, and they don't even care. They're so %#&@ stupid. The dirt I've got on all of them would bury the biggest coffin. Seriously. Nobody can touch me. Because I might have all the money—more than Charles Xavier, I bet—but I also have all the secrets. And secrets are the most valuable commodity. By the way, I think I want a place on the moon. Like those mutant #%&@$. Let's look into that. Yeah. I want the moon."

Countertops in the kitchen of [redacted] at his ski villa in the French Alps.

"Hey, Patsy. What do you think of this Bordeaux? You like it? I like it too. It's just that...maybe I'm crazy, but it really tastes more like a Left Bank than a Right Bank to me. Hmm. Anyway. Just to keep the crazy going for a second... I'm starting to think something screwy is going on with Krakoa. I mean beyond the whole big swinging #$%@ treaty business. I'm talking about their numbers. I've been tabulating accounts of their deaths...and comparing it with their current population, and...the math just doesn't add up."

Cross mounted on the wall of the private quarters of [redacted].

"We're worried, Your Grace. About rumors of a new religion. We fear it may seed doubt in both our Lord and savior...and man."

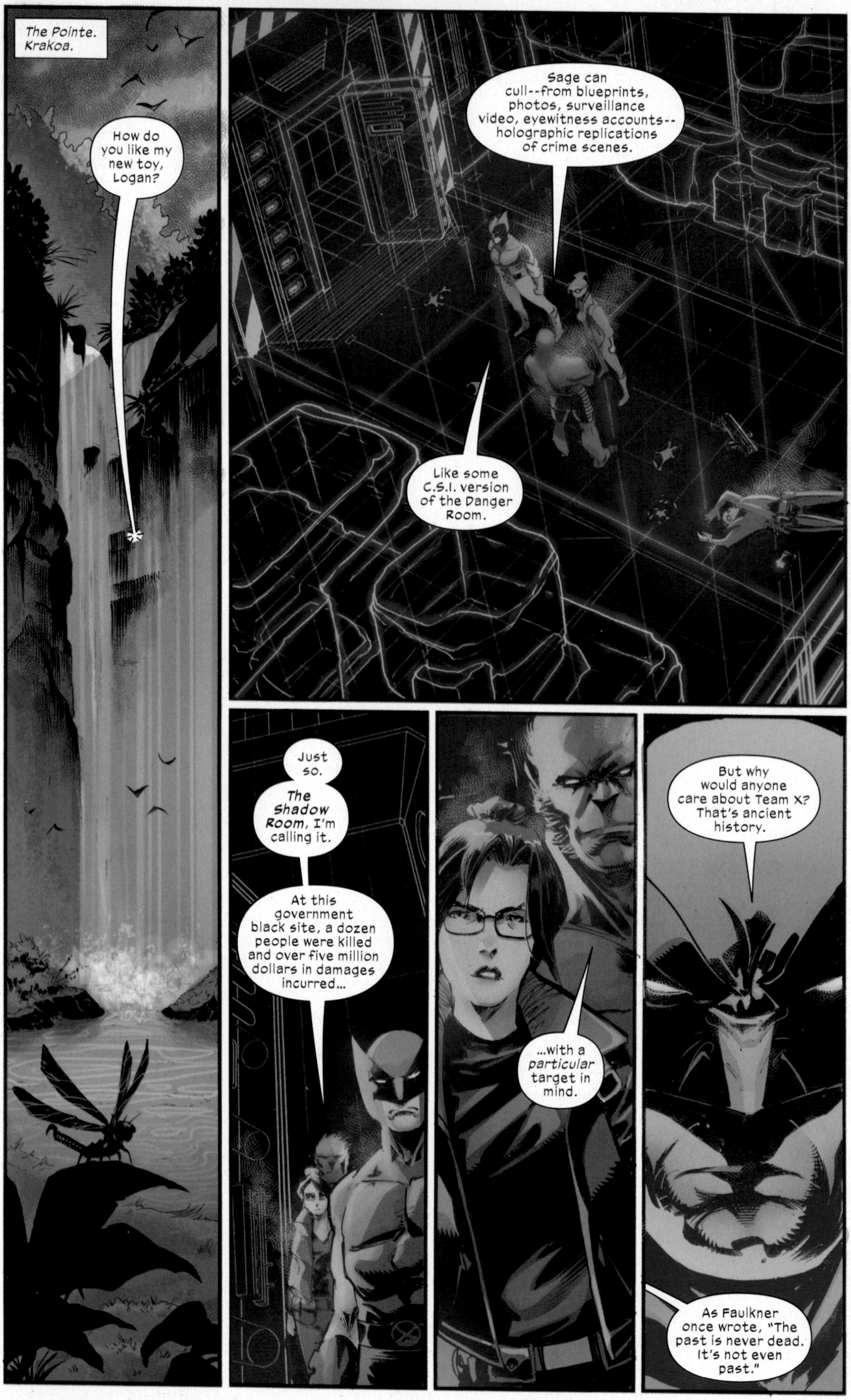

The Pointe. Krakoa.
How do you like my new toy, Logan?
Sage can cull--from blueprints, photos, surveillance video, eyewitness accounts--holographic replications of crime scenes.
Like some C.S.I. version of the Danger Room.
Just so.
The Shadow Room, I'm calling it.
At this government black site, a dozen people were killed and over five million dollars in damages incurred...
...with a *particular* target in mind.
But why would anyone care about Team X? That's ancient history.
As Faulkner once wrote, "The past is never dead. It's not even past."

Make sense, Beast.

We might be living in the future. But the past is very much with us... ...as your little encounter with Omega Red proves.

How do you even know about that? It is my business to know things.

The D.O.D. has reached out. They want to know if you can help them understand why the vault was targeted.

I ain't got nothing to do with this. Let them wipe their own asses.

If you'll allow me to finish my thought? A federal crime has been committed. America wants answers, and I'm afraid we are, in fact, accountable. We've examined the blood profile...

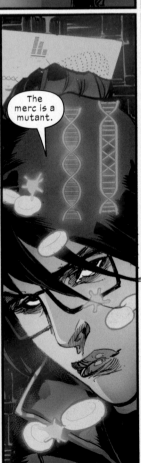

The merc is a mutant.

Besides you, there are only two other mutants who might have an interest in Team X. One of them--Creed--is accounted for.

The other is missing. Agent Zero, A.K.A. David North, A.K.A.--

--Maverick.

BEAST'S LOGBOOK:

THE MERCS

I have been keeping a close watch on the mercenaries (or so-called Mercs) responsible for the attacks on several of Xavier's businesses last year.

They appear to be a financially motivated private security firm -- composed of former soldiers from many nations -- which claims no political affiliation. Their work for the Man with the Peacock Tattoo -- the apparent leader of the anti-mutant cabal known as XENO -- was a money-grab, nothing more.

They can -- and will -- work for us as well. I've made certain of that.

After interrogating one of their members -- one Trevor Crosby, a former Green Beret, dishonorably discharged for desertion -- I returned him to his home in coastal California. I could have easily terminated him, but I am not a barbarian, after all. And I also saw that he might benefit us. I secretly tagged him with a surveillance tracker. And, for the sake of insurance, took his beloved dog, Rufus.

The last I checked, Rufus is currently wandering happily about Krakoa. And the last I checked, Crosby was part of a mission to raid a U.S. government black site.

Any attempts at audio surveillance have been inconveniently interrupted by a jammer their team leader seems to carry on him.

Their current location is Los Angeles, where it appears they are prepping for their next mission.

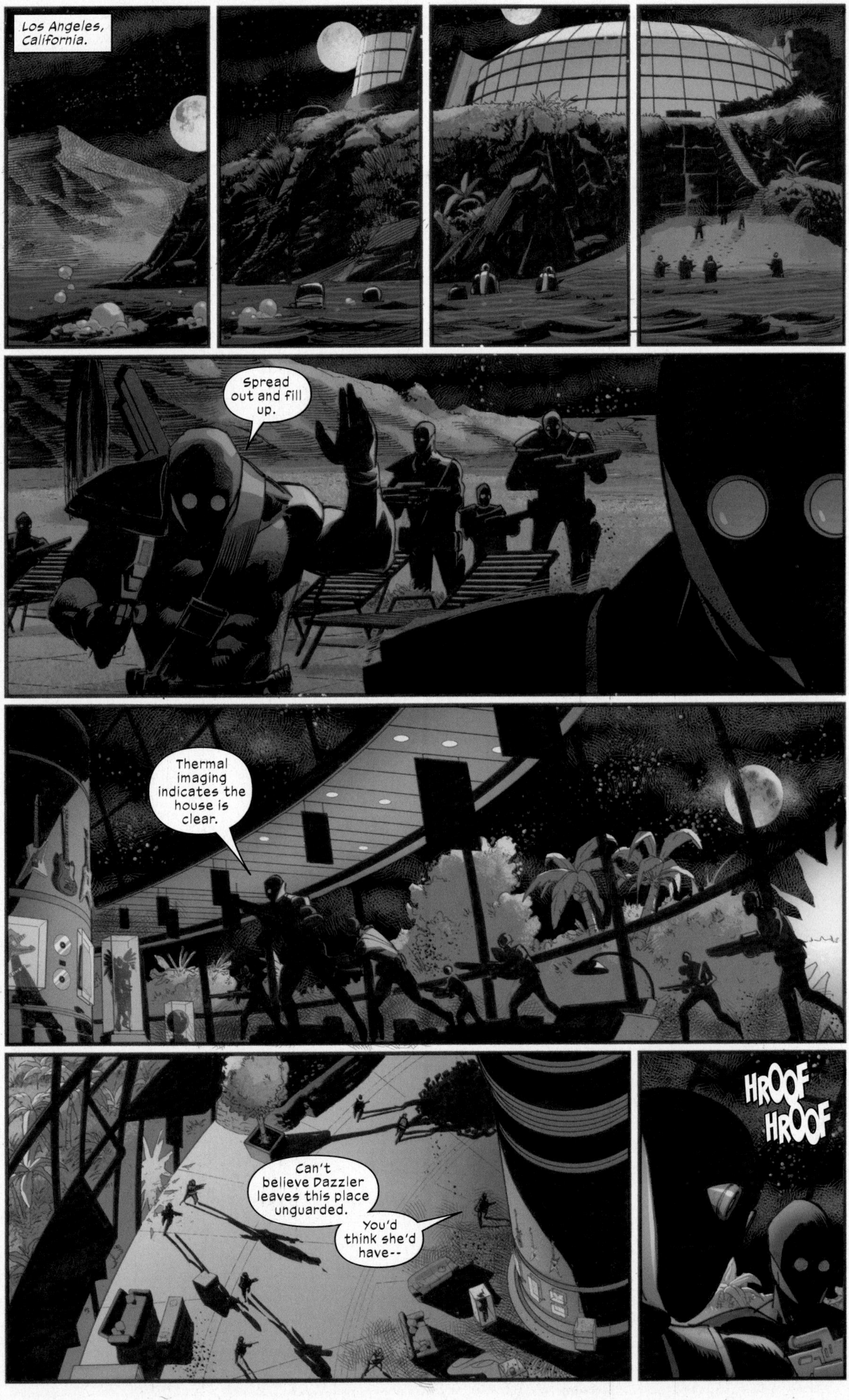
Los Angeles, California.
Spread out and fill up.
Thermal imaging indicates the house is clear.
Can't believe Dazzler leaves this place unguarded.
You'd think she'd have--
HROOF HROOF

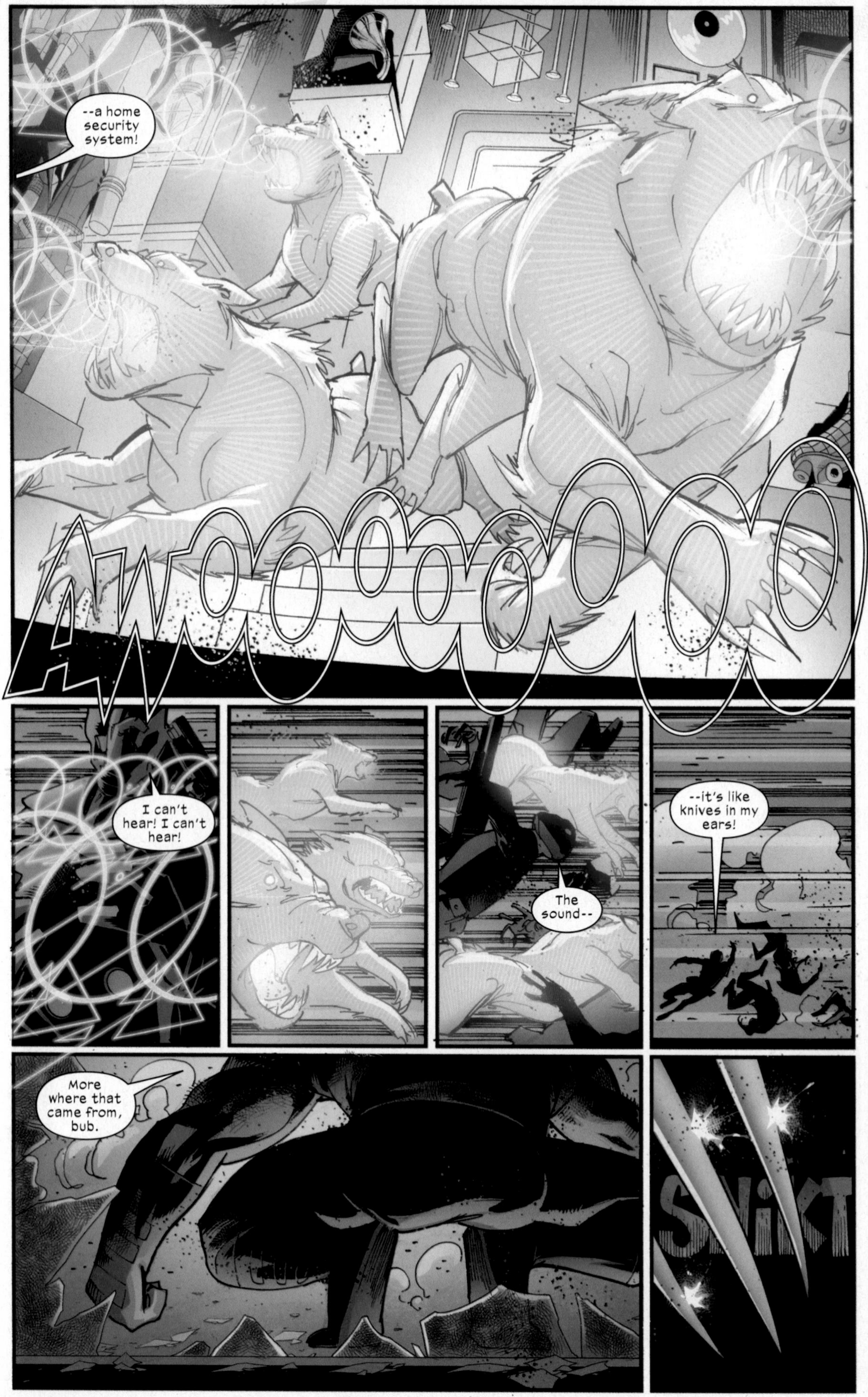
--a home security system!
AWOOOOOOOOOO
I can't hear! I can't hear!
The sound--
--it's like knives in my ears!
More where that came from, bub.
SNIKT

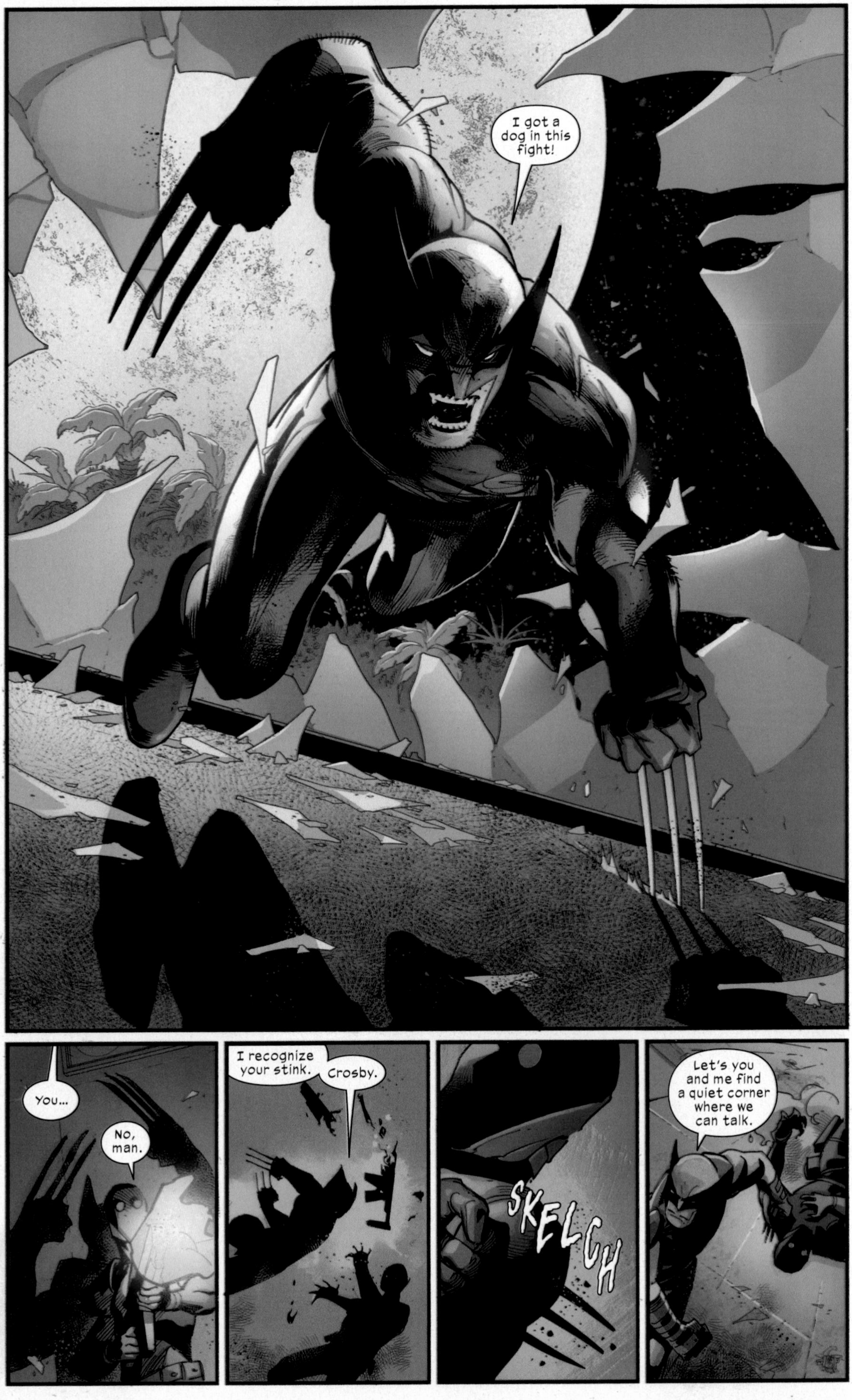
I got a dog in this fight!
You...
No, man.
I recognize your stink.
Crosby.
SKELCH
Let's you and me find a quiet corner where we can talk.

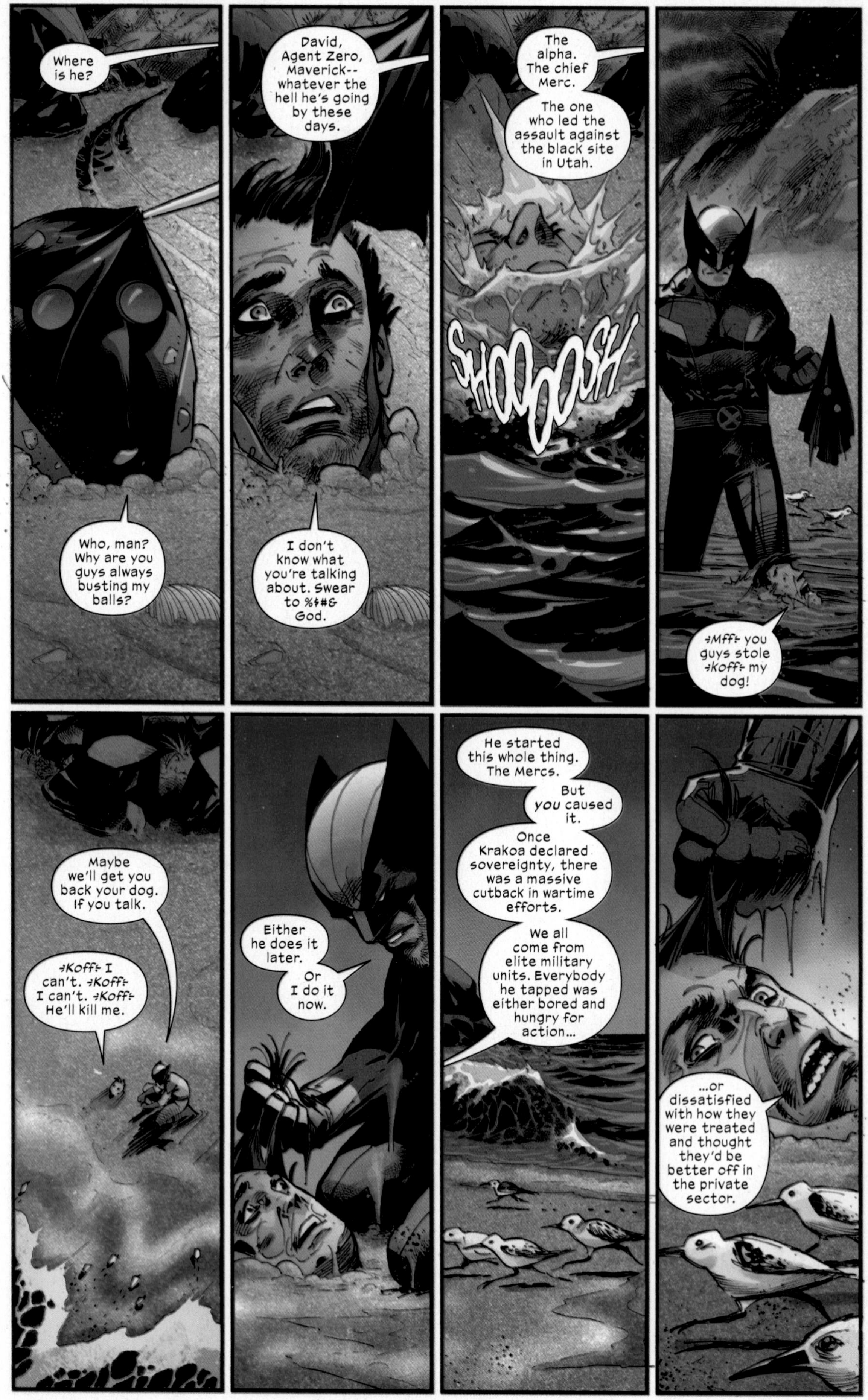
Where is he?
Who, man? Why are you guys always busting my balls?
David, Agent Zero, Maverick--whatever the hell he's going by these days.
I don't know what you're talking about. Swear to %$#& God.
The alpha. The chief Merc.
The one who led the assault against the black site in Utah.
SHOOOOSH
=Mff= you guys stole =Koff= my dog!
Maybe we'll get you back your dog. If you talk.
=Koff= I can't. =Koff= I can't. =Koff= He'll kill me.
Either he does it later.
Or I do it now.
He started this whole thing. The Mercs.
But *you* caused it.
Once Krakoa declared sovereignty, there was a massive cutback in wartime efforts.
We all come from elite military units. Everybody he tapped was either bored and hungry for action...
...or dissatisfied with how they were treated and thought they'd be better off in the private sector.

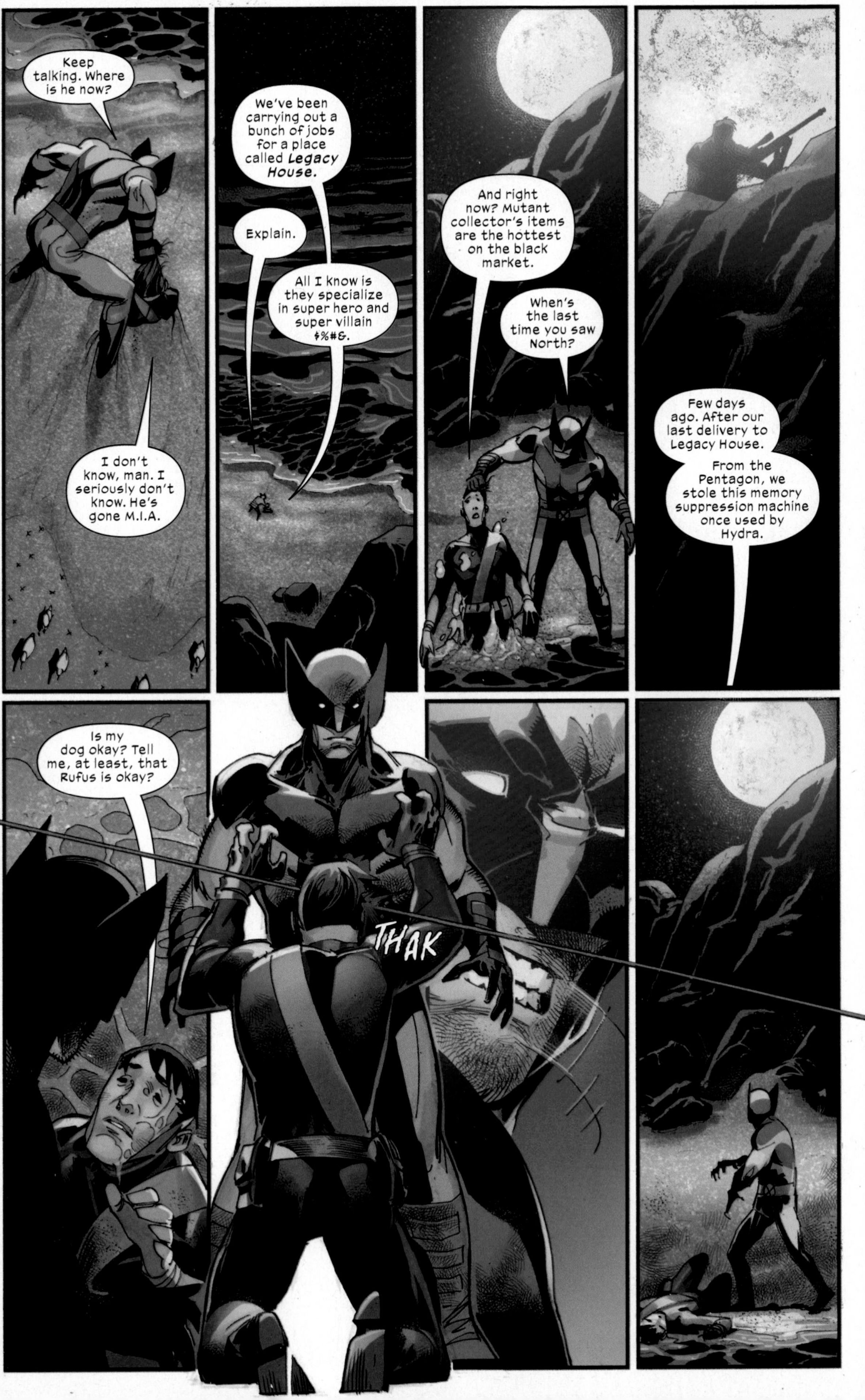

Keep talking. Where is he now?
I don't know, man. I seriously don't know. He's gone M.I.A.
We've been carrying out a bunch of jobs for a place called *Legacy House.*
Explain.
All I know is they specialize in super hero and super villain $%#&.
And right now? Mutant collector's items are the hottest on the black market.
When's the last time you saw North?
Few days ago. After our last delivery to Legacy House.
From the Pentagon, we stole this memory suppression machine once used by Hydra.
Is my dog okay? Tell me, at least, that Rufus is okay?
THAK

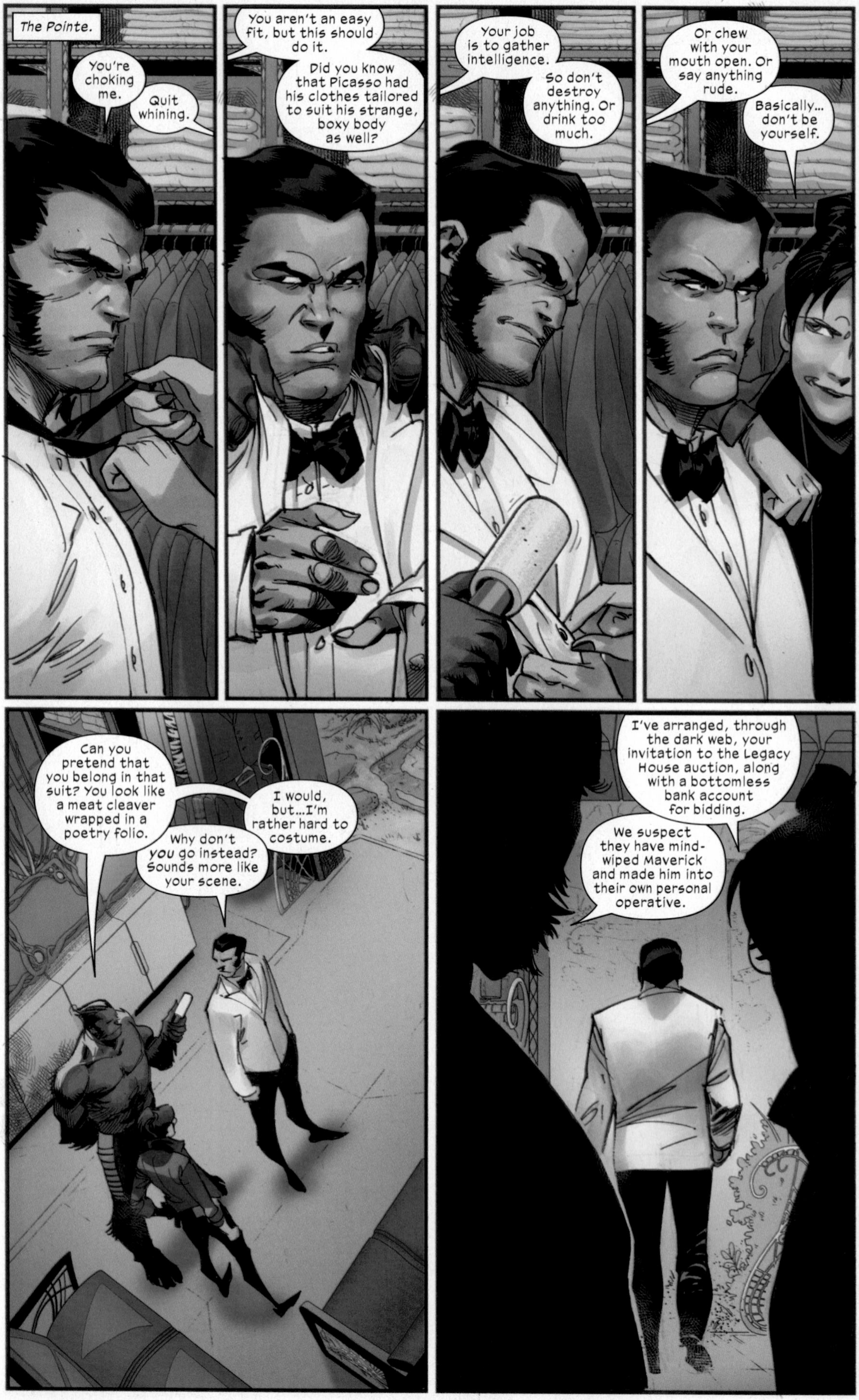
The Pointe.
You're choking me.
Quit whining.
You aren't an easy fit, but this should do it.
Did you know that Picasso had his clothes tailored to suit his strange, boxy body as well?
Your job is to gather intelligence.
So don't destroy anything. Or drink too much.
Or chew with your mouth open. Or say anything rude.
Basically... don't be yourself.
Can you pretend that you belong in that suit? You look like a meat cleaver wrapped in a poetry folio.
Why don't *you* go instead? Sounds more like your scene.
I would, but...I'm rather hard to costume.
I've arranged, through the dark web, your invitation to the Legacy House auction, along with a bottomless bank account for bidding.
We suspect they have mind-wiped Maverick and made him into their own personal operative.

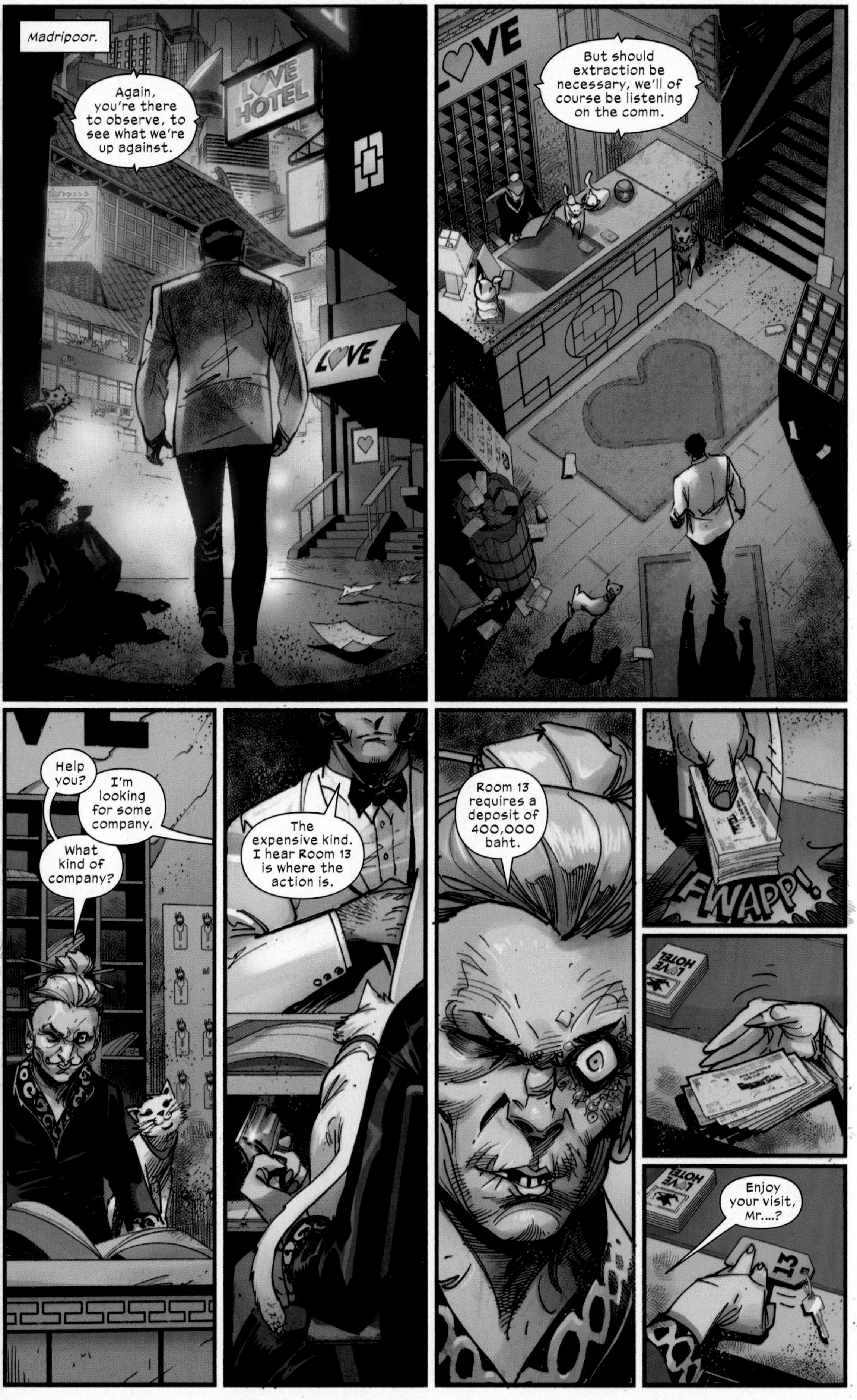
Madripoor.
LOVE HOTEL
Again, you're there to observe, to see what we're up against.
LOVE
LOVE
But should extraction be necessary, we'll of course be listening on the comm.
Help you?
I'm looking for some company.
What kind of company?
The expensive kind. I hear Room 13 is where the action is.
Room 13 requires a deposit of 400,000 baht.
FWAPP!
LOVE HOTEL
Enjoy your visit, Mr....?
13

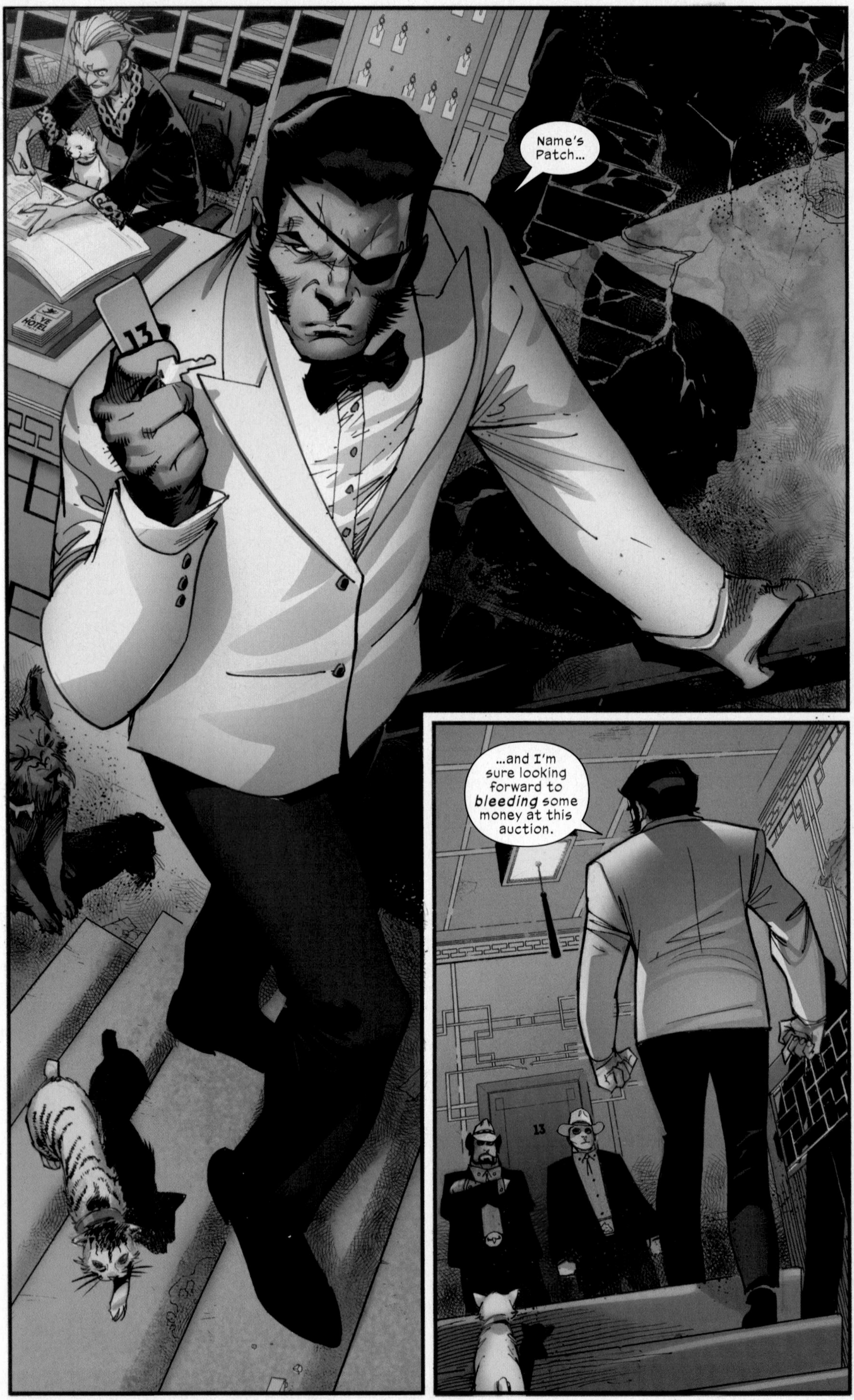

Name's Patch...
13
...and I'm sure looking forward to *bleeding* some money at this auction.
13

[reign_of_x]

[best__]
[there_]

[is__]
[bub_]

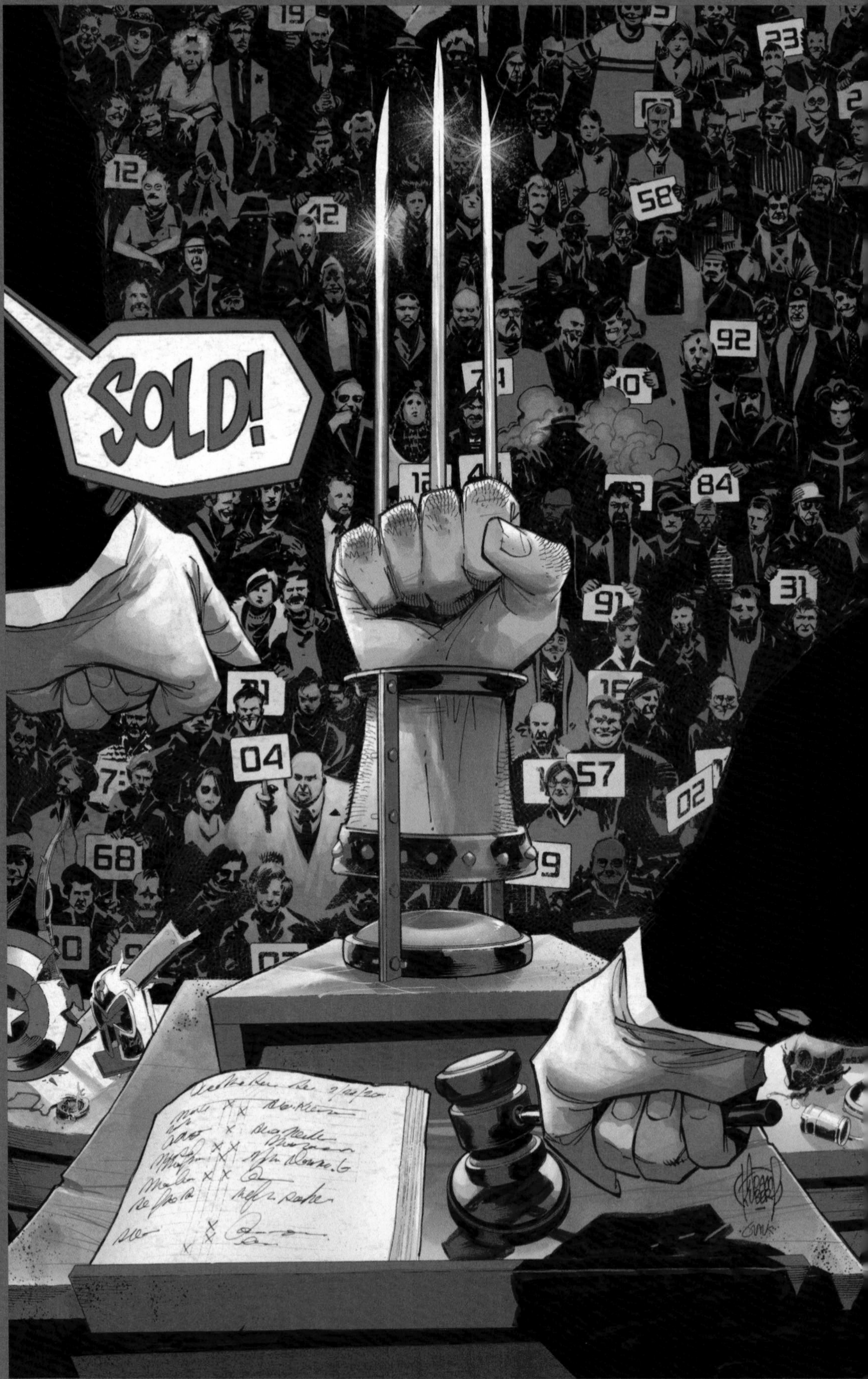
SOLD!

Bidding War

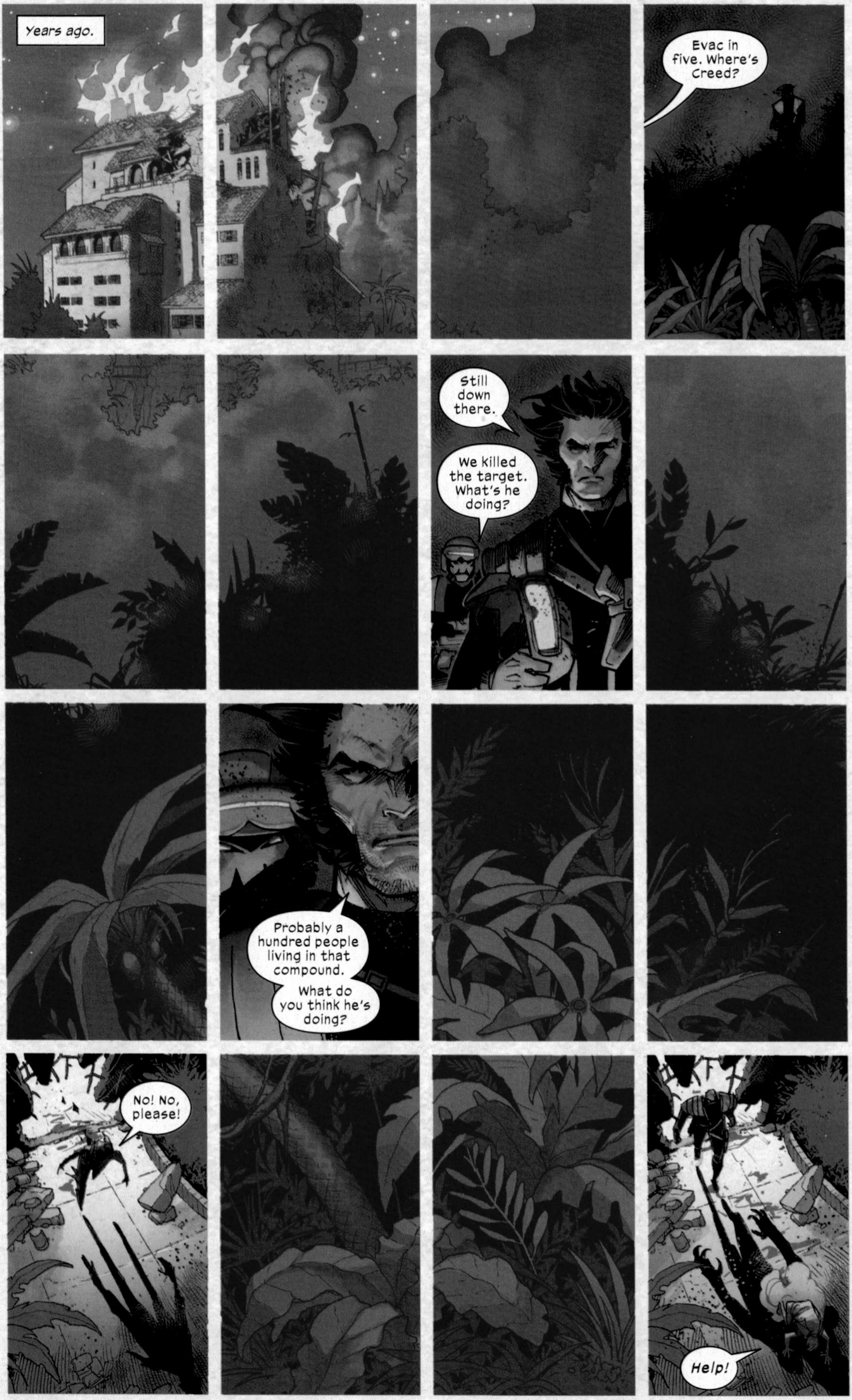
Years ago.
Evac in five. Where's Creed?
Still down there.
We killed the target. What's he doing?
Probably a hundred people living in that compound.
What do you think he's doing?
No! No, please!
Help!

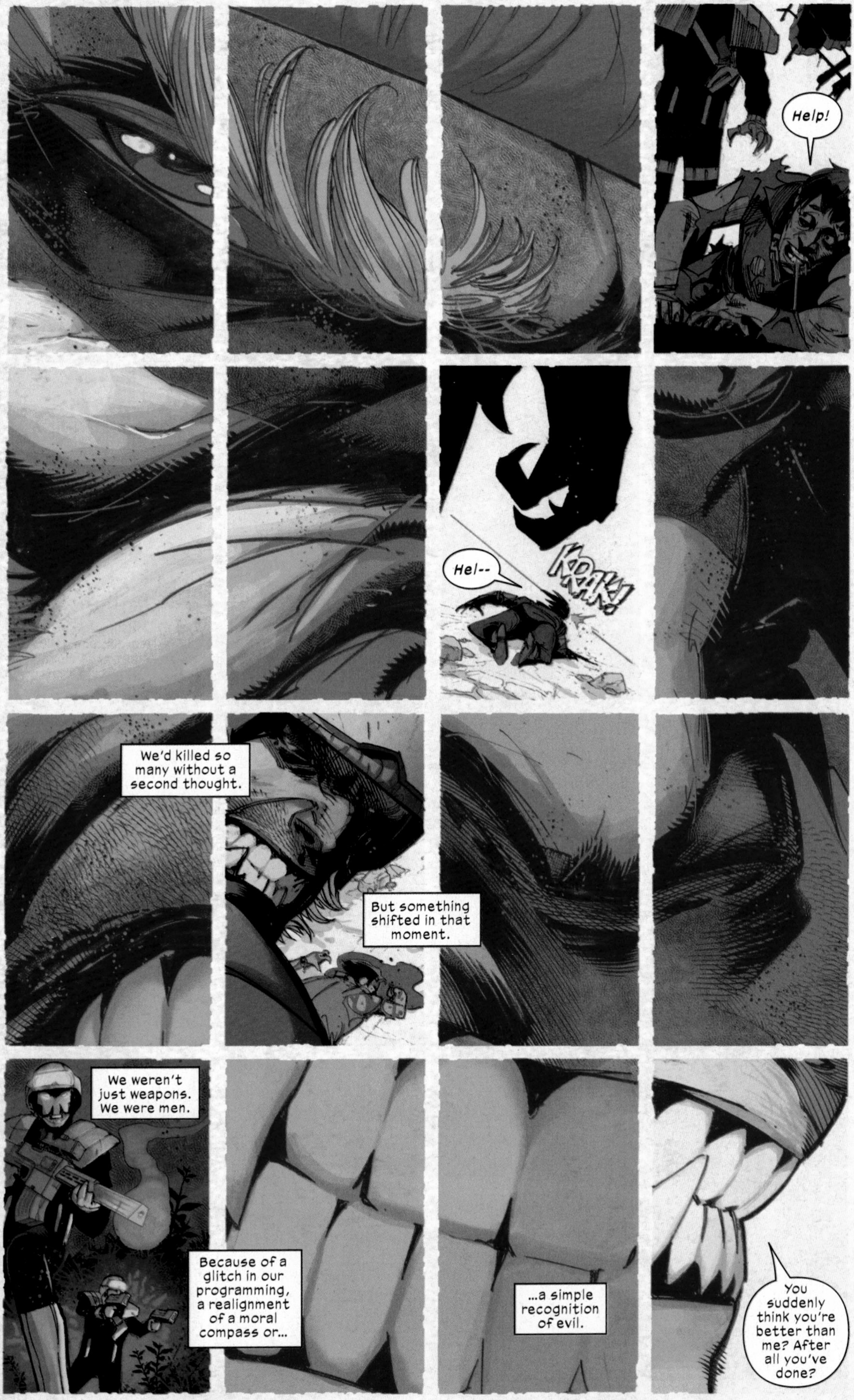
Help!
Hel--
KRAK!
We'd killed so many without a second thought.
But something shifted in that moment.
We weren't just weapons. We were men.
Because of a glitch in our programming, a realignment of a moral compass or...
...a simple recognition of evil.
You suddenly think you're better than me? After all you've done?

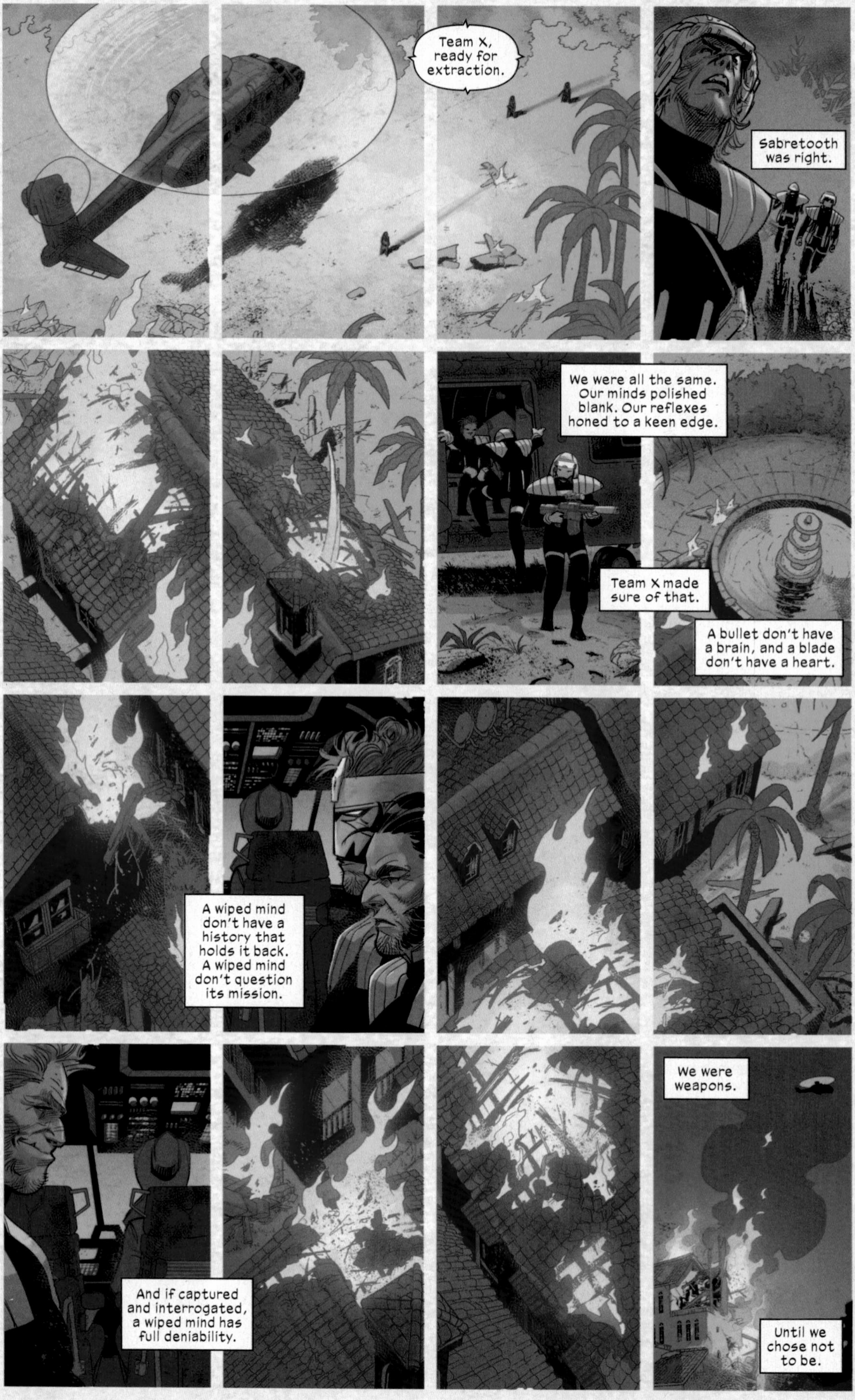

Team X, ready for extraction.
Sabretooth was right.
We were all the same. Our minds polished blank. Our reflexes honed to a keen edge.
Team X made sure of that.
A bullet don't have a brain, and a blade don't have a heart.
A wiped mind don't have a history that holds it back. A wiped mind don't question its mission.
And if captured and interrogated, a wiped mind has full deniability.
We were weapons.
Until we chose not to be.

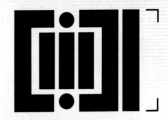

FROM *THE SECRET HISTORY OF WOLVERINE*
BY ▮▮▮▮▮▮▮▮.

They had done terrible things. Of this they were certain.

Professor Thornton tried to keep them clean. The mindwipes were frequent enough to ensure obedience, mollify guilt and keep them focused on the task ahead.

A coup. An assassination. A drug shipment. An arms deal.

But if a week or more passed, the brain found a way to recover. The memories were still there, hazed over like the writing on an erased chalkboard.

After that night, Wolverine and Maverick made a pact. They would never be the same as Sabretooth. They would escape the arsenal of Team X.

Maybe they would never really know who they were -- in the time before the black-ops program -- but they could control who they might become.

On one of their missions, Wolverine stole a book from a nightstand. *The Book of Five Rings* by Miyamoto Musashi. He recognized it without knowing why. He kept it hidden in his bunk. How many times he read it, he doesn't know, but he jotted down notes in its margins. Notes about those he had killed. So that he wouldn't forget.

Wolverine and Maverick developed a mnemonic device borrowed from the book. "Today is a victory over yourself of yesterday." It was meant to bring them back, to anchor them in the present, to help them recognize the loss of a thousand yesterdays. A way to find their way back from indoctrination.

They didn't know why they were going to Lebanon or Myanmar or Egypt or Colombia. They didn't understand the motions of violence that defined their days. They didn't even know who they were.

They only knew the hope that they might save each other. "Today is a victory over yourself of yesterday. Today is a victory over yourself of yesterday. Today is a victory over yourself of yesterday."

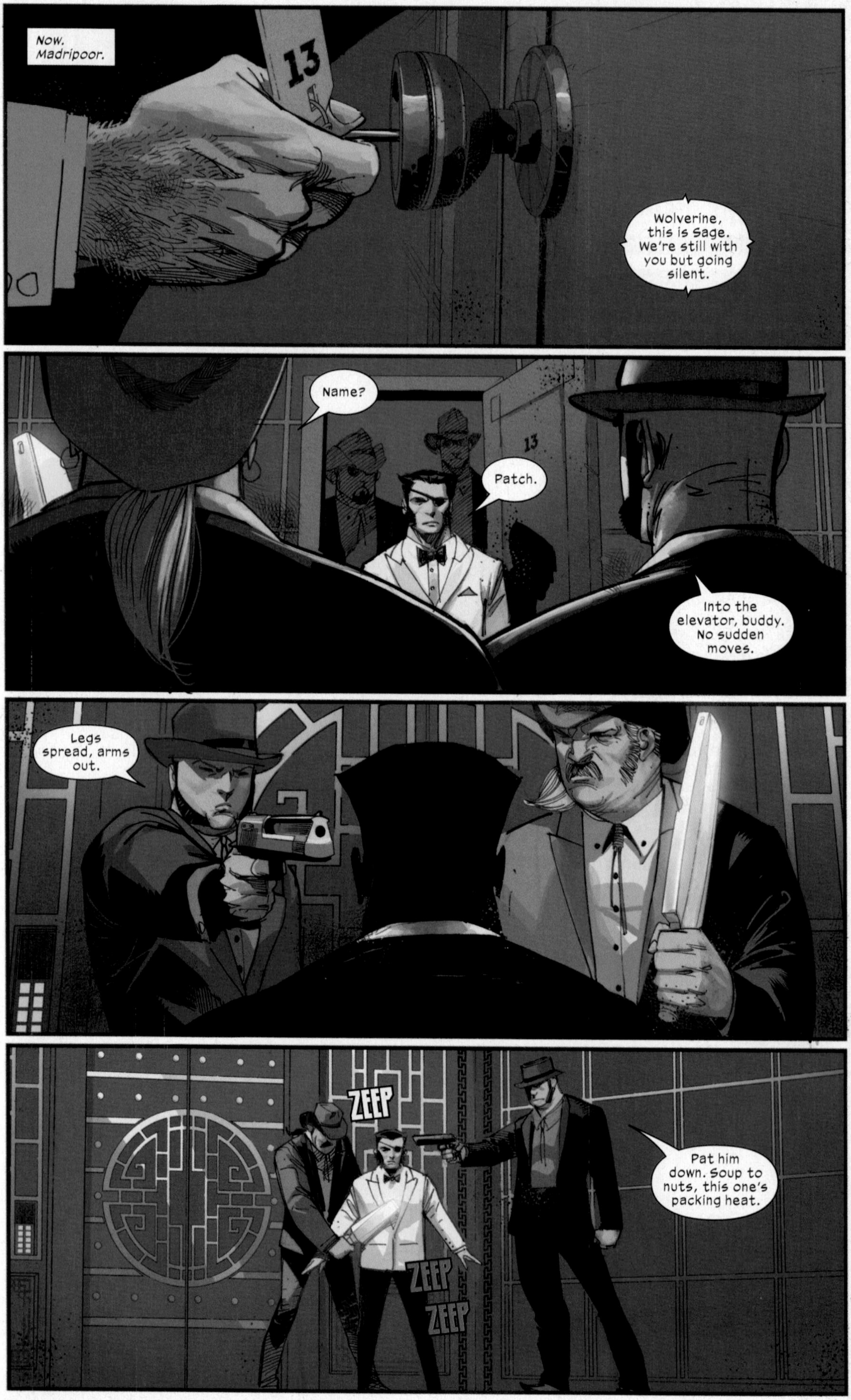
Now.
Madripoor.
13
Wolverine, this is Sage. We're still with you but going silent.
Name?
13
Patch.
Into the elevator, buddy. No sudden moves.
Legs spread, arms out.
ZEEP
Pat him down. Soup to nuts, this one's packing heat.
ZEEP
ZEEP

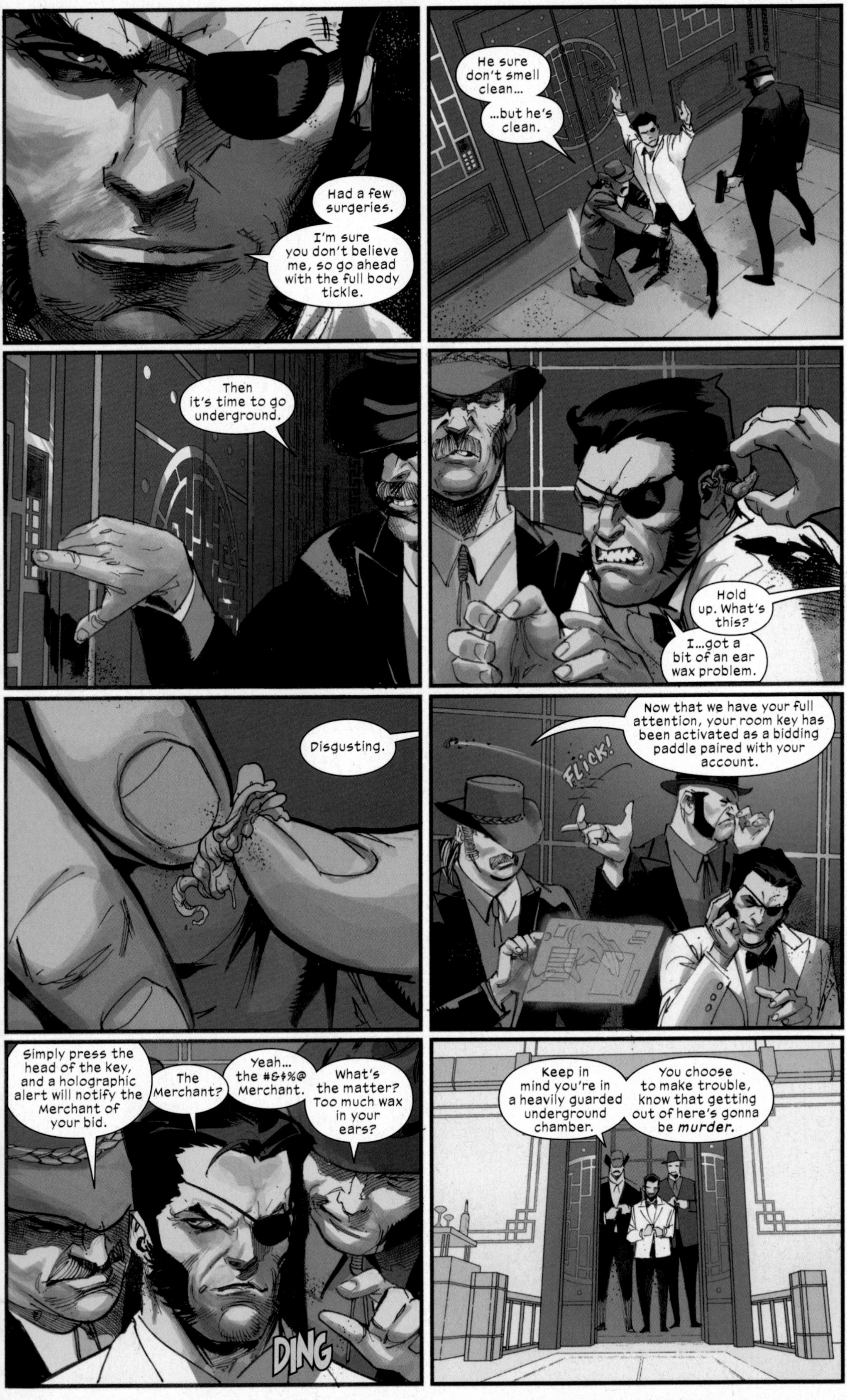
Had a few surgeries.
I'm sure you don't believe me, so go ahead with the full body tickle.
He sure don't smell clean...
...but he's clean.
Then it's time to go underground.
Hold up. What's this?
I...got a bit of an ear wax problem.
Disgusting.
Now that we have your full attention, your room key has been activated as a bidding paddle paired with your account.
FLICK!
Simply press the head of the key, and a holographic alert will notify the Merchant of your bid.
The Merchant?
Yeah... the #&$%@ Merchant.
What's the matter? Too much wax in your ears?
DING
Keep in mind you're in a heavily guarded underground chamber.
You choose to make trouble, know that getting out of here's gonna be *murder.*

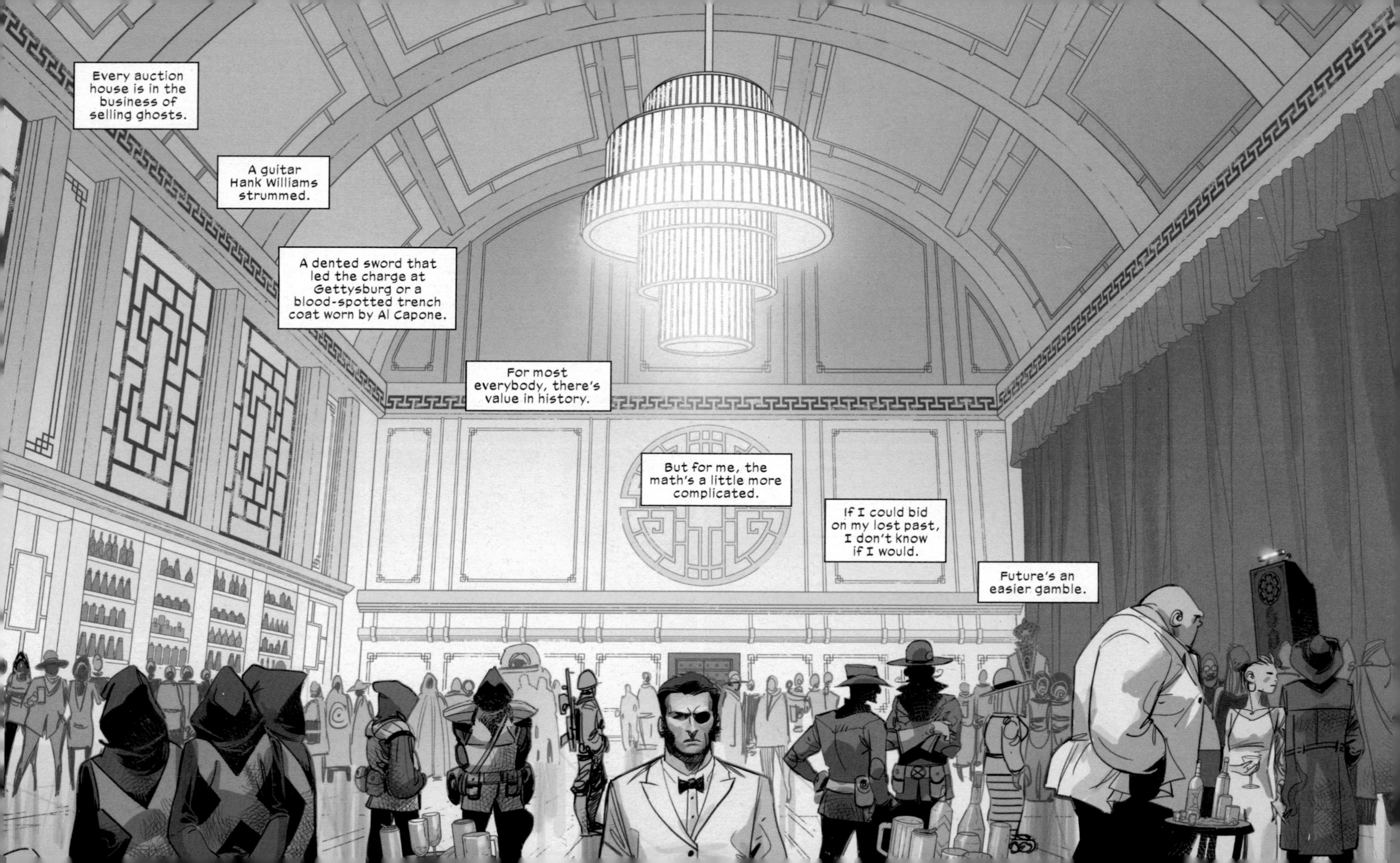
Every auction house is in the business of selling ghosts.
A guitar Hank Williams strummed.
A dented sword that led the charge at Gettysburg or a blood-spotted trench coat worn by Al Capone.
For most everybody, there's value in history.
But for me, the math's a little more complicated.
If I could bid on my lost past, I don't know if I would.
Future's an easier gamble.

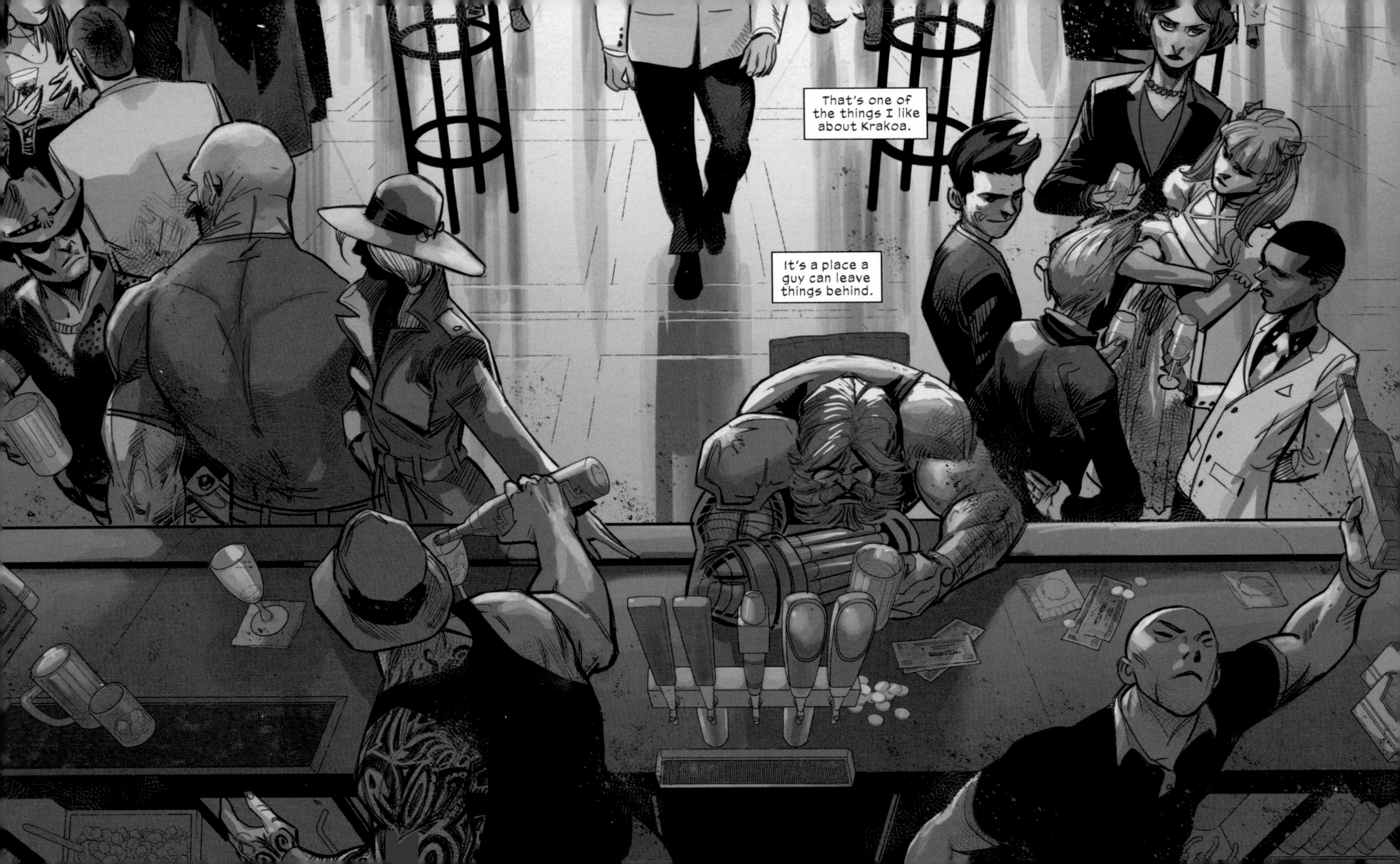
That's one of the things I like about Krakoa.
It's a place a guy can leave things behind.

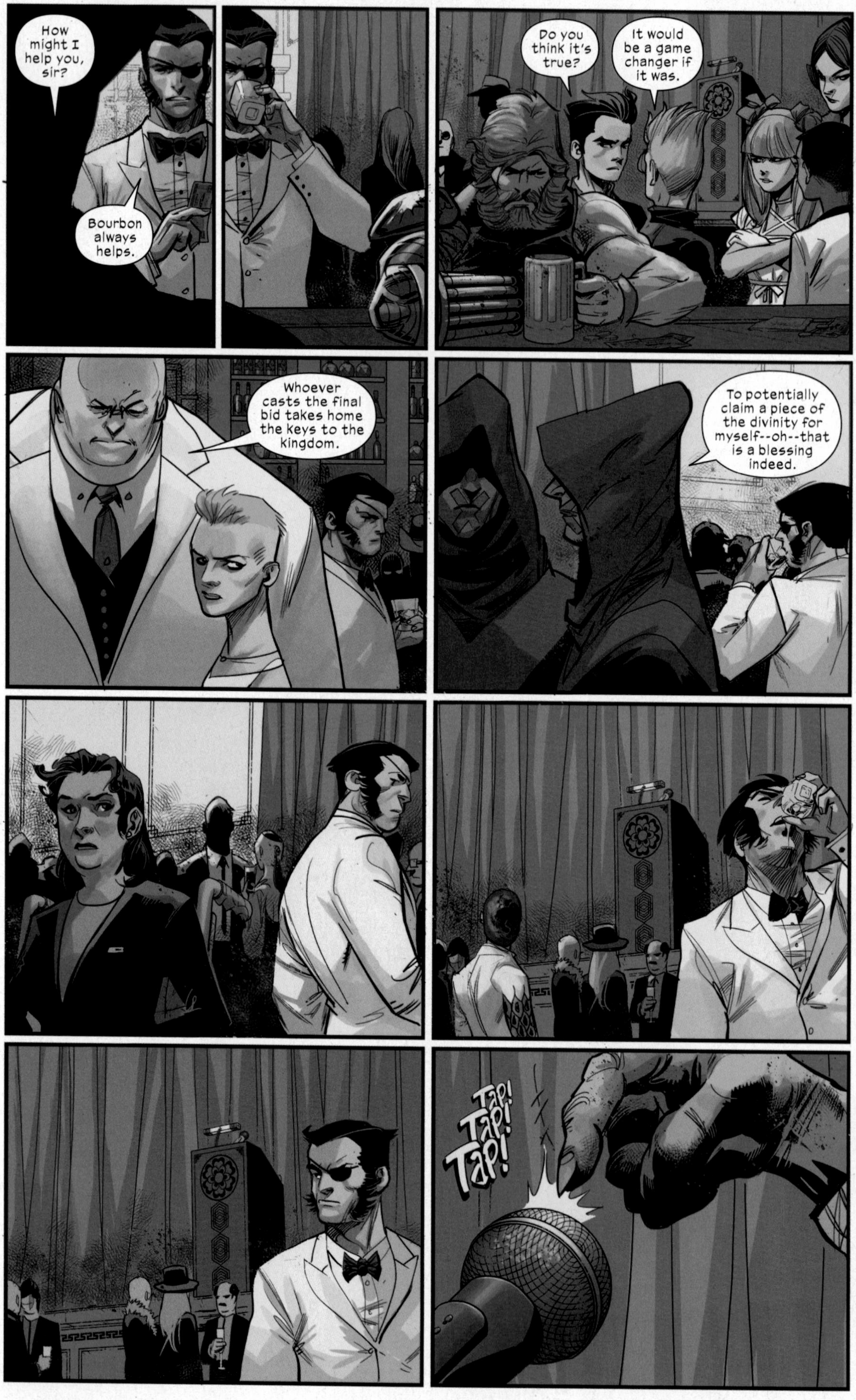
How might I help you, sir?
Bourbon always helps.
Do you think it's true?
It would be a game changer if it was.
Whoever casts the final bid takes home the keys to the kingdom.
To potentially claim a piece of the divinity for myself--oh--that is a blessing indeed.
TAP! TAP! TAP!

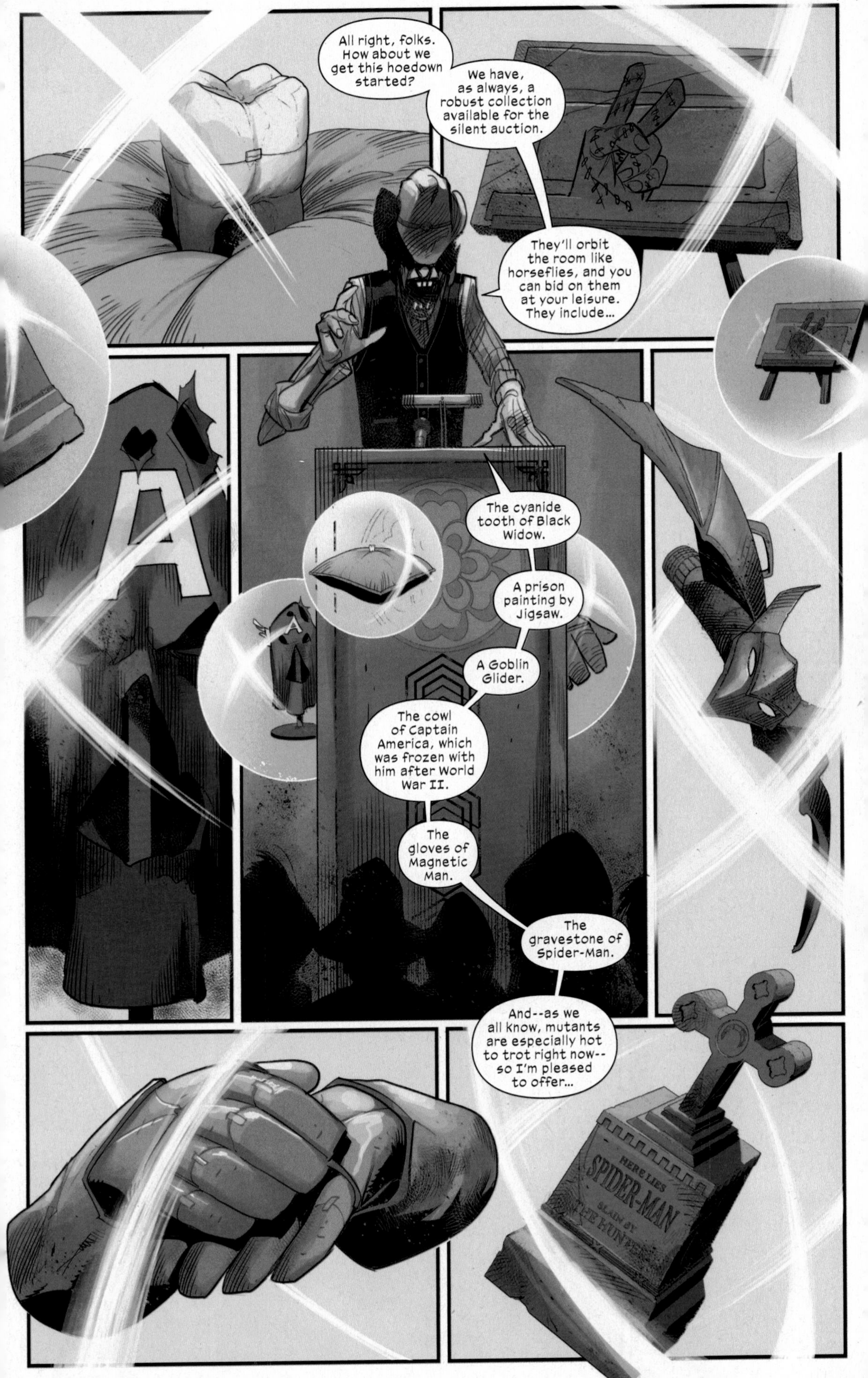

All right, folks. How about we get this hoedown started?
We have, as always, a robust collection available for the silent auction.
They'll orbit the room like horseflies, and you can bid on them at your leisure. They include...
The cyanide tooth of Black Widow.
A prison painting by Jigsaw.
A Goblin Glider.
The cowl of Captain America, which was frozen with him after World War II.
The gloves of Magnetic Man.
The gravestone of Spider-Man.
And--as we all know, mutants are especially hot to trot right now--so I'm pleased to offer...
HERE LIES SPIDER-MAN SLAIN BY THE HUNTER

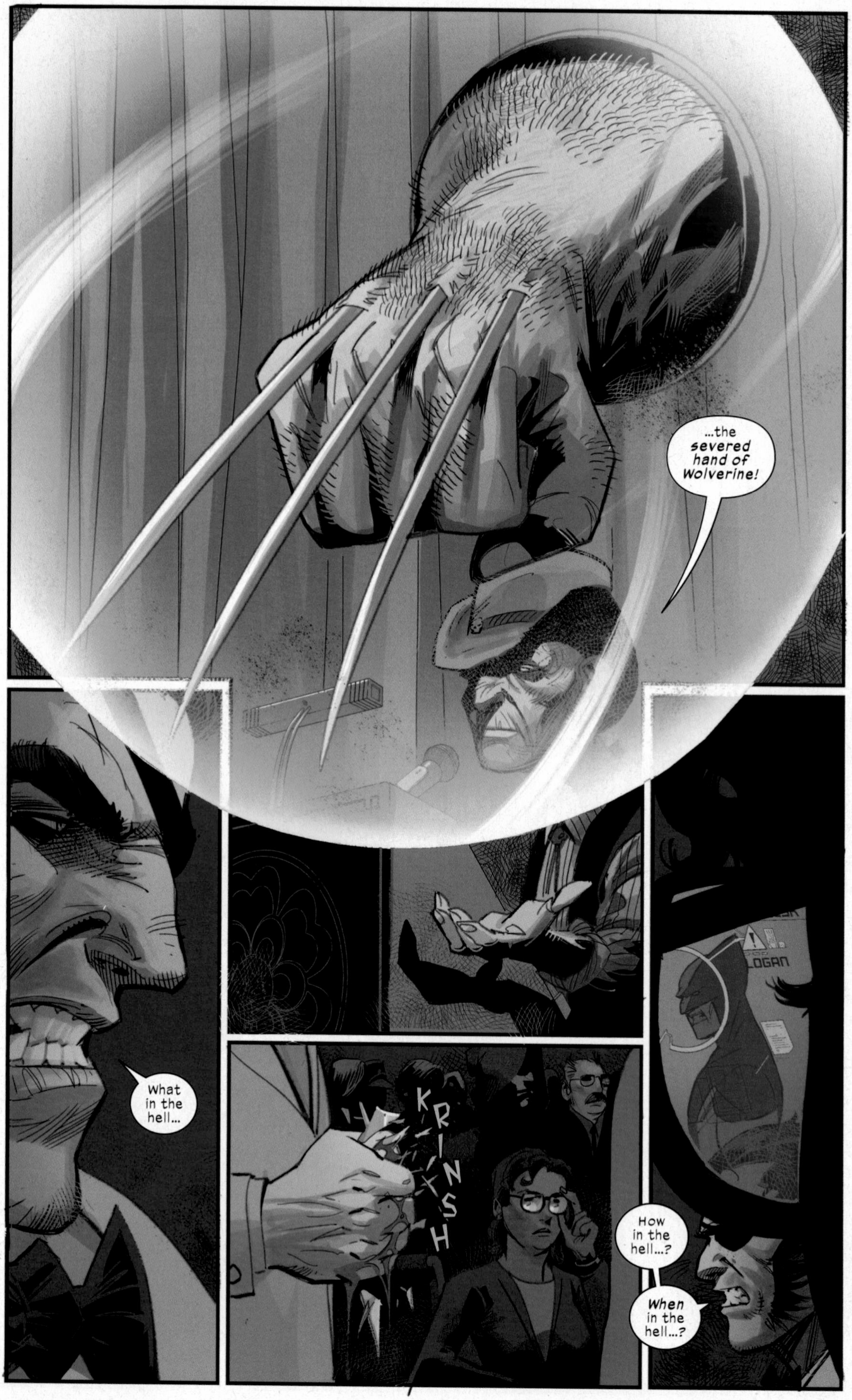
...the severed hand of Wolverine!
What in the hell...
KRINSH
How in the hell...?
When in the hell...?
LOGAN

That's the thing about my broken brain.

Whole sections of time have been rearranged or carved away or planted.

Some things I don't remember.

And the things I do remember might've never happened.

Even when I think I've finally found my way back to clarity, things go haywire again.

It's like time itself is broken, the way the past is always coming back to surprise and haunt me.

History has its own strange life and power.

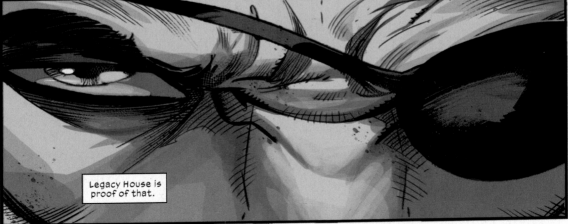

Legacy House is proof of that.

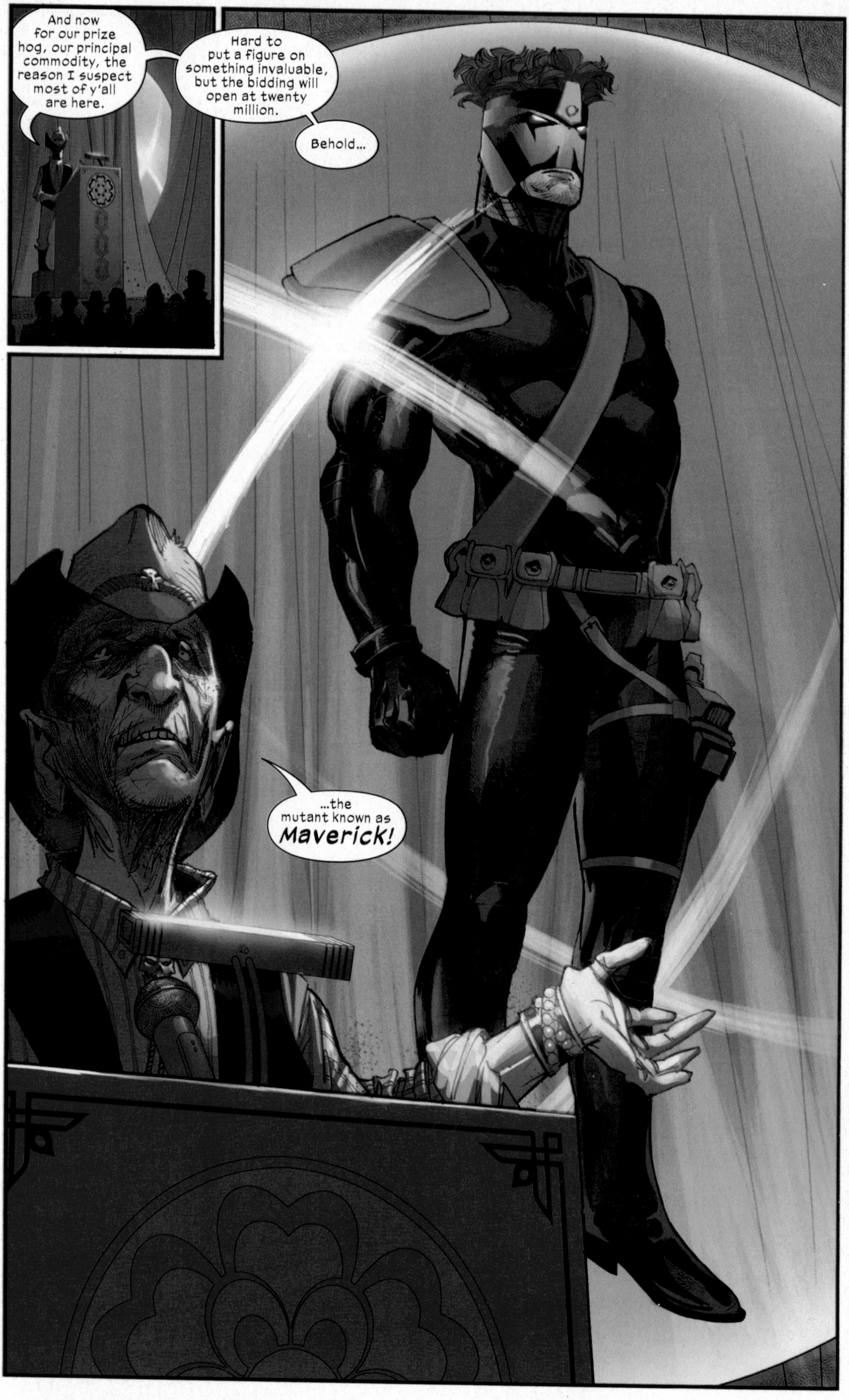
And now for our prize hog, our principal commodity, the reason I suspect most of y'all are here.
Hard to put a figure on something invaluable, but the bidding will open at twenty million.
Behold...
...the mutant known as Maverick!

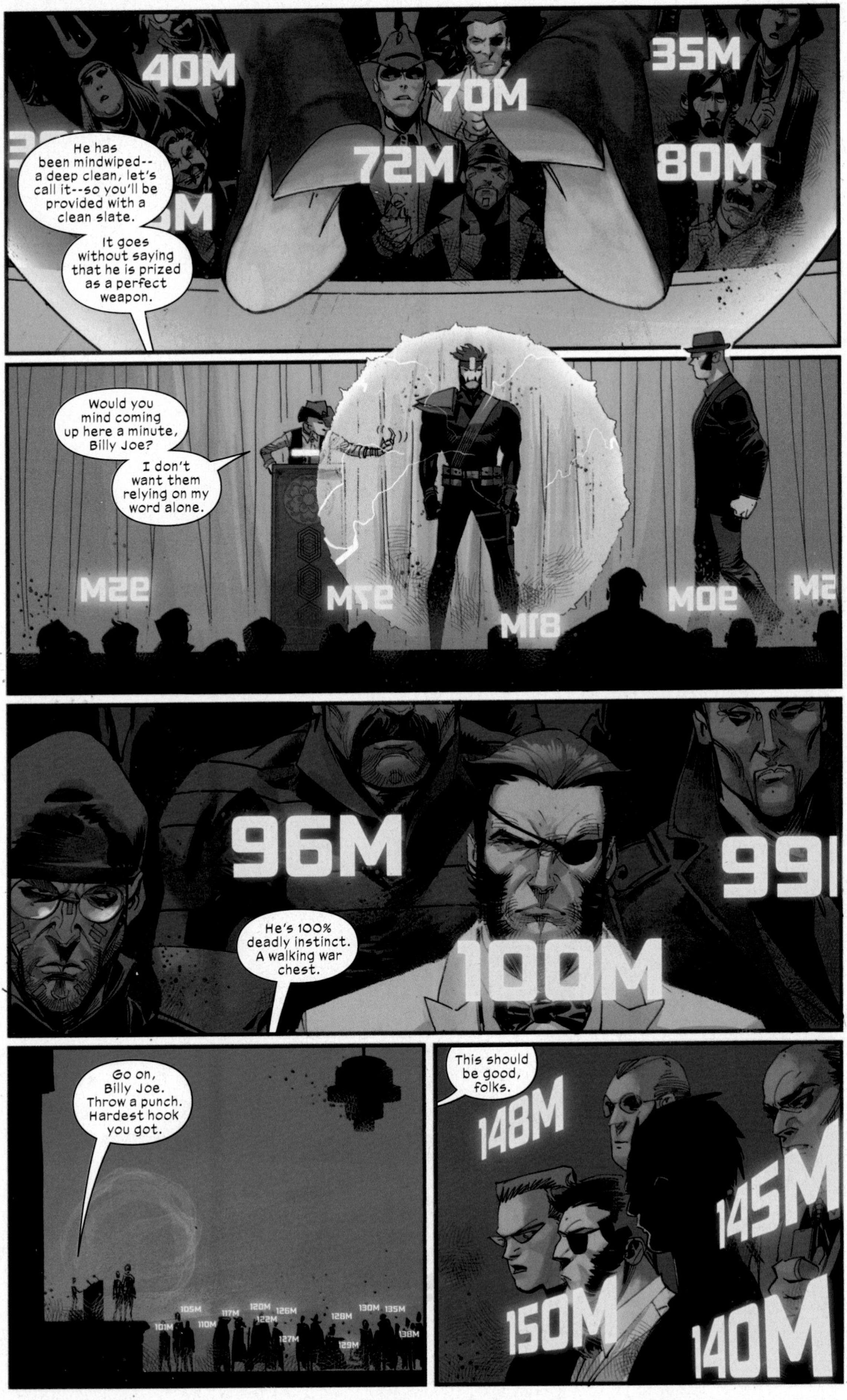
40M
70M
35M
72M
80M
He has been mindwiped--a deep clean, let's call it--so you'll be provided with a clean slate.
It goes without saying that he is prized as a perfect weapon.
Would you mind coming up here a minute, Billy Joe?
I don't want them relying on my word alone.
96M
He's 100% deadly instinct. A walking war chest.
100M
Go on, Billy Joe. Throw a punch. Hardest hook you got.
This should be good, folks.
148M
145M
150M
140M

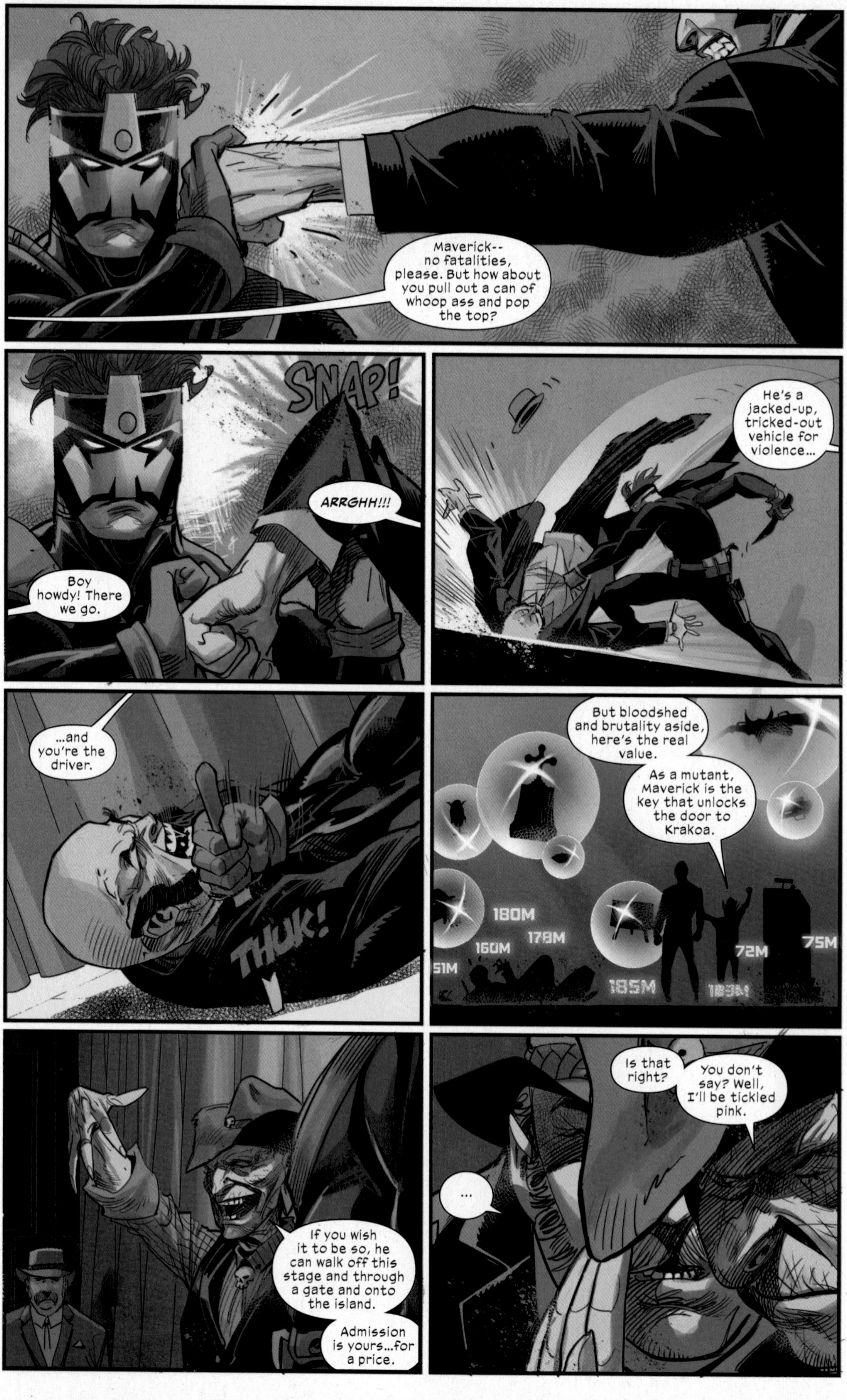
Maverick--
no fatalities, please. But how about you pull out a can of whoop ass and pop the top?
SNAP!
ARRGHH!!!
Boy howdy! There we go.
He's a jacked-up, tricked-out vehicle for violence...
...and you're the driver.
THUK!
But bloodshed and brutality aside, here's the real value.
As a mutant, Maverick is the key that unlocks the door to Krakoa.
180M
178M
160M
51M
185M
72M
75M
If you wish it to be so, he can walk off this stage and through a gate and onto the island.
Admission is yours...for a price.
Is that right?
You don't say? Well, I'll be tickled pink.
...

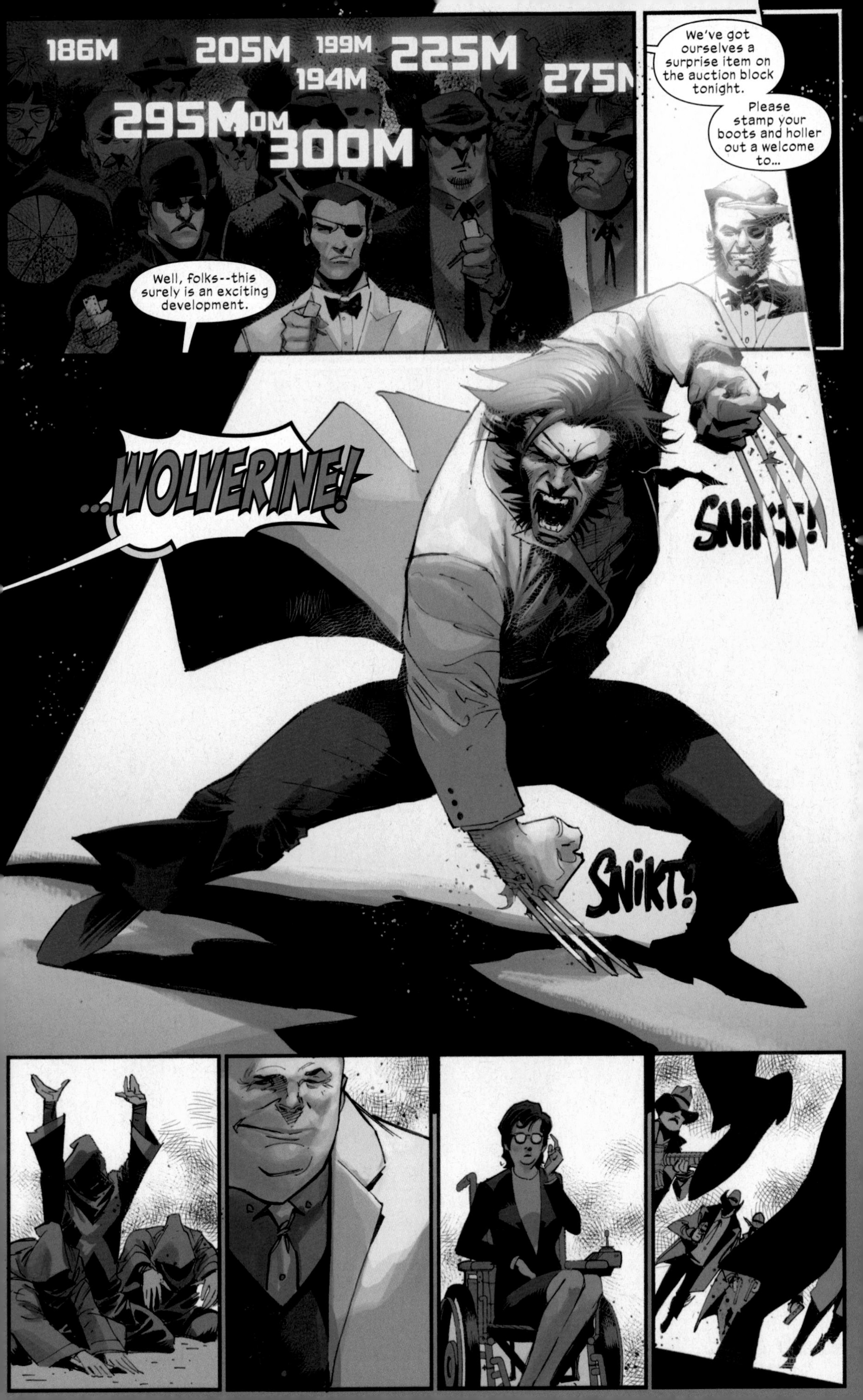
186M
205M
199M
225M
194M
275M
295M
300M
Well, folks--this surely is an exciting development.
We've got ourselves a surprise item on the auction block tonight.
Please stamp your boots and holler out a welcome to...
...WOLVERINE!
SNIKT!
SNIKT!

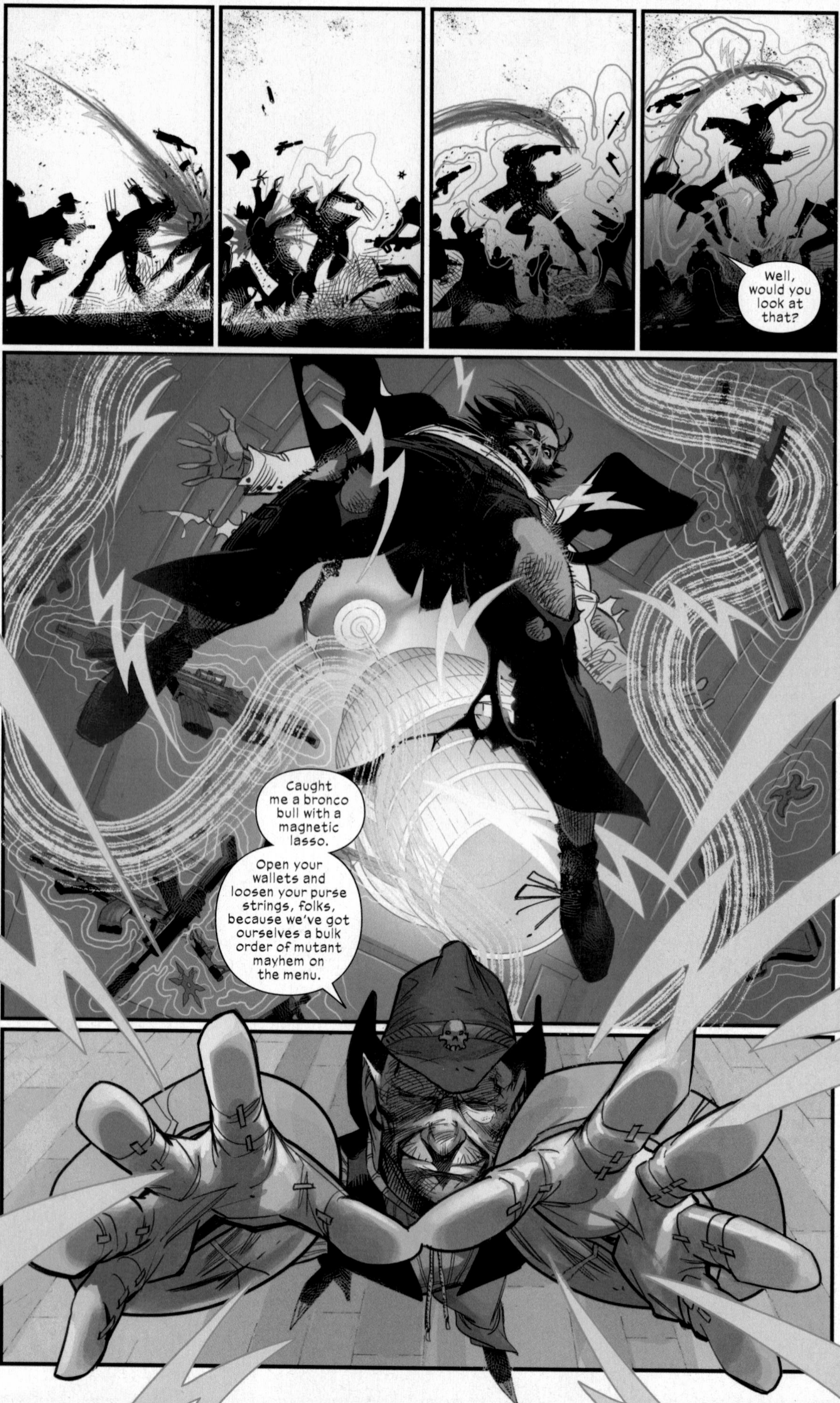
Well, would you look at that?
Caught me a bronco bull with a magnetic lasso.
Open your wallets and loosen your purse strings, folks, because we've got ourselves a bulk order of mutant mayhem on the menu.

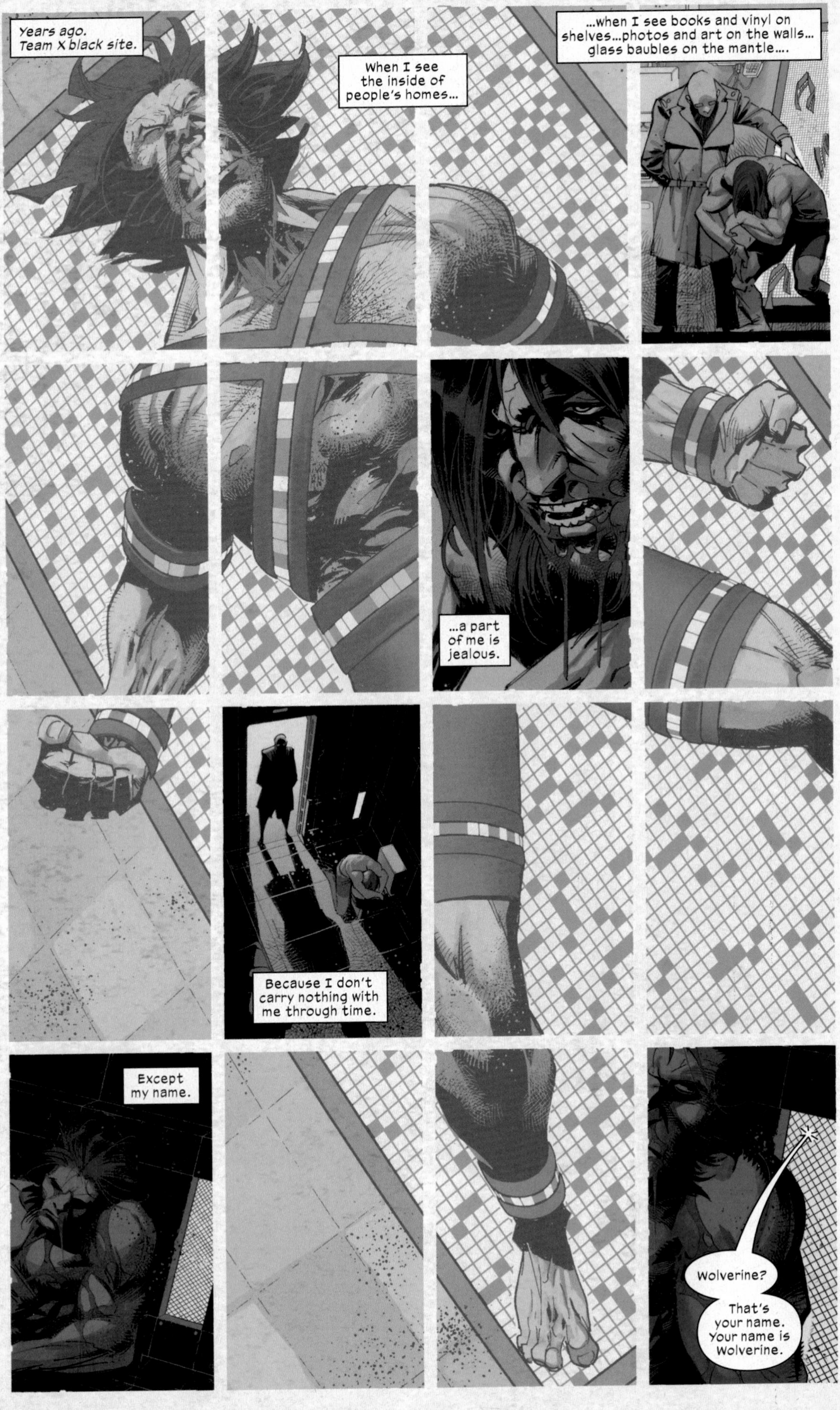
Years ago.
Team X black site.
When I see the inside of people's homes...
...when I see books and vinyl on shelves...photos and art on the walls... glass baubles on the mantle....
...a part of me is jealous.
Because I don't carry nothing with me through time.
Except my name.
Wolverine?
That's your name. Your name is Wolverine.

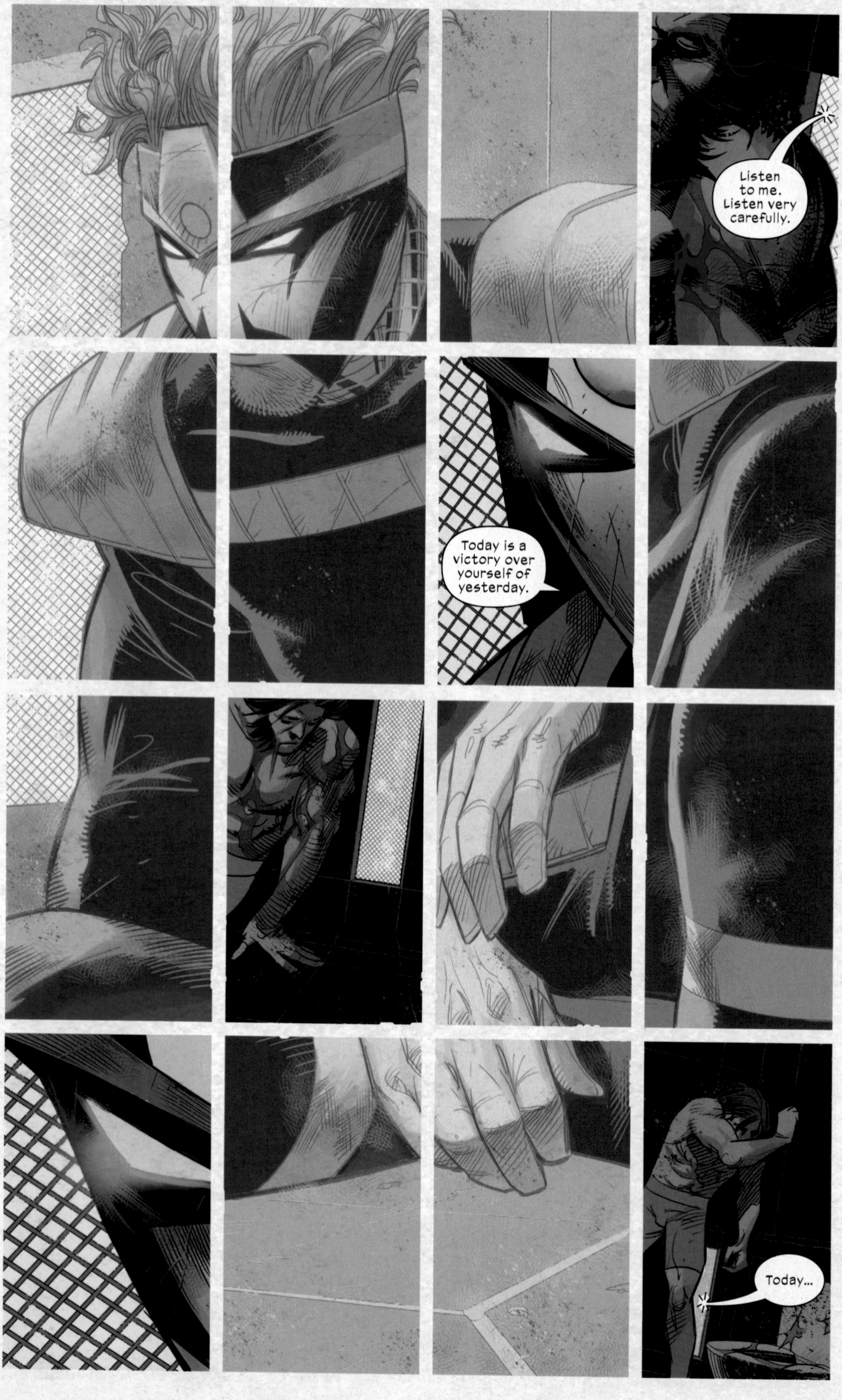
Listen to me. Listen very carefully.
Today is a victory over yourself of yesterday.
Today...

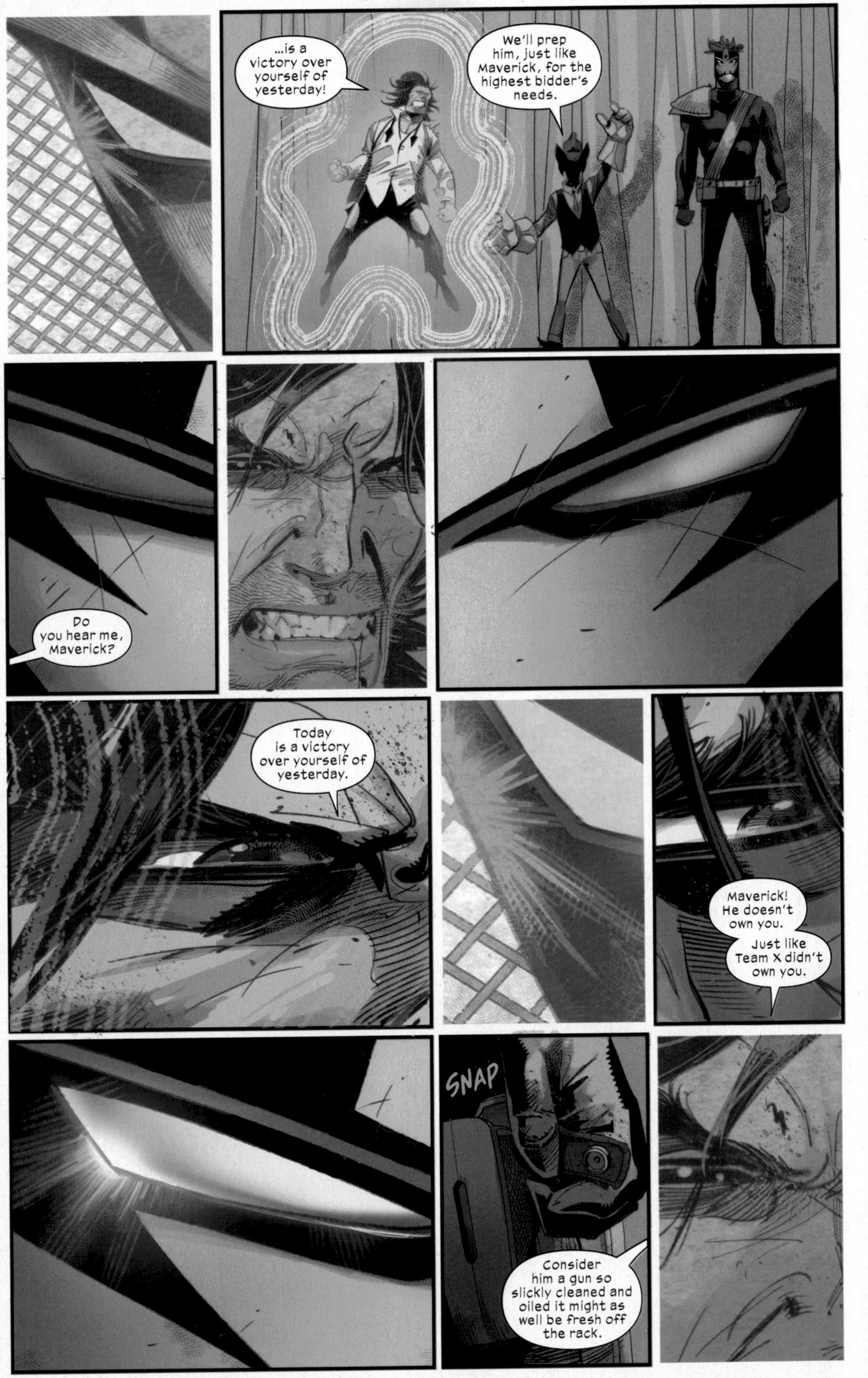

...is a victory over yourself of yesterday!
We'll prep him, just like Maverick, for the highest bidder's needs.
Do you hear me, Maverick?
Today is a victory over yourself of yesterday.
Maverick! He doesn't own you.
Just like Team X didn't own you.
SNAP
Consider him a gun so slickly cleaned and oiled it might as well be fresh off the rack.

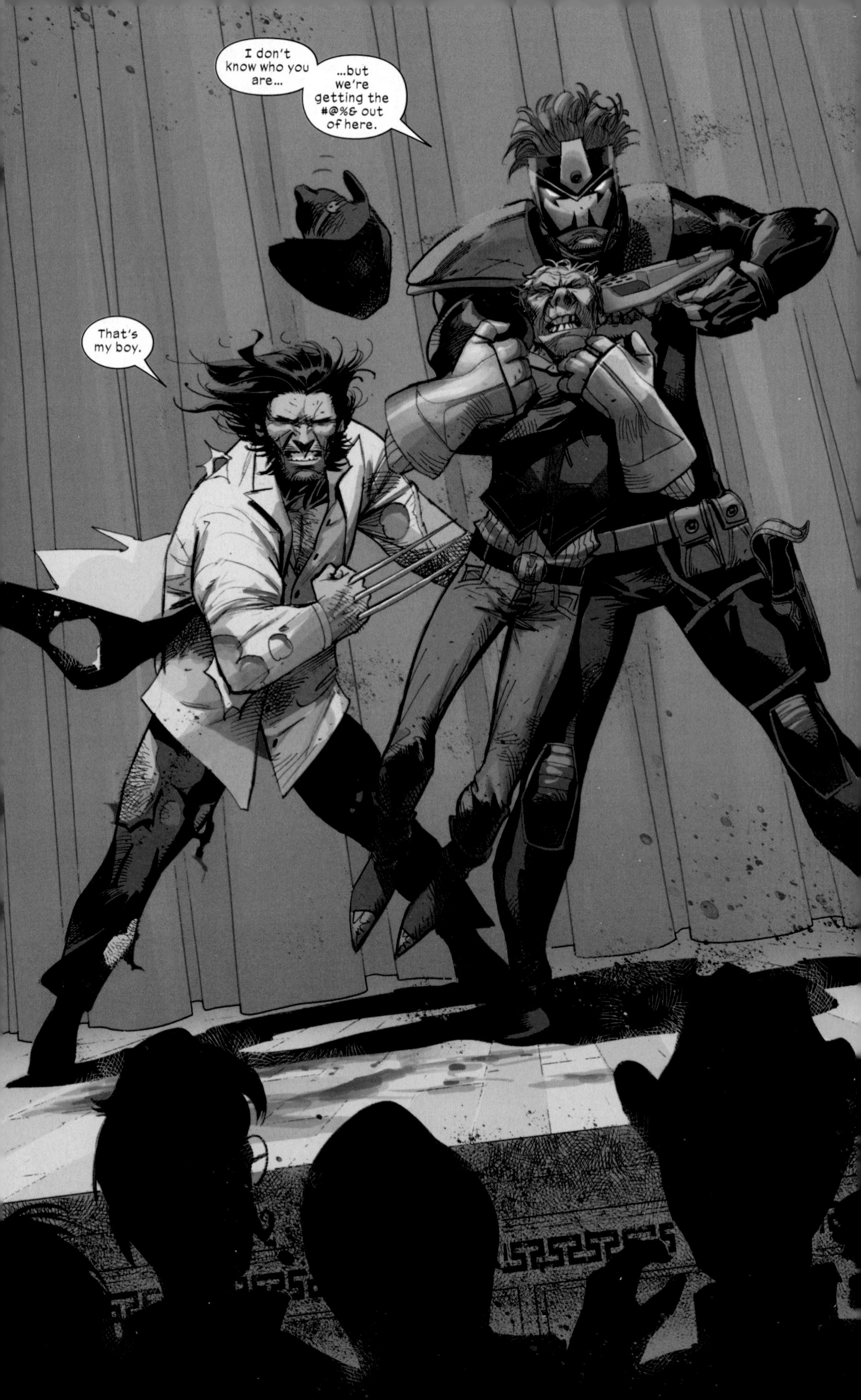
I don't know who you are...
...but we're getting the #@%& out of here.
That's my boy.

[Wolve.....[0.09]
[rine......[0.09]

Maverick is the best kind of bastard.

The best kind of bastard is worth having around, but only if there's beers to be drank or bullets to be dodged.

"You can't trust him with your wife but you can trust him with your life" kind of deal.

Long as you're playing for the same team, that is. Long as you're dodging the same bullets.

But like every pretty boy, he only really cares about one person, and that's numero uno.

-- WOLVERINE

[Wolve.....[0.09]
[rine......[0.09]

[wolve..[0.09]...]
[rine...[0.09]...]

[wolverine_09]

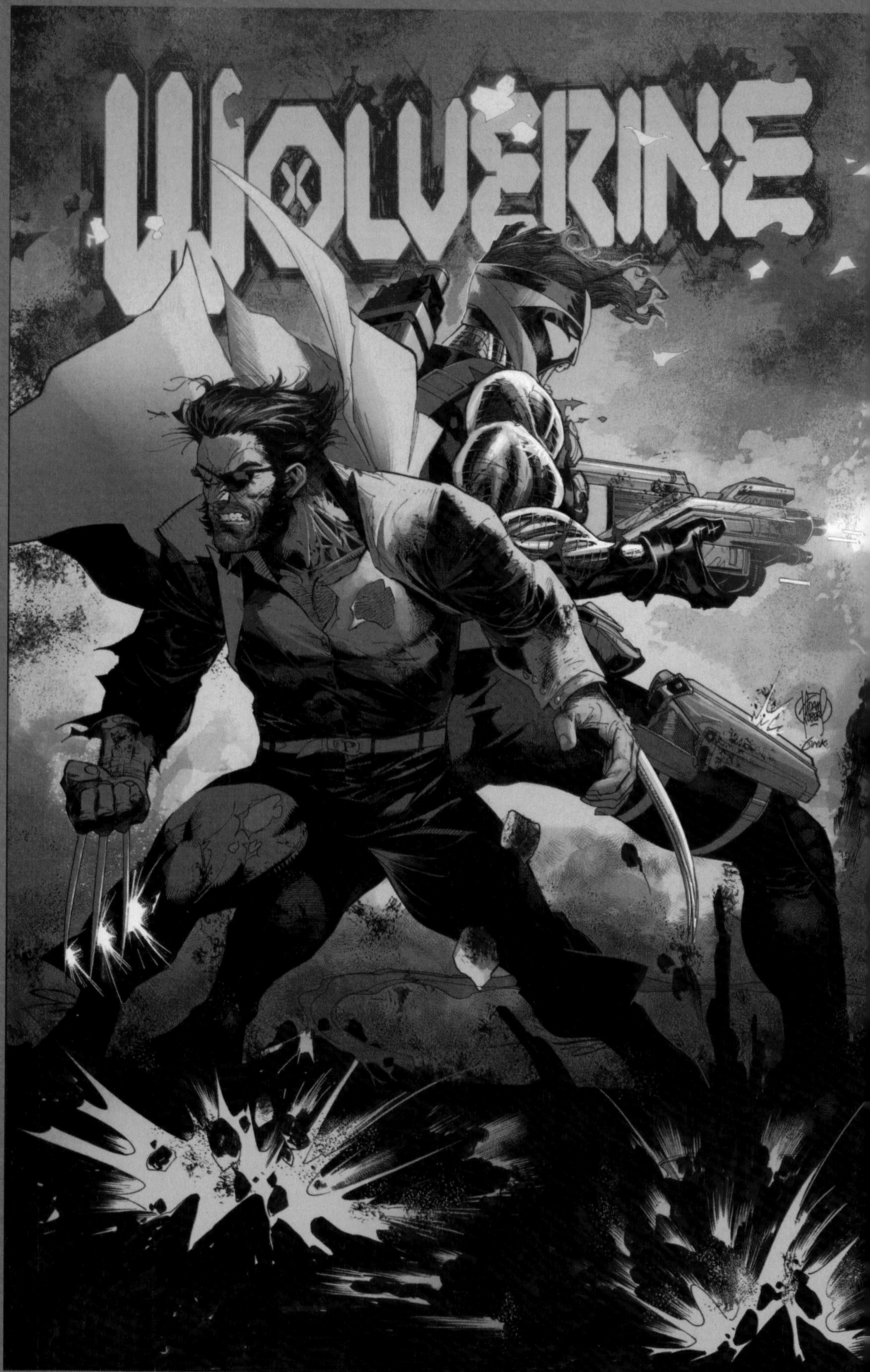
WOLVERINE

Mercenaries

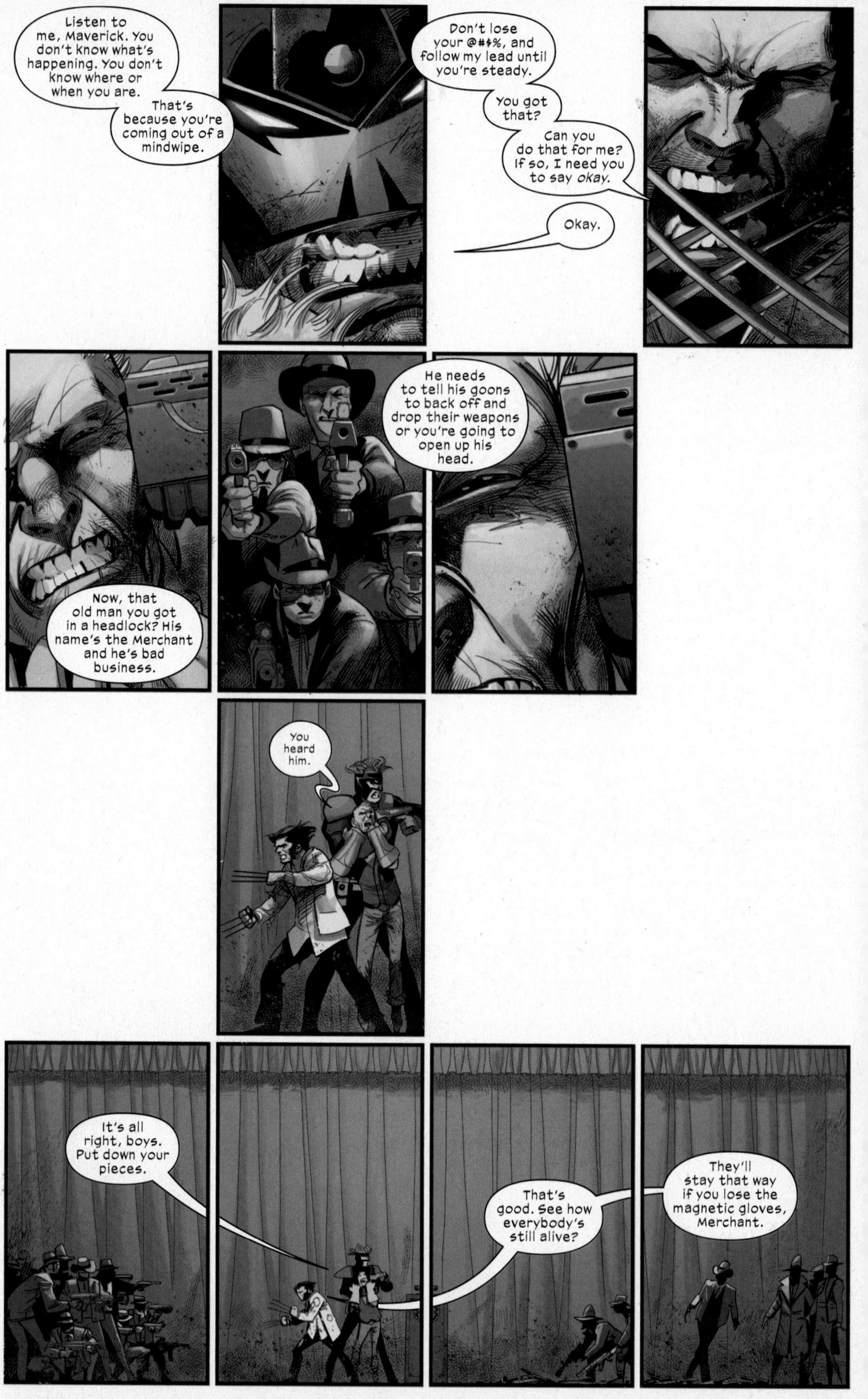
Listen to me, Maverick. You don't know what's happening. You don't know where or when you are.
That's because you're coming out of a mindwipe.
Don't lose your @#$%, and follow my lead until you're steady.
You got that?
Can you do that for me? If so, I need you to say *okay*.
Okay.
Now, that old man you got in a headlock? His name's the Merchant and he's bad business.
He needs to tell his goons to back off and drop their weapons or you're going to open up his head.
You heard him.
It's all right, boys. Put down your pieces.
That's good. See how everybody's still alive?
They'll stay that way if you lose the magnetic gloves, Merchant.

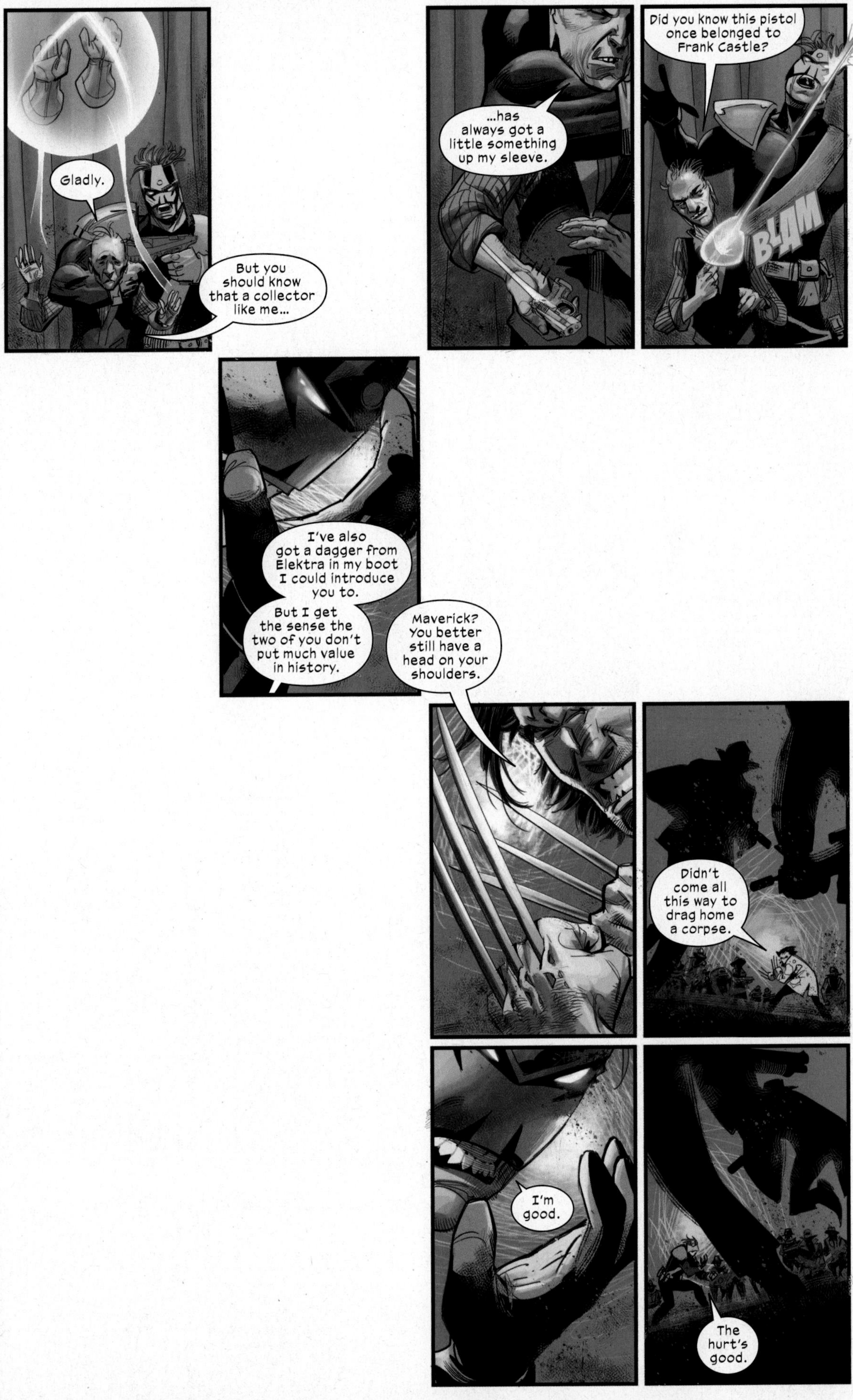
Gladly.
But you should know that a collector like me...
...has always got a little something up my sleeve.
Did you know this pistol once belonged to Frank Castle?
BLAM
I've also got a dagger from Elektra in my boot I could introduce you to.
But I get the sense the two of you don't put much value in history.
Maverick? You better still have a head on your shoulders.
Didn't come all this way to drag home a corpse.
I'm good.
The hurt's good.

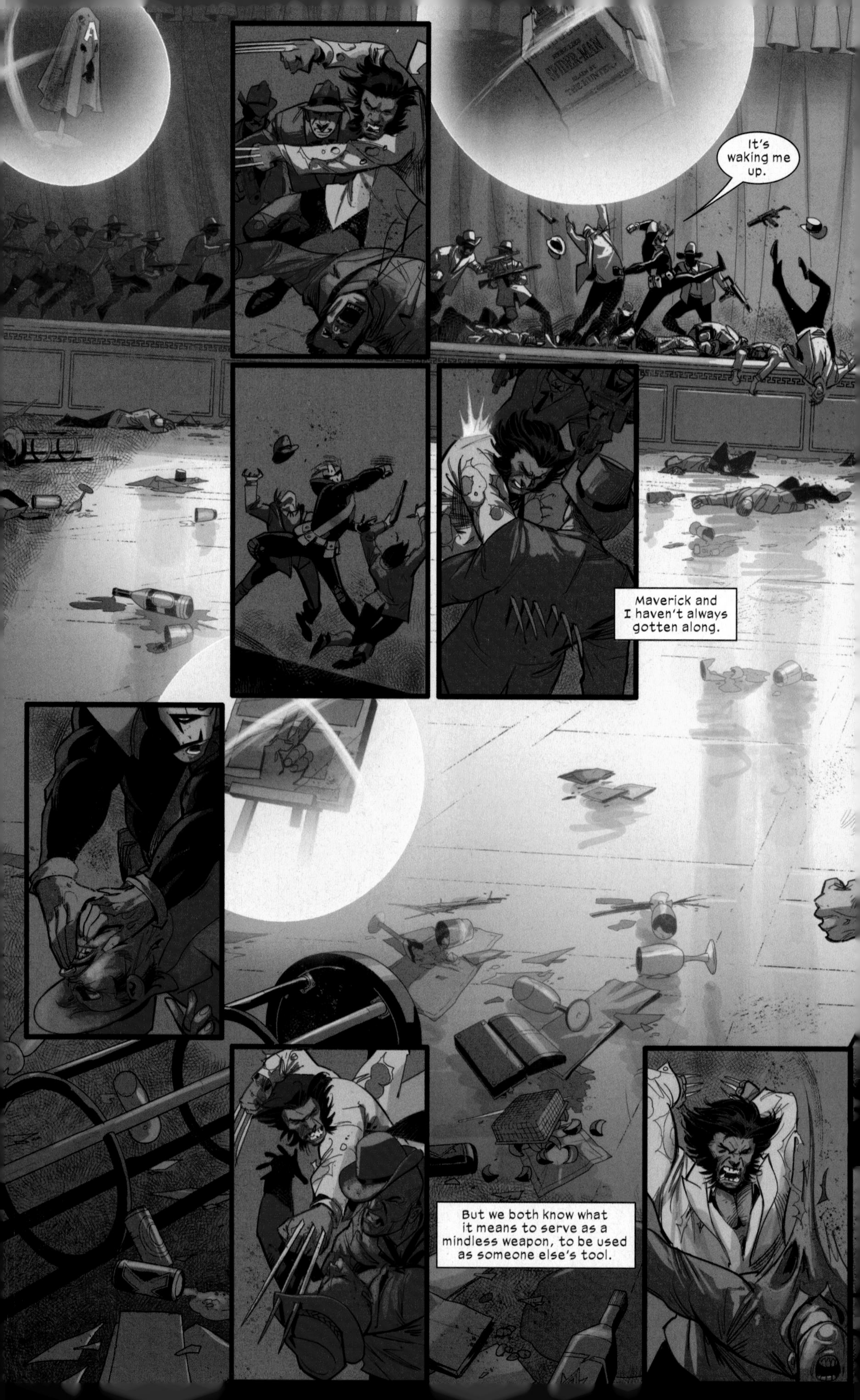
It's waking me up.
Maverick and I haven't always gotten along.
But we both know what it means to serve as a mindless weapon, to be used as someone else's tool.

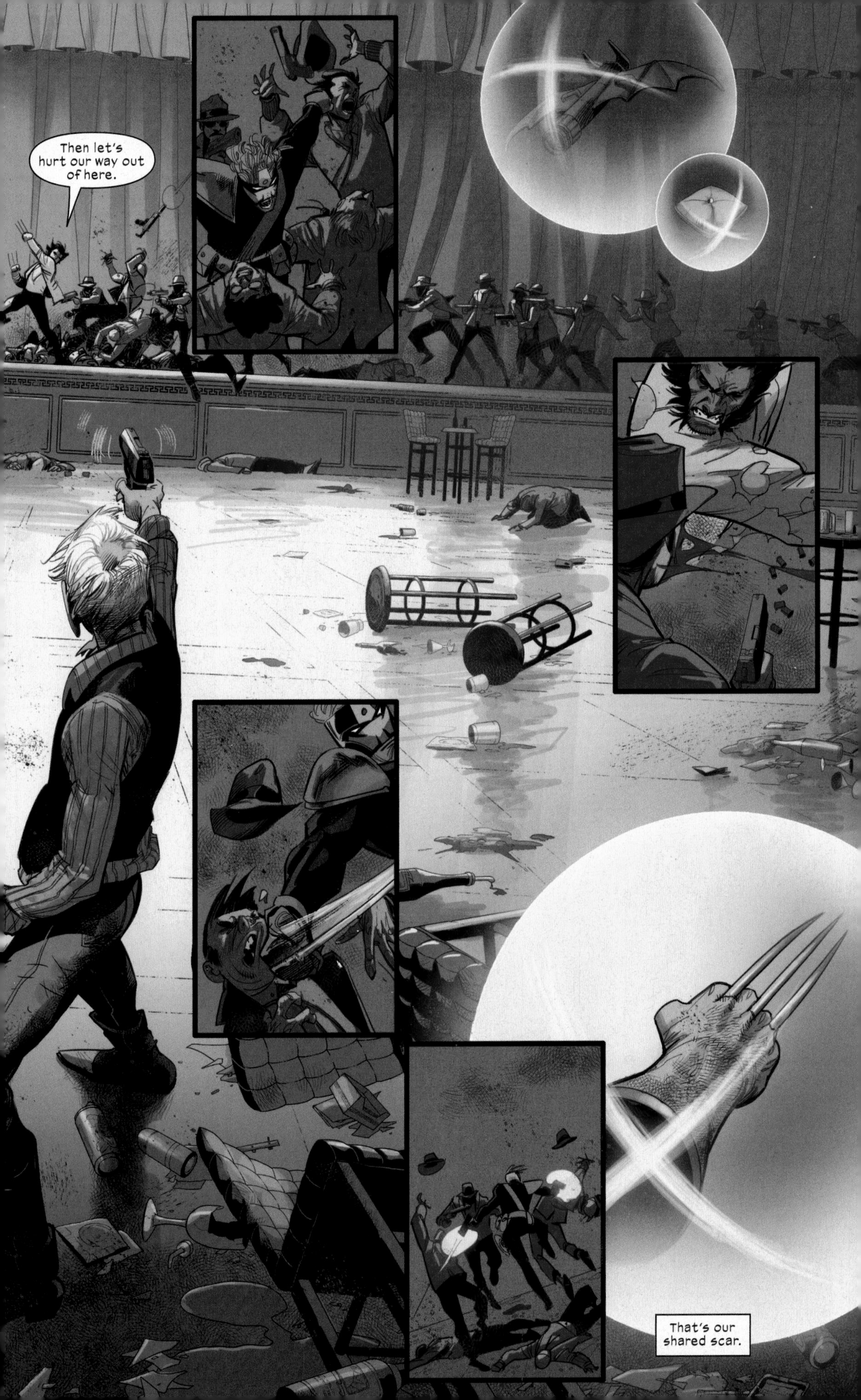
Then let's hurt our way out of here.
That's our shared scar.

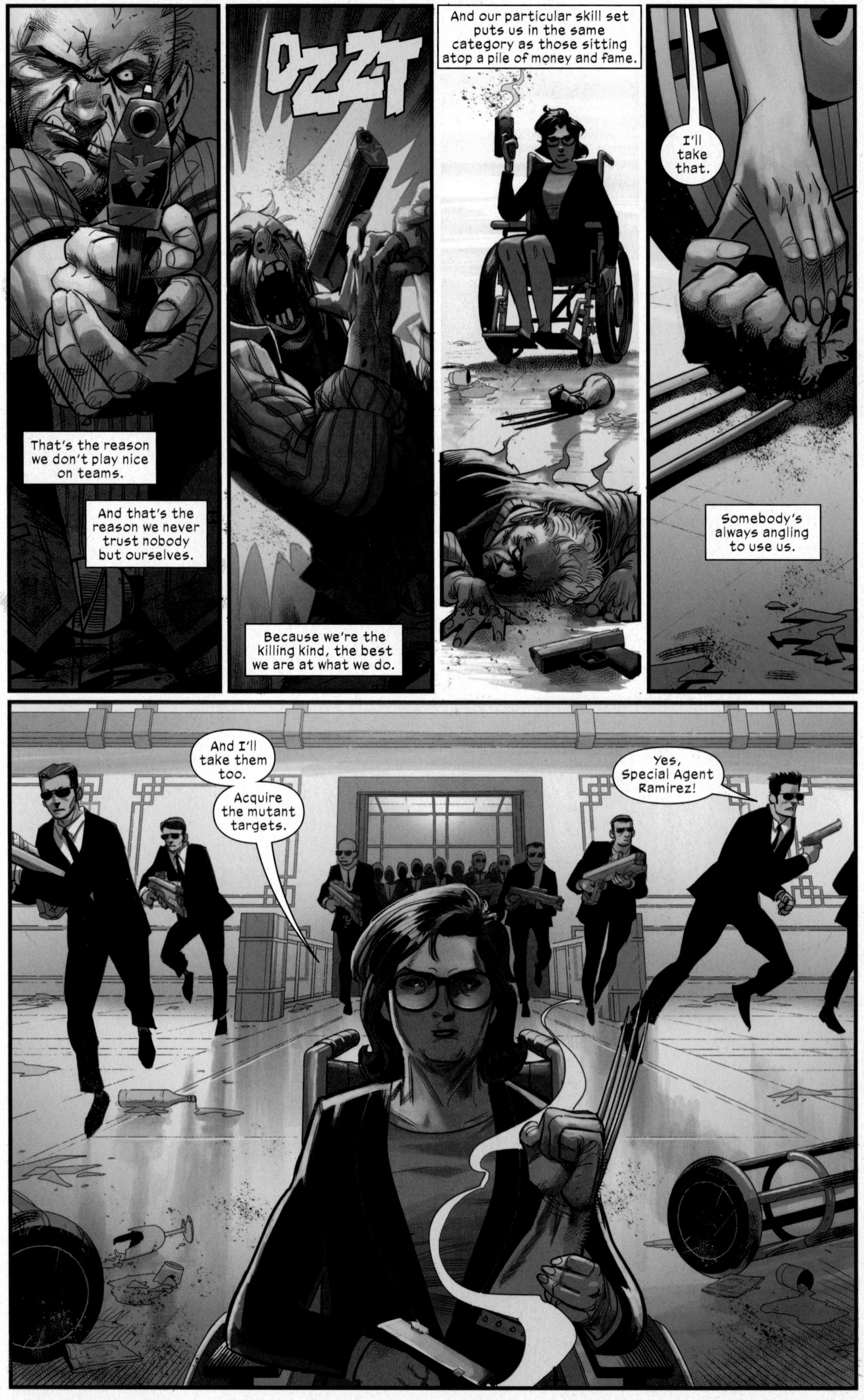
That's the reason we don't play nice on teams.
And that's the reason we never trust nobody but ourselves.
DZZT
Because we're the killing kind, the best we are at what we do.
And our particular skill set puts us in the same category as those sitting atop a pile of money and fame.
I'll take that.
Somebody's always angling to use us.
And I'll take them too.
Acquire the mutant targets.
Yes, Special Agent Ramirez!

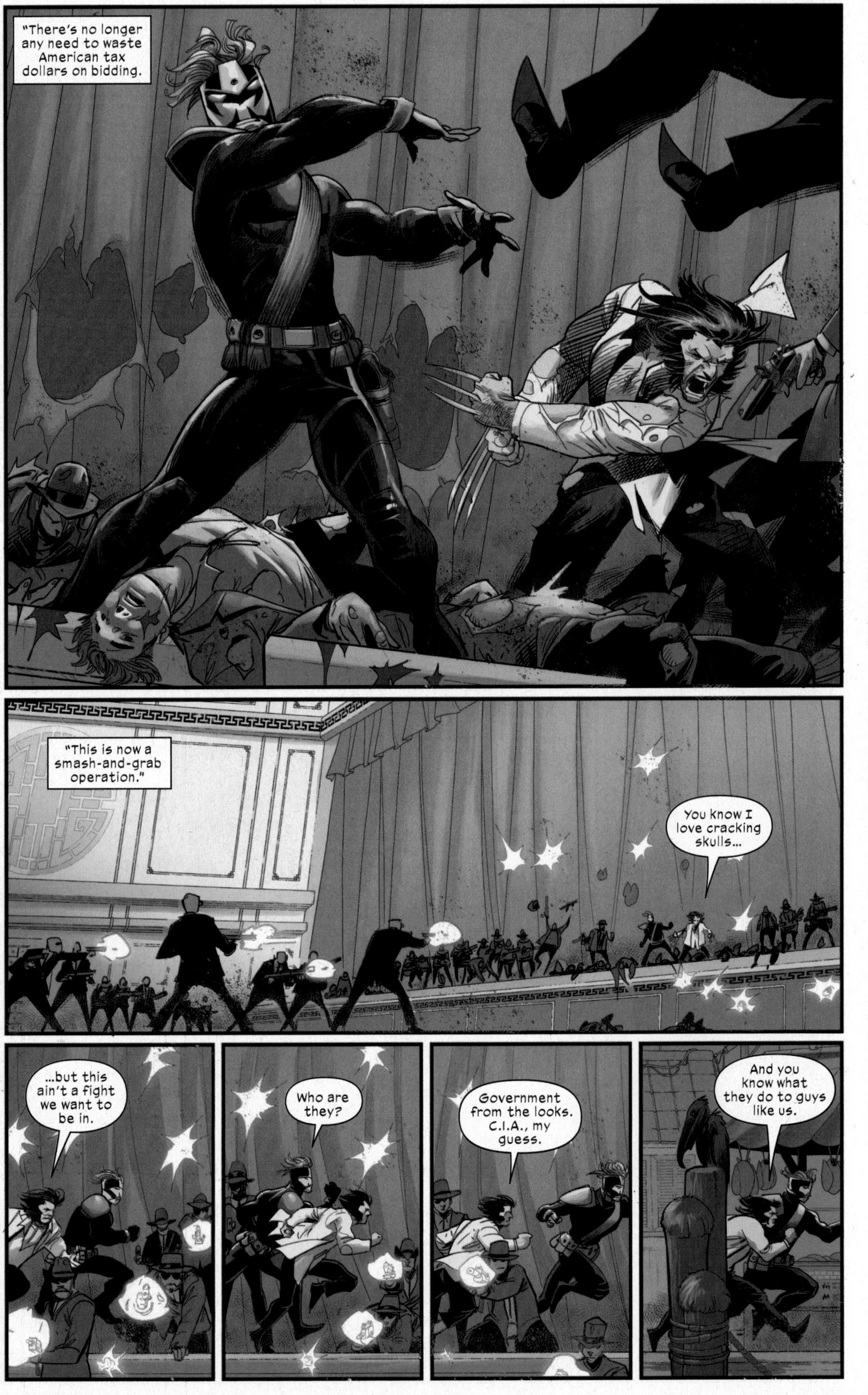
"There's no longer any need to waste American tax dollars on bidding.
"This is now a smash-and-grab operation."
You know I love cracking skulls...
...but this ain't a fight we want to be in.
Who are they?
Government from the looks. C.I.A., my guess.
And you know what they do to guys like us.

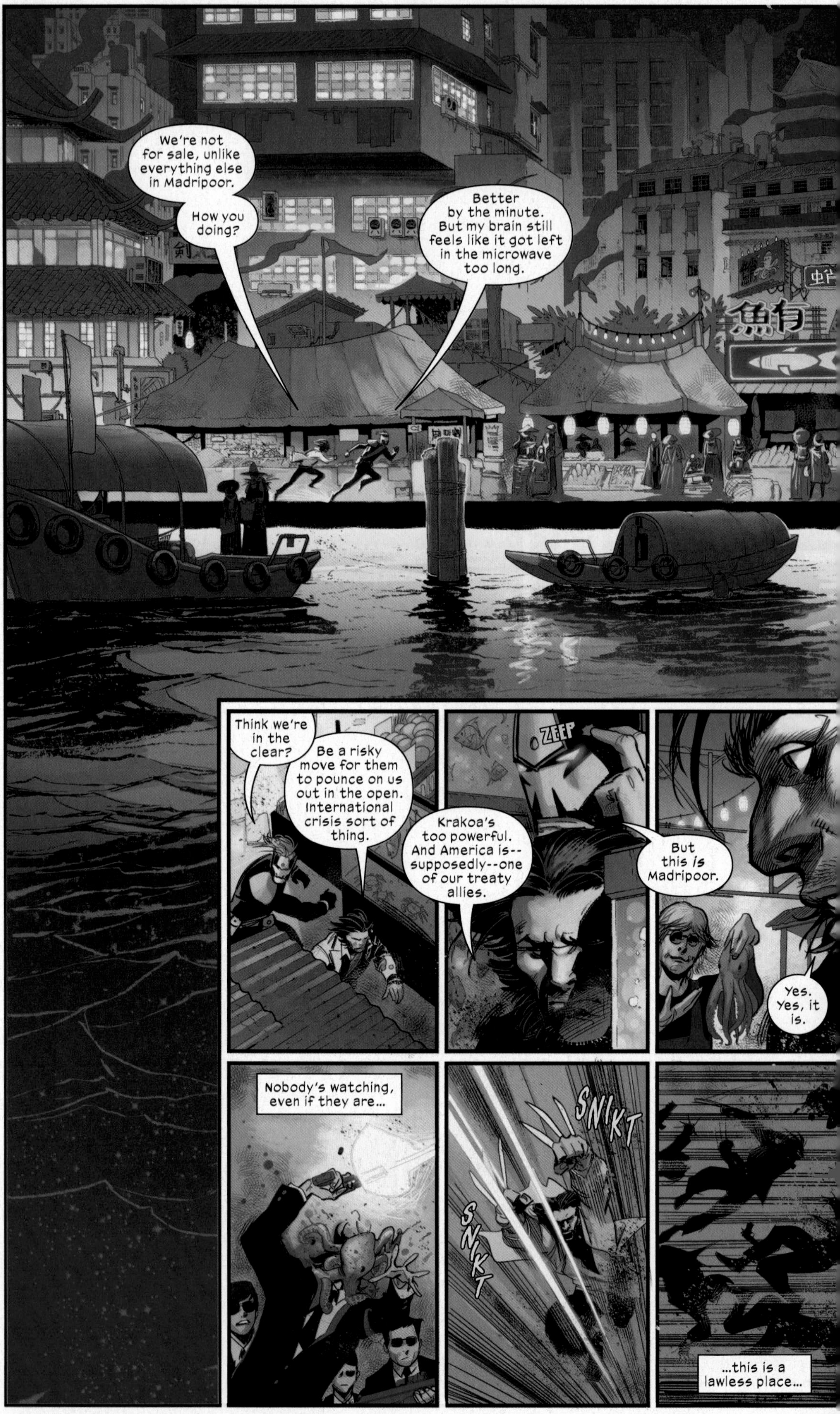

We're not for sale, unlike everything else in Madripoor.
How you doing?
Better by the minute. But my brain still feels like it got left in the microwave too long.
Think we're in the clear?
Be a risky move for them to pounce on us out in the open. International crisis sort of thing.
ZEEP
Krakoa's too powerful. And America is--supposedly--one of our treaty allies.
But this *is* Madripoor.
Yes. Yes, it is.
Nobody's watching, even if they are...
SNIKT
SNIKT
...this is a lawless place...

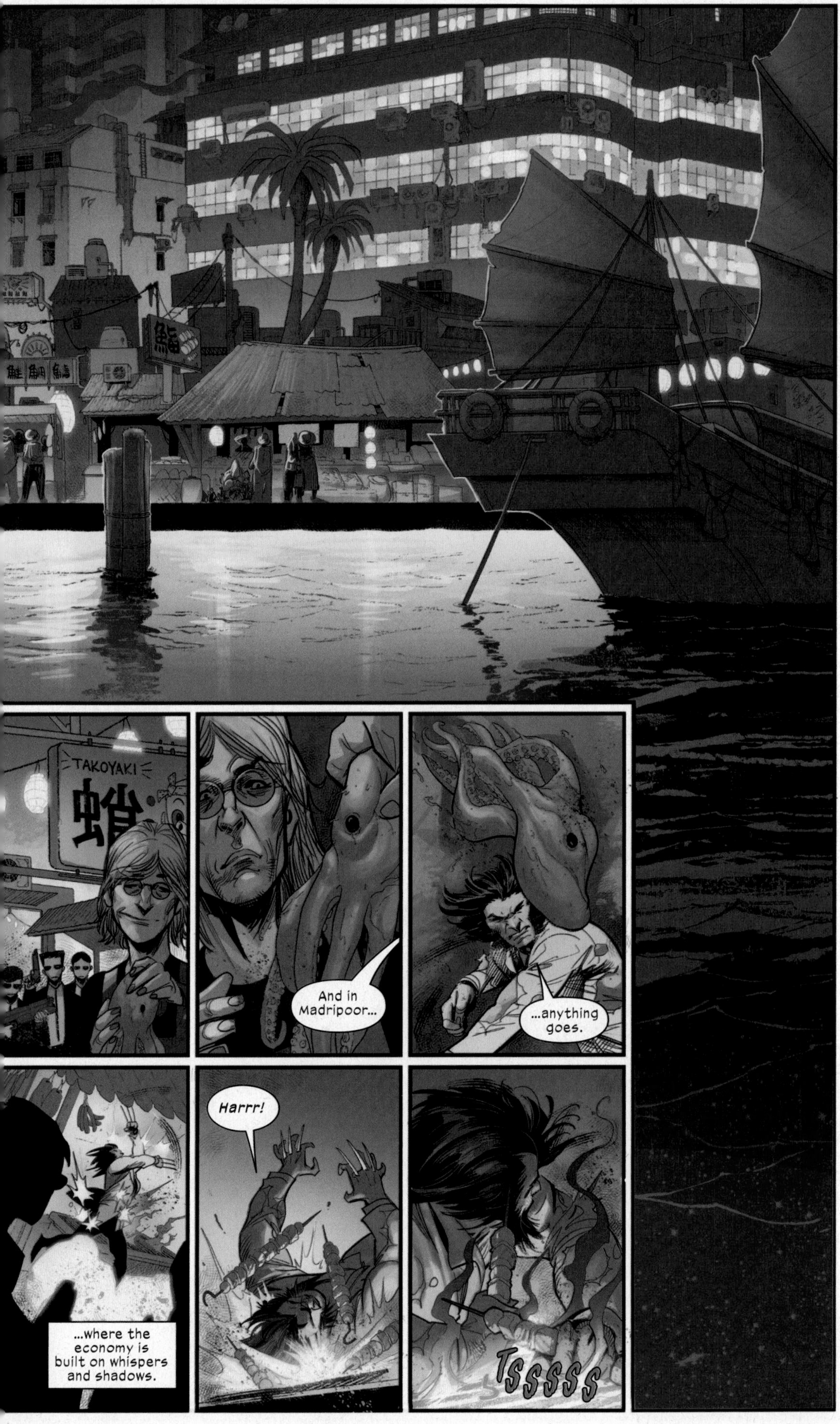
TAKOYAKI
And in Madripoor...
...anything goes.
...where the economy is built on whispers and shadows.
Harrr!
TSSSSS

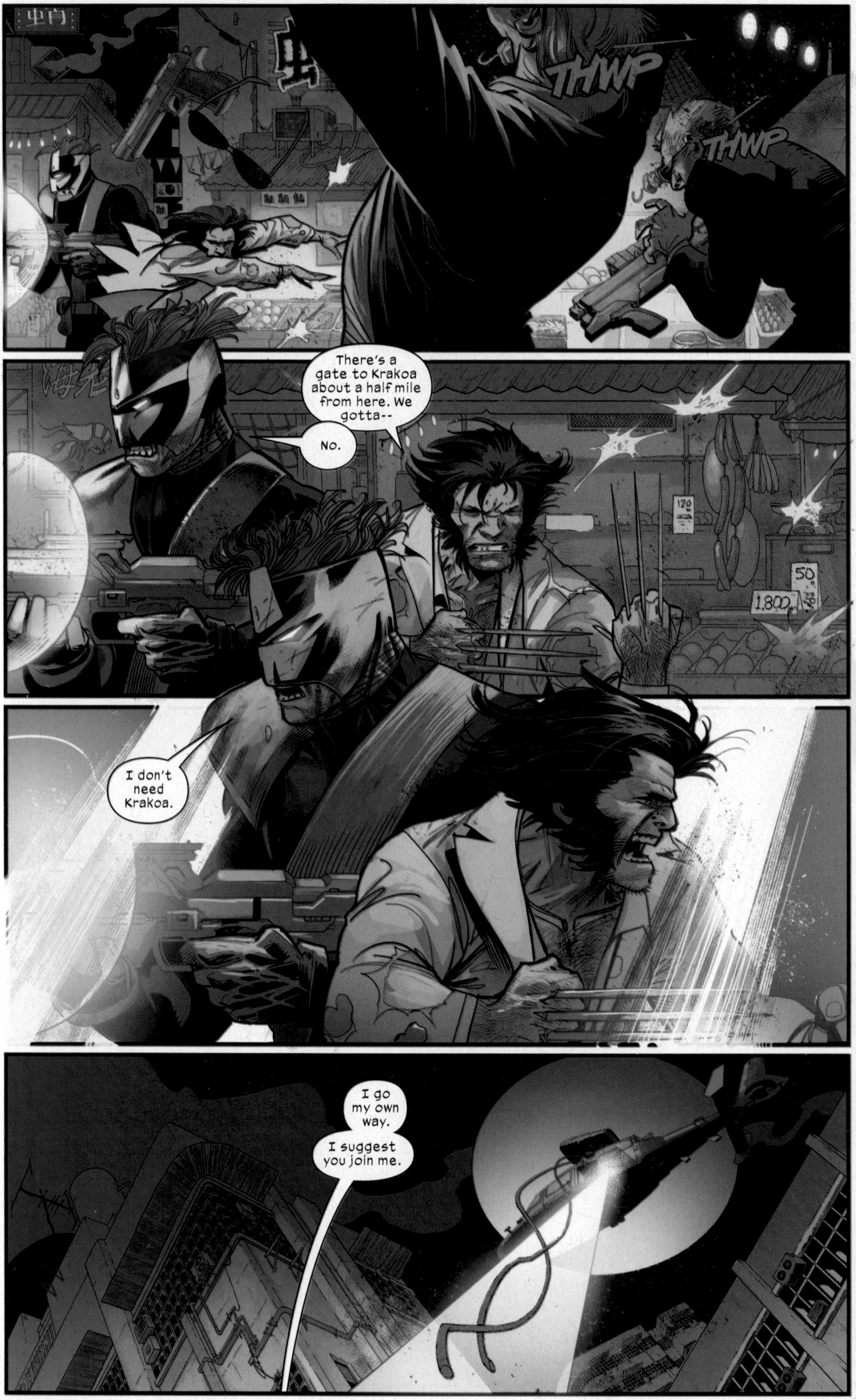
THWP
THWP
There's a gate to Krakoa about a half mile from here. We gotta--
No.
I don't need Krakoa.
I go my own way.
I suggest you join me.

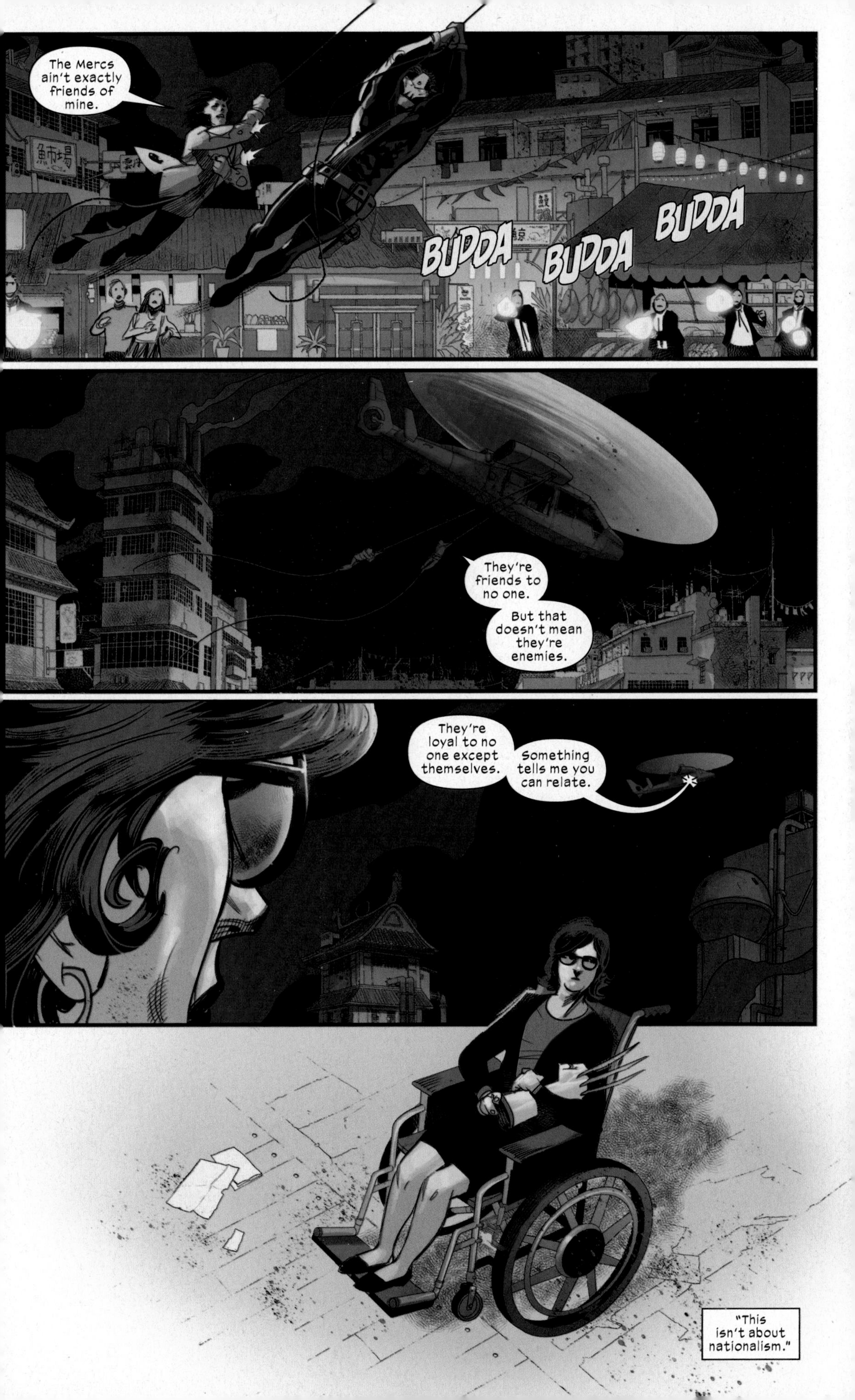
The Mercs ain't exactly friends of mine.
BUDDA
BUDDA
BUDDA
They're friends to no one.
But that doesn't mean they're enemies.
They're loyal to no one except themselves.
Something tells me you can relate.
"This isn't about nationalism."

[reign_of_x]

[best__]
[there_]

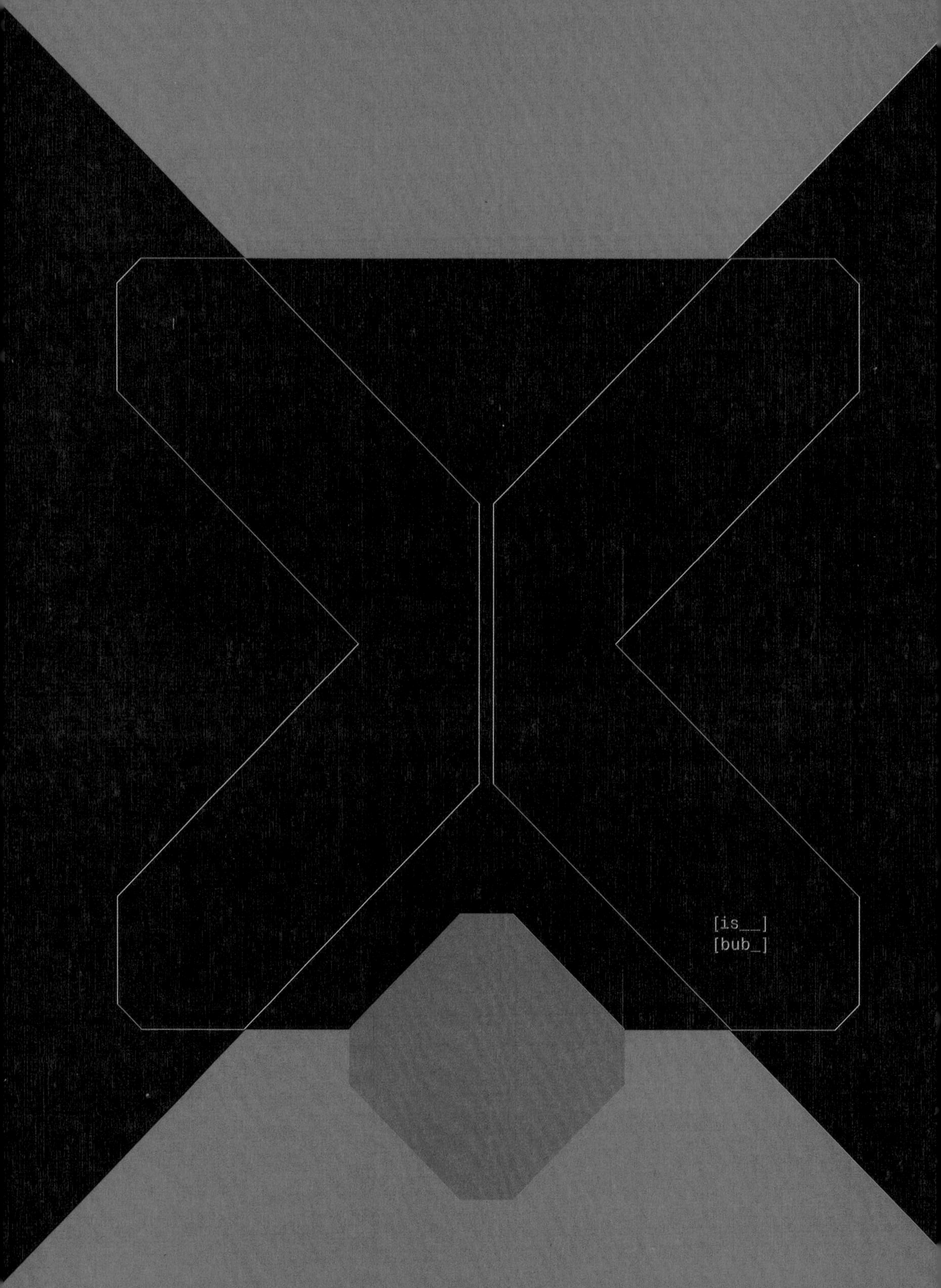
[is__]
[bub_]

C.I.A. PHONE LOG

Decrypted /// Analog Scramble///

Caller Identification: Special Agent Delores Ramirez /// X-Desk

Ramirez: We failed to acquire the target.

Director: You were outbid?

Ramirez: Outgunned.

<Silence lasting ten seconds>

Director: You assured me this would be a quiet operation.

Ramirez: I didn't anticipate Wolverine's presence. He's an agent of chaos.

Director: Please tell me you haven't jeopardized the treaty?

Ramirez: Not exactly.

Director: Not exactly? That's a half-assed answer to what could be a politically and economically calamitous reality. You assured me --

Ramirez: I assured you that anything goes in Madripoor. What happens there stays there. We're fine.

Director: We are far from fine.

Ramirez: Yes, the mutants will know we made a move, but they're not going to do anything about it. Because they're back-alleying on their promises as much as we are. That's why the X-Desk is so necessary.

Director: I'm honestly starting to question whether that's true. The last thing I need is --

Ramirez: I know how to rectify the situation.

Director: Oh?

Ramirez: Our goal was to buy Maverick, yes?

Director: Your goal.

Ramirez: I believe a more transactional approach is still possible. If the auction funds are still available to me?

Director: Keep talking.

<Signal lost>

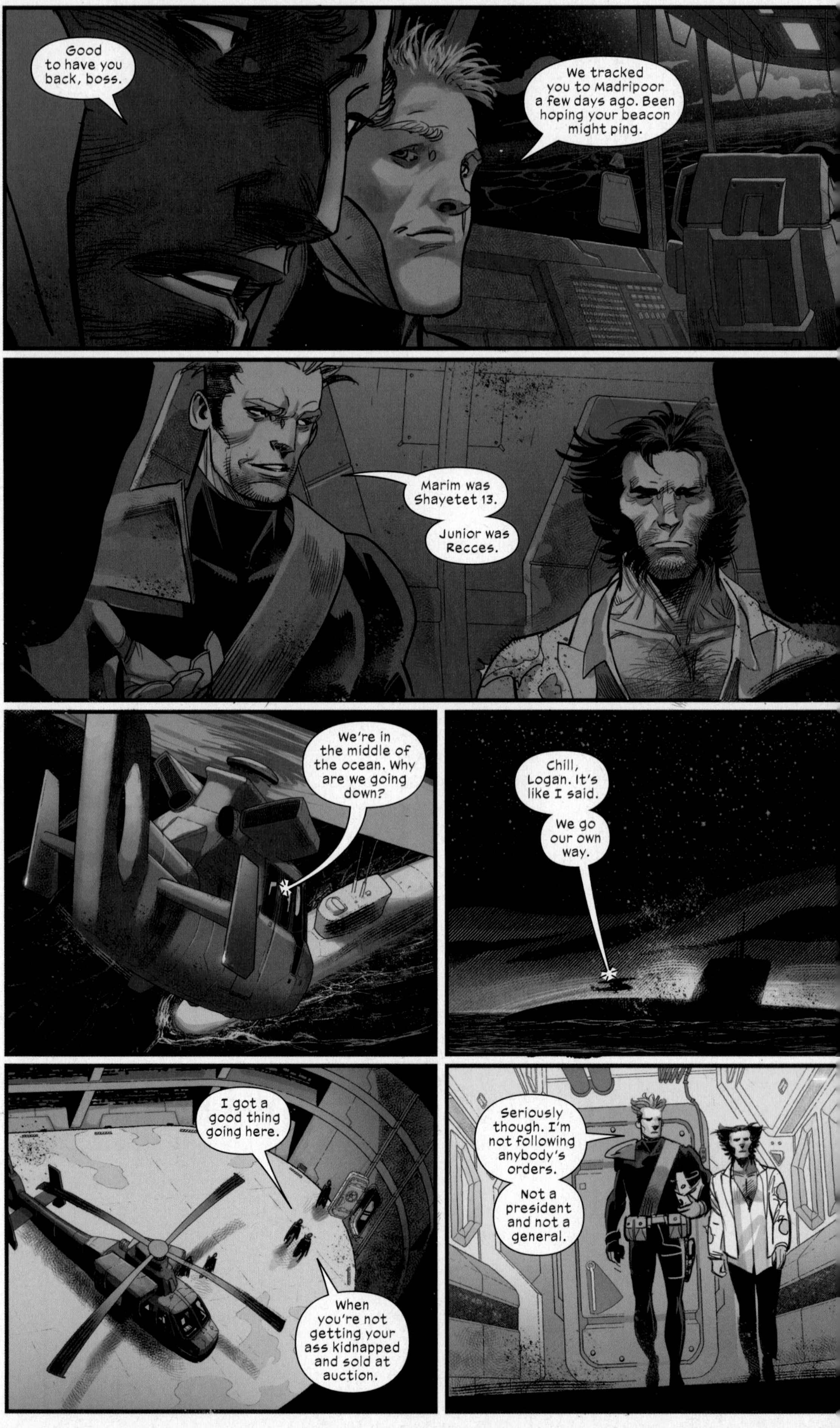
Good to have you back, boss.
We tracked you to Madripoor a few days ago. Been hoping your beacon might ping.
Marim was Shayetet 13.
Junior was Recces.
We're in the middle of the ocean. Why are we going down?
Chill, Logan. It's like I said.
We go our own way.
I got a good thing going here.
When you're not getting your ass kidnapped and sold at auction.
Seriously though. I'm not following anybody's orders.
Not a president and not a general.

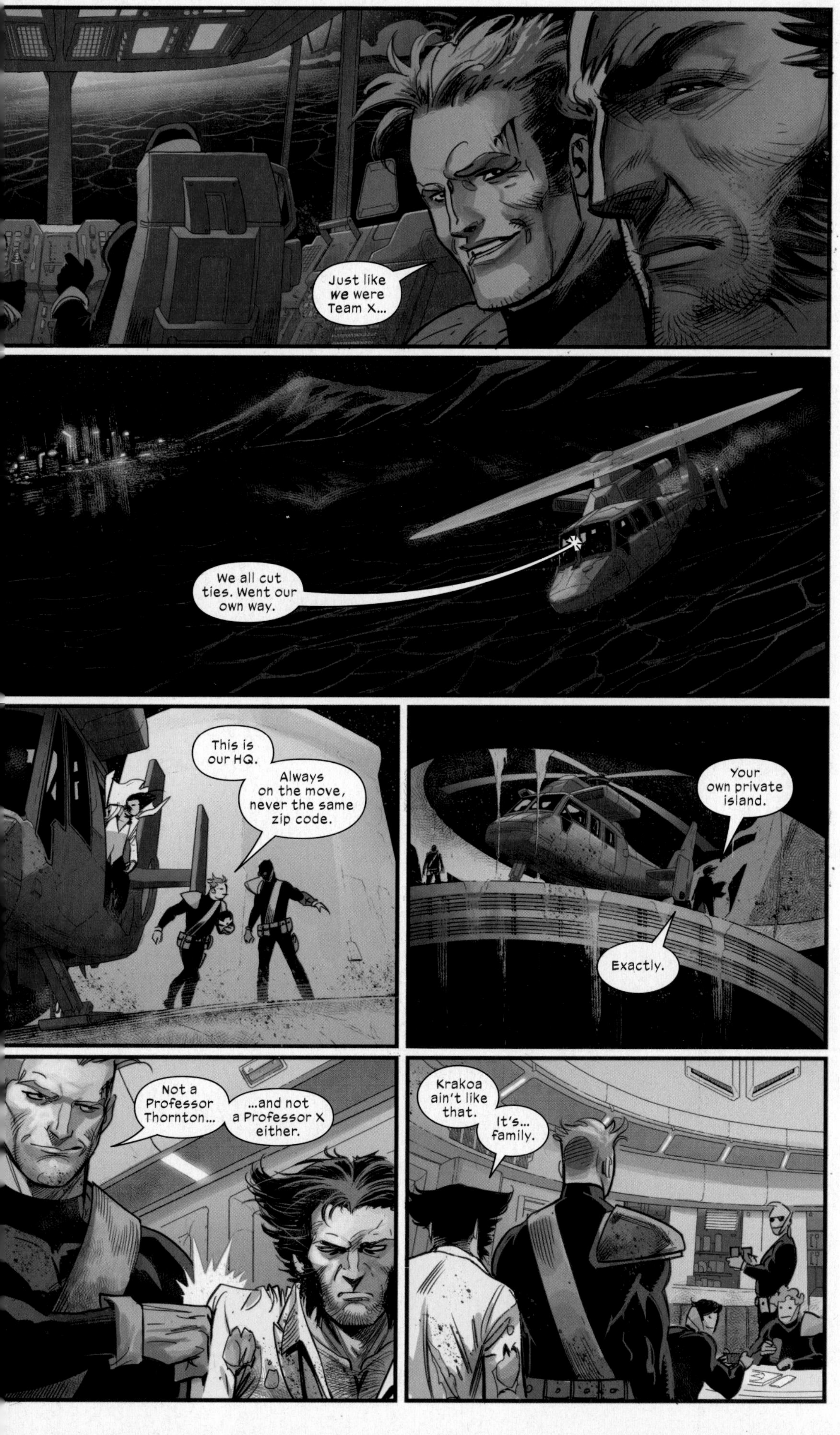
Just like we were Team X...
We all cut ties. Went our own way.
This is our HQ.
Always on the move, never the same zip code.
Your own private island.
Exactly.
Not a Professor Thornton...
...and not a Professor X either.
Krakoa ain't like that.
It's... family.

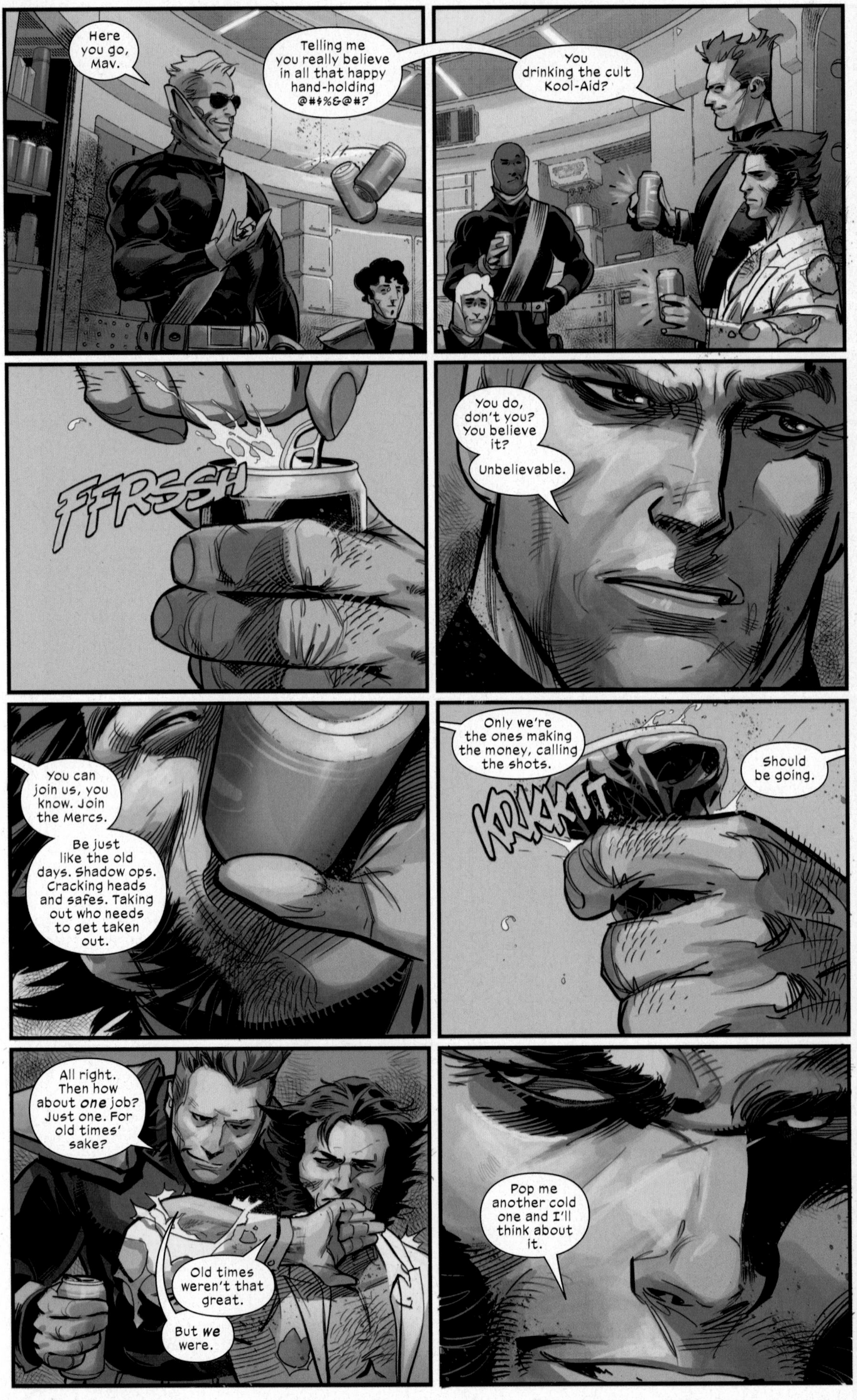
Here you go, Mav.
Telling me you really believe in all that happy hand-holding @#$%&@#?
You drinking the cult Kool-Aid?
FFRSSH
You do, don't you? You believe it?
Unbelievable.
You can join us, you know. Join the Mercs.
Be just like the old days. Shadow ops. Cracking heads and safes. Taking out who needs to get taken out.
Only we're the ones making the money, calling the shots.
KRUKTT
Should be going.
All right. Then how about *one* job? Just one. For old times' sake?
Old times weren't that great.
But *we* were.
Pop me another cold one and I'll think about it.

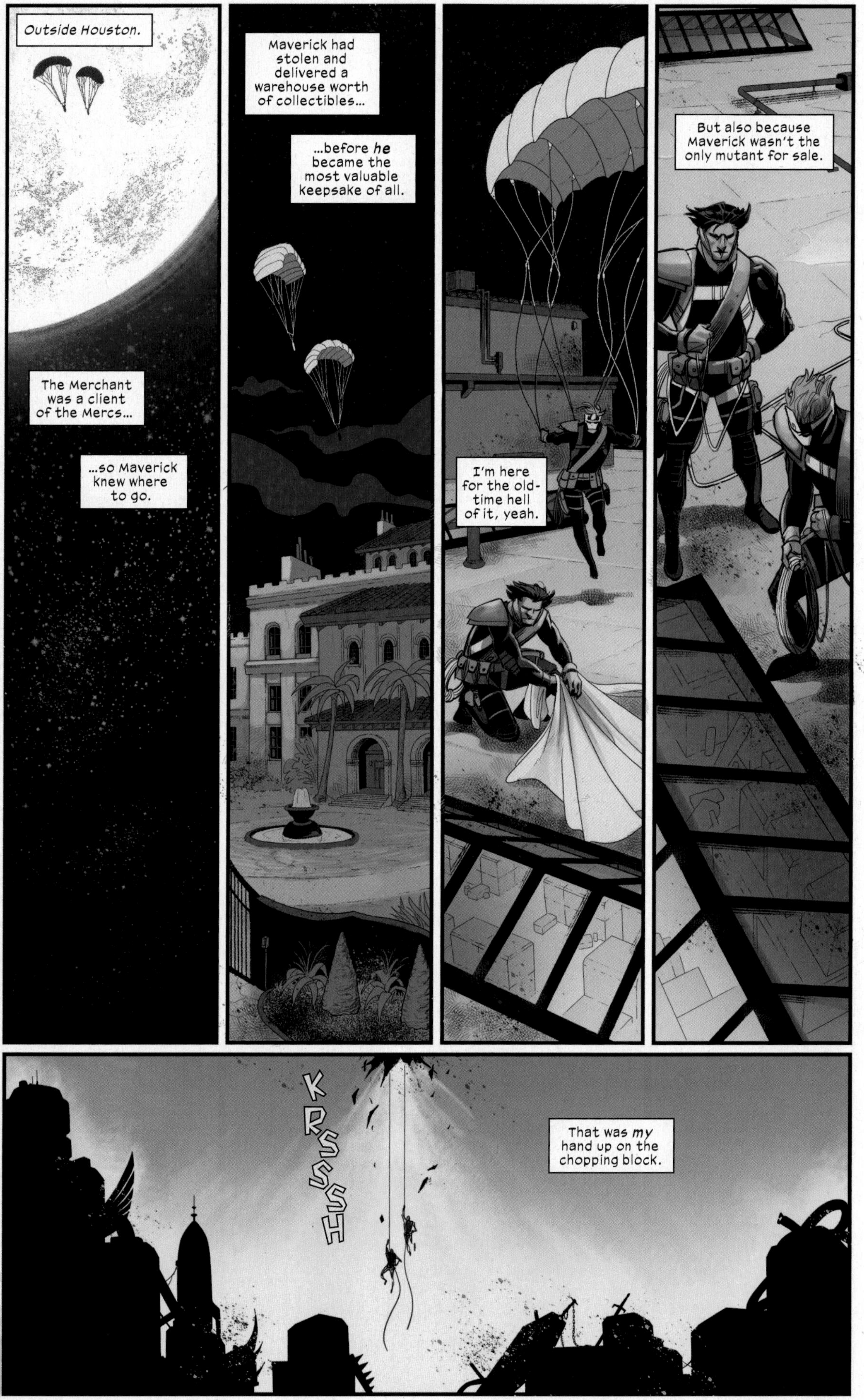

Outside Houston.
The Merchant was a client of the Mercs...
...so Maverick knew where to go.
Maverick had stolen and delivered a warehouse worth of collectibles...
...before he became the most valuable keepsake of all.
I'm here for the old-time hell of it, yeah.
But also because Maverick wasn't the only mutant for sale.
KRSSSH
That was my hand up on the chopping block.

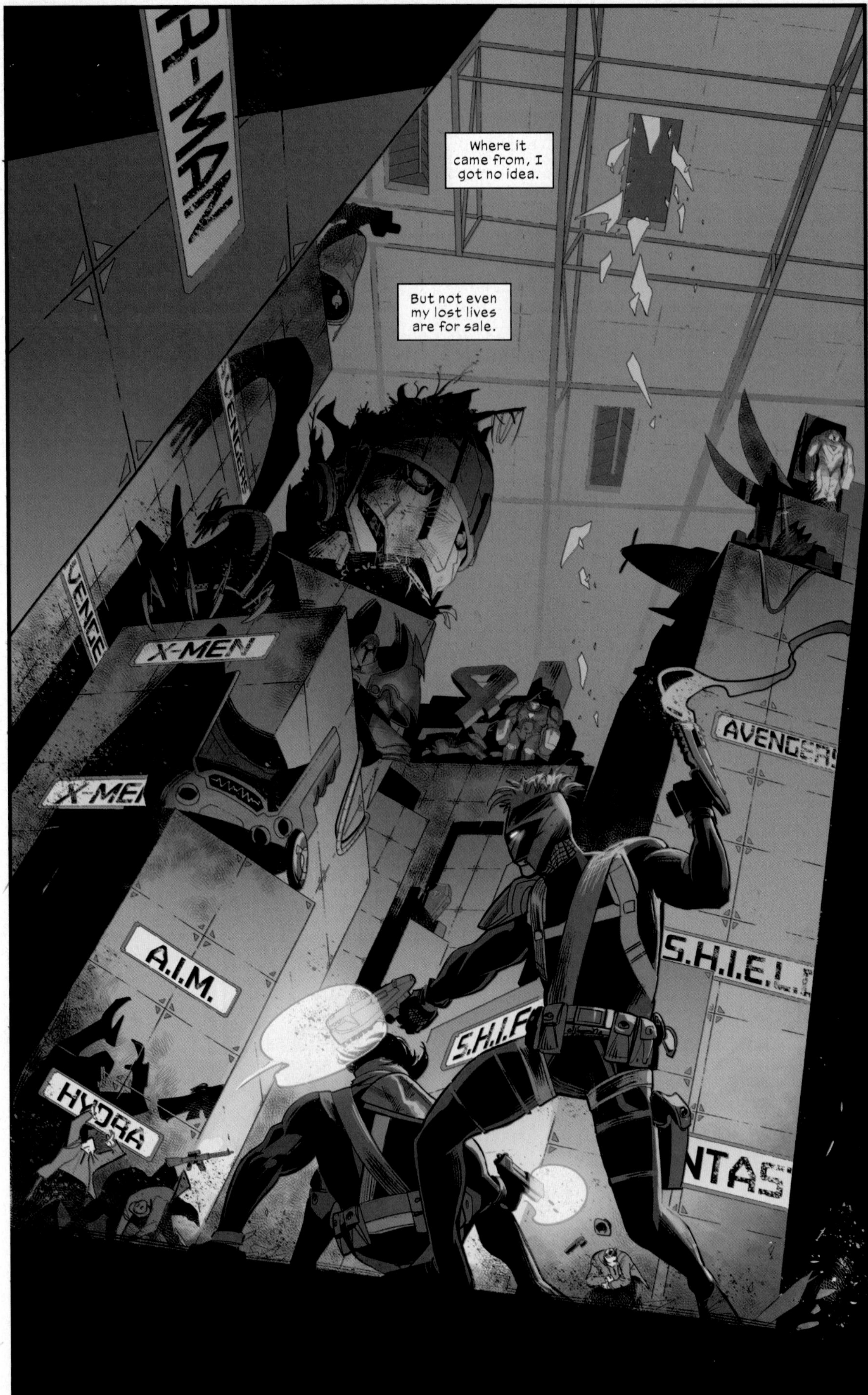
Where it came from, I got no idea.
But not even my lost lives are for sale.
X-MEN
AVENGERS
X-MEN
A.I.M.
S.H.I.E.L.D.
HYDRA

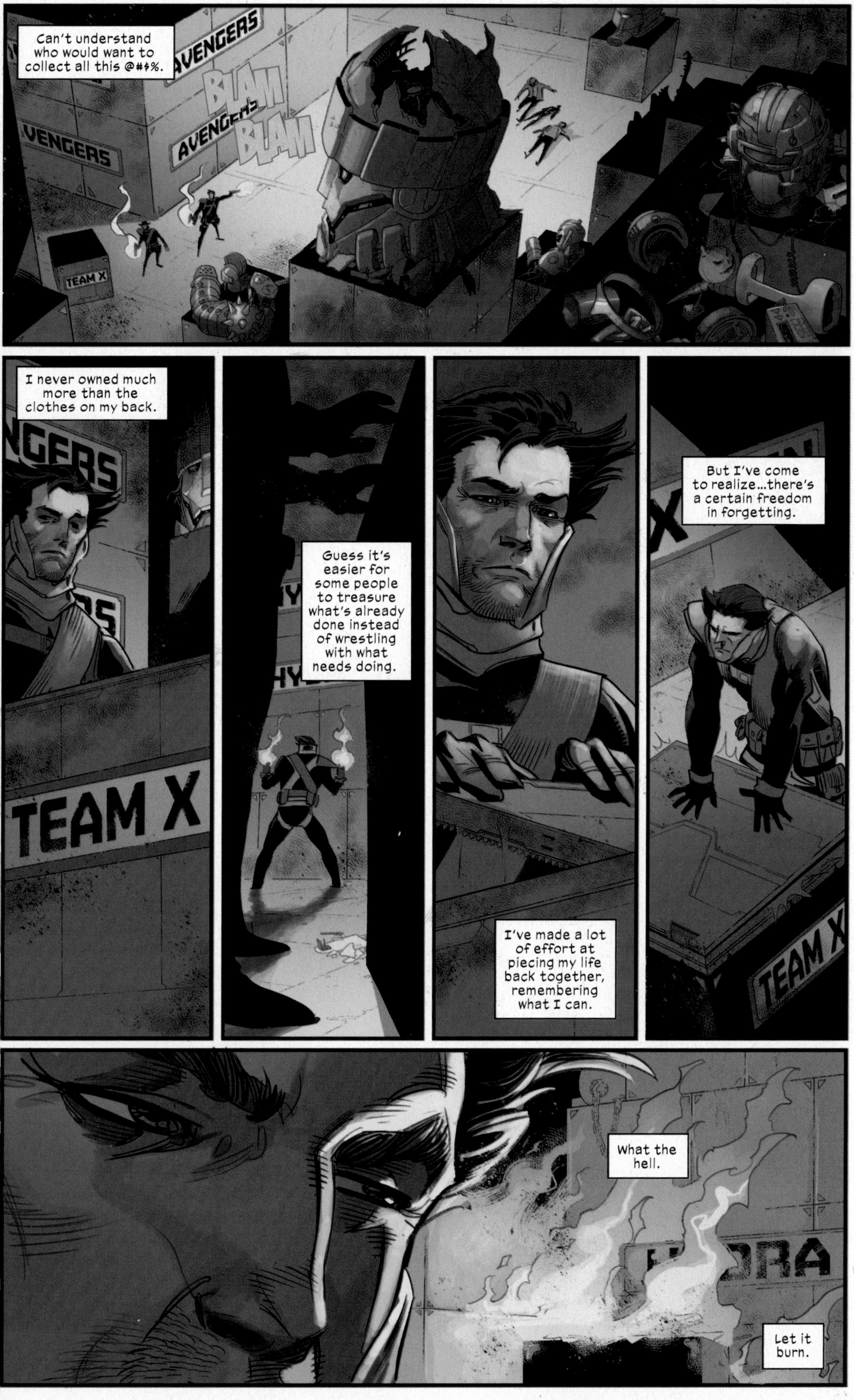
Can't understand who would want to collect all this @#$%.
AVENGERS
BLAM
AVENGERS
BLAM
VENGERS
TEAM X
I never owned much more than the clothes on my back.
TEAM X
Guess it's easier for some people to treasure what's already done instead of wrestling with what needs doing.
I've made a lot of effort at piecing my life back together, remembering what I can.
But I've come to realize...there's a certain freedom in forgetting.
TEAM X
What the hell.
Let it burn.

[reign_of_x]

[best__]
[there_]

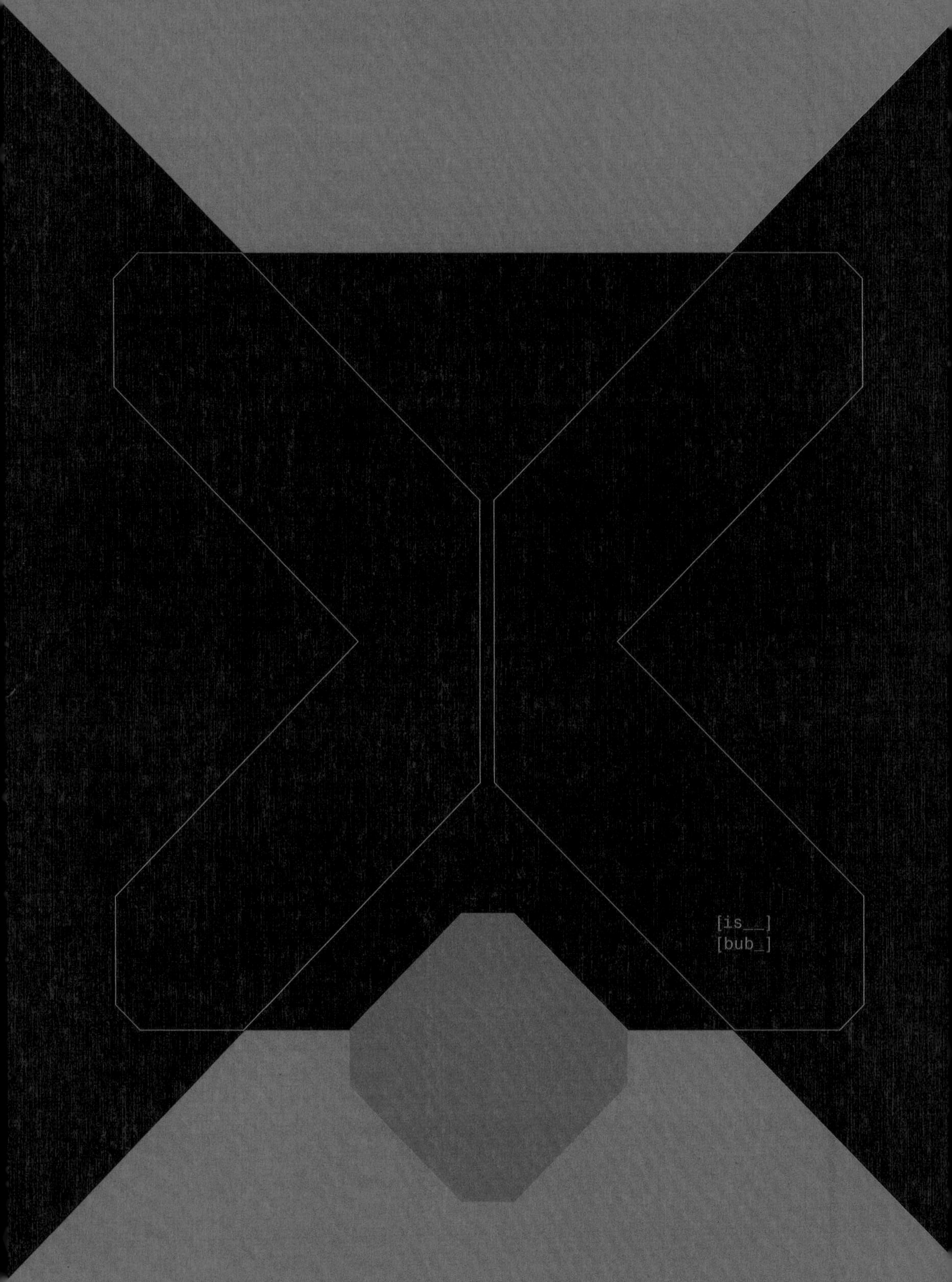
[is__]
[bub_]

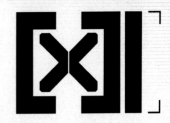

X-FACTOR LOGBOOK

Mutant: Wolverine

Subject: Lost Lives

Resurrection Query: Logan requests a full review of his resurrection log, citing an aberration encountered during a recent operation.

The presence of a severed hand -- allegedly his own -- indicates:

>> possible anomaly in death logs >>

>> possible relic of Weapon X clone >>

>> possible genomic experiment by XENO >>

>> *collating* >>

>> *collating* >>

>> *collating* >>

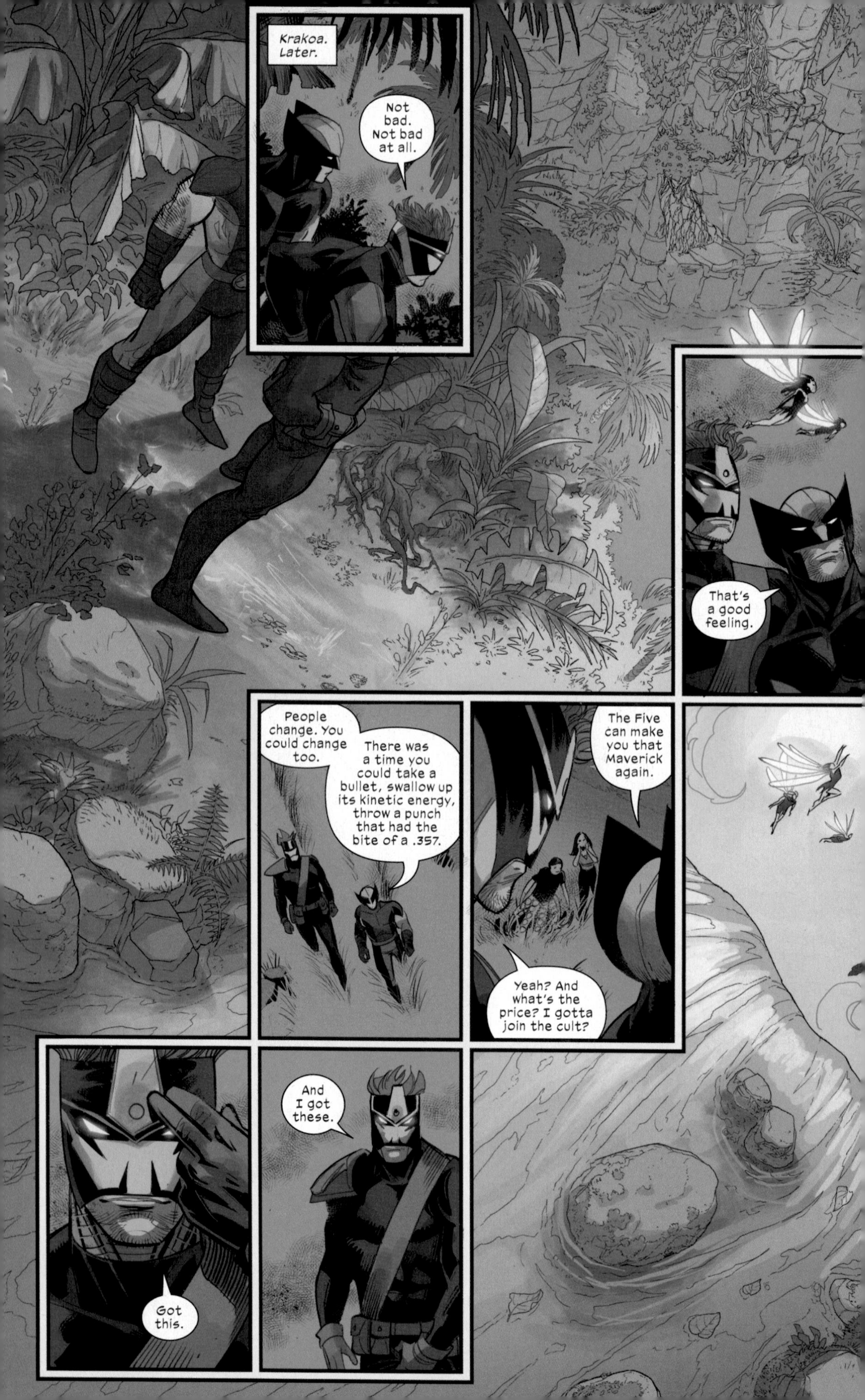
Krakoa. Later.
Not bad. Not bad at all.
That's a good feeling.
People change. You could change too.
There was a time you could take a bullet, swallow up its kinetic energy, throw a punch that had the bite of a .357.
The Five can make you that Maverick again.
Yeah? And what's the price? I gotta join the cult?
Got this.
And I got these.

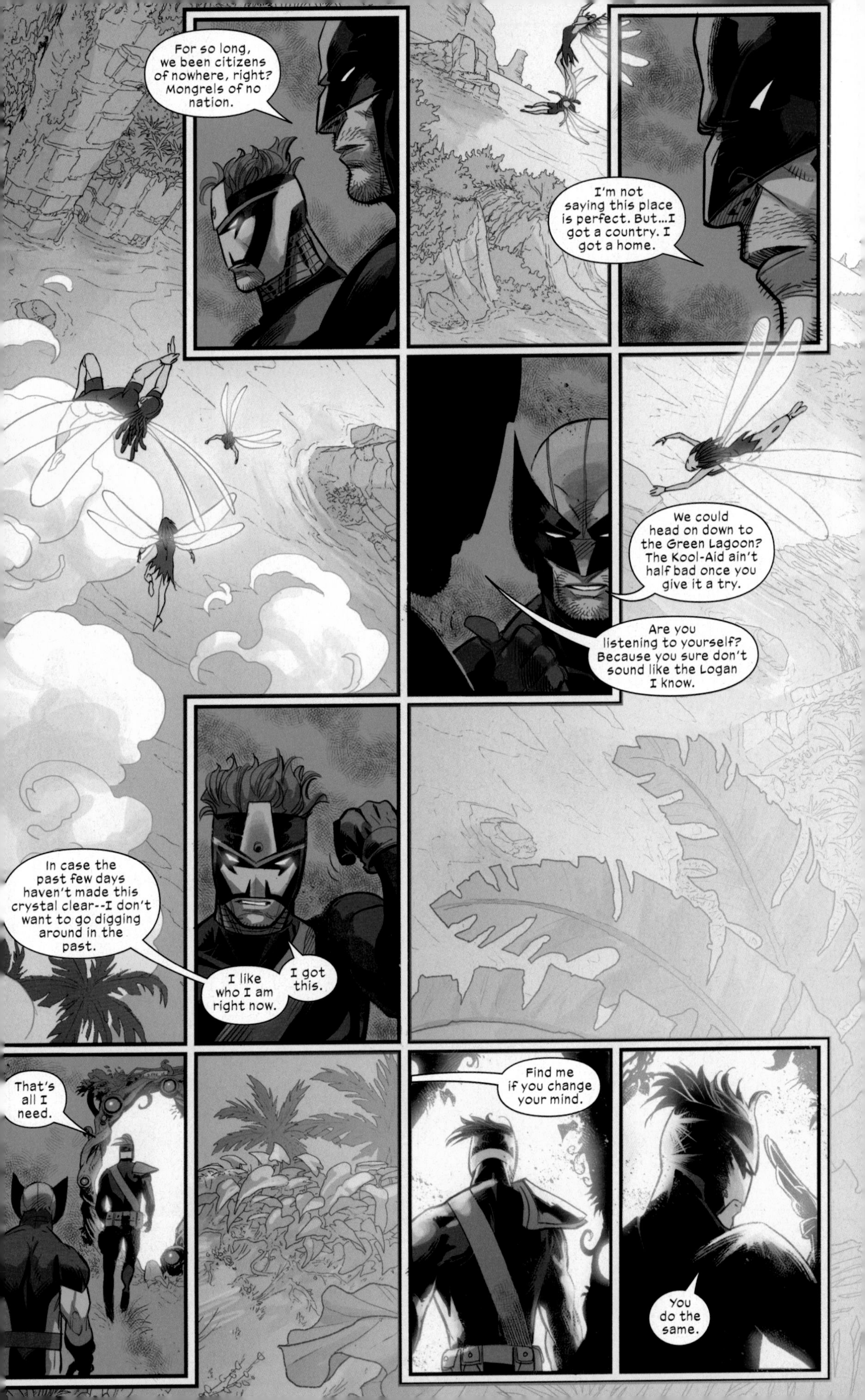
For so long, we been citizens of nowhere, right? Mongrels of no nation.
I'm not saying this place is perfect. But...I got a country. I got a home.
We could head on down to the Green Lagoon? The Kool-Aid ain't half bad once you give it a try.
Are you listening to yourself? Because you sure don't sound like the Logan I know.
In case the past few days haven't made this crystal clear--I don't want to go digging around in the past.
I like who I am right now.
I got this.
That's all I need.
Find me if you change your mind.
You do the same.

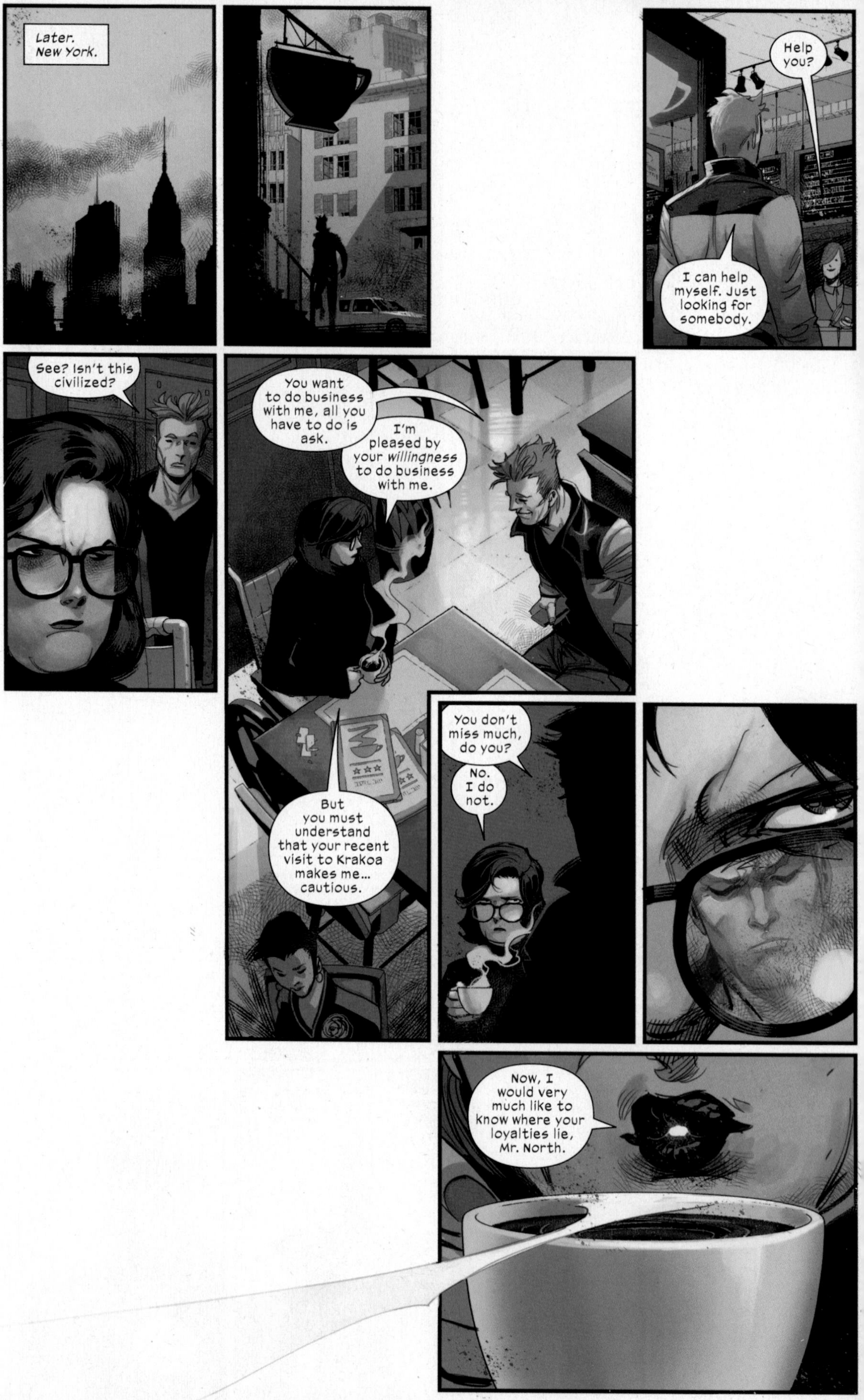
Later. New York.
Help you?
I can help myself. Just looking for somebody.
See? Isn't this civilized?
You want to do business with me, all you have to do is ask.
I'm pleased by your *willingness* to do business with me.
But you must understand that your recent visit to Krakoa makes me... cautious.
You don't miss much, do you?
No. I do not.
Now, I would very much like to know where your loyalties lie, Mr. North.

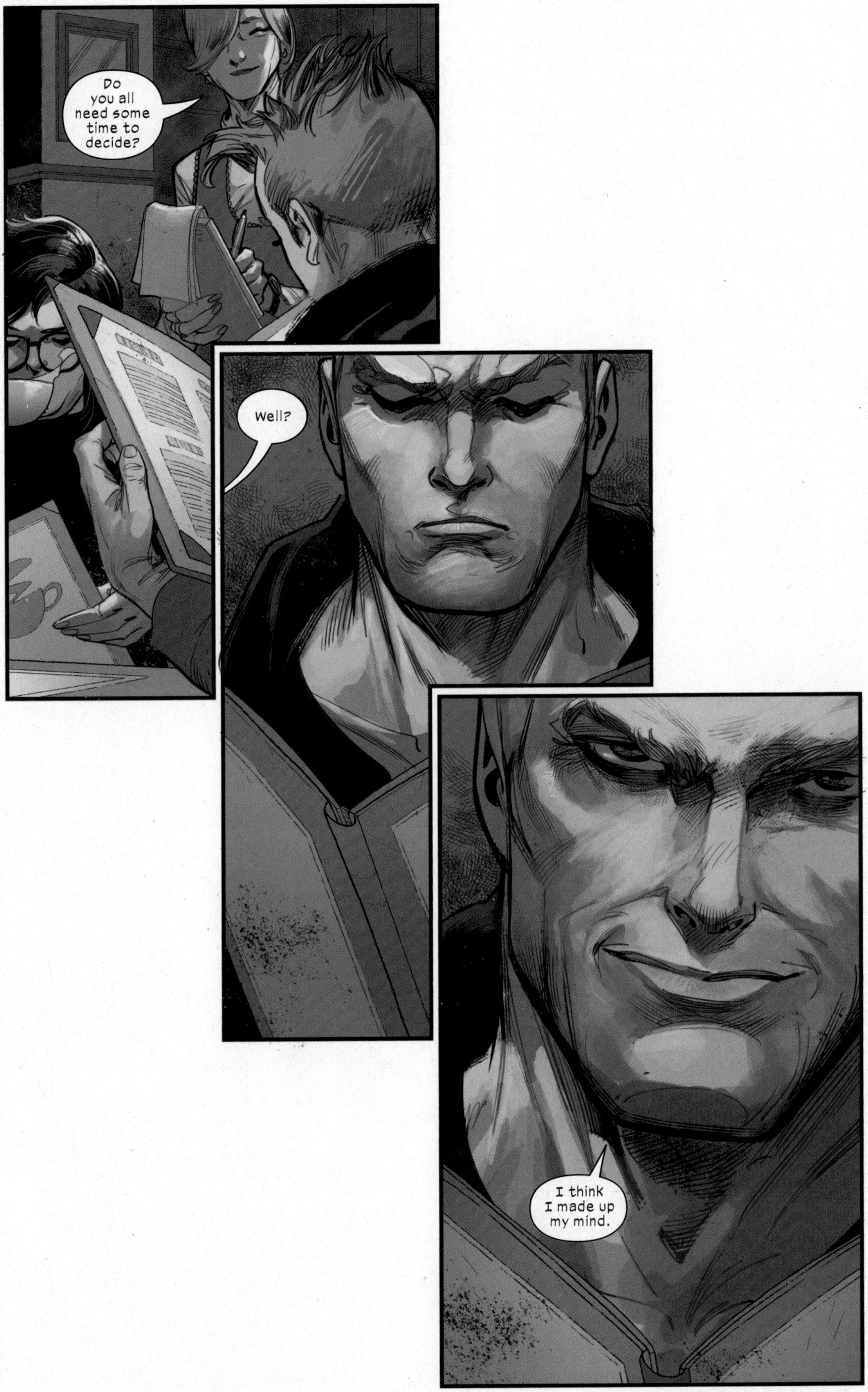
Do you all need some time to decide?
Well?
I think I made up my mind.

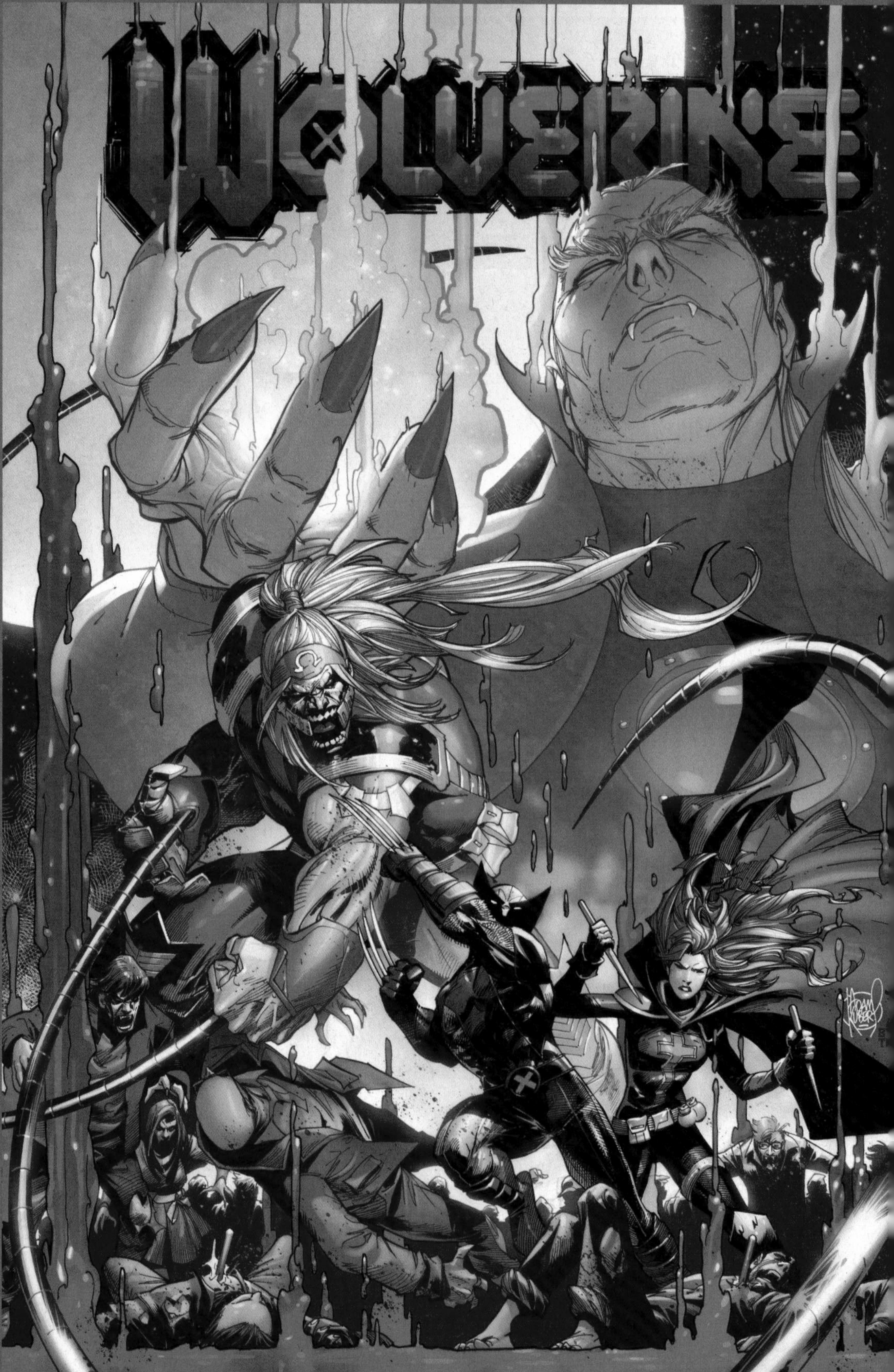
WOLVERINE

A Confusion of Mercenaria

11

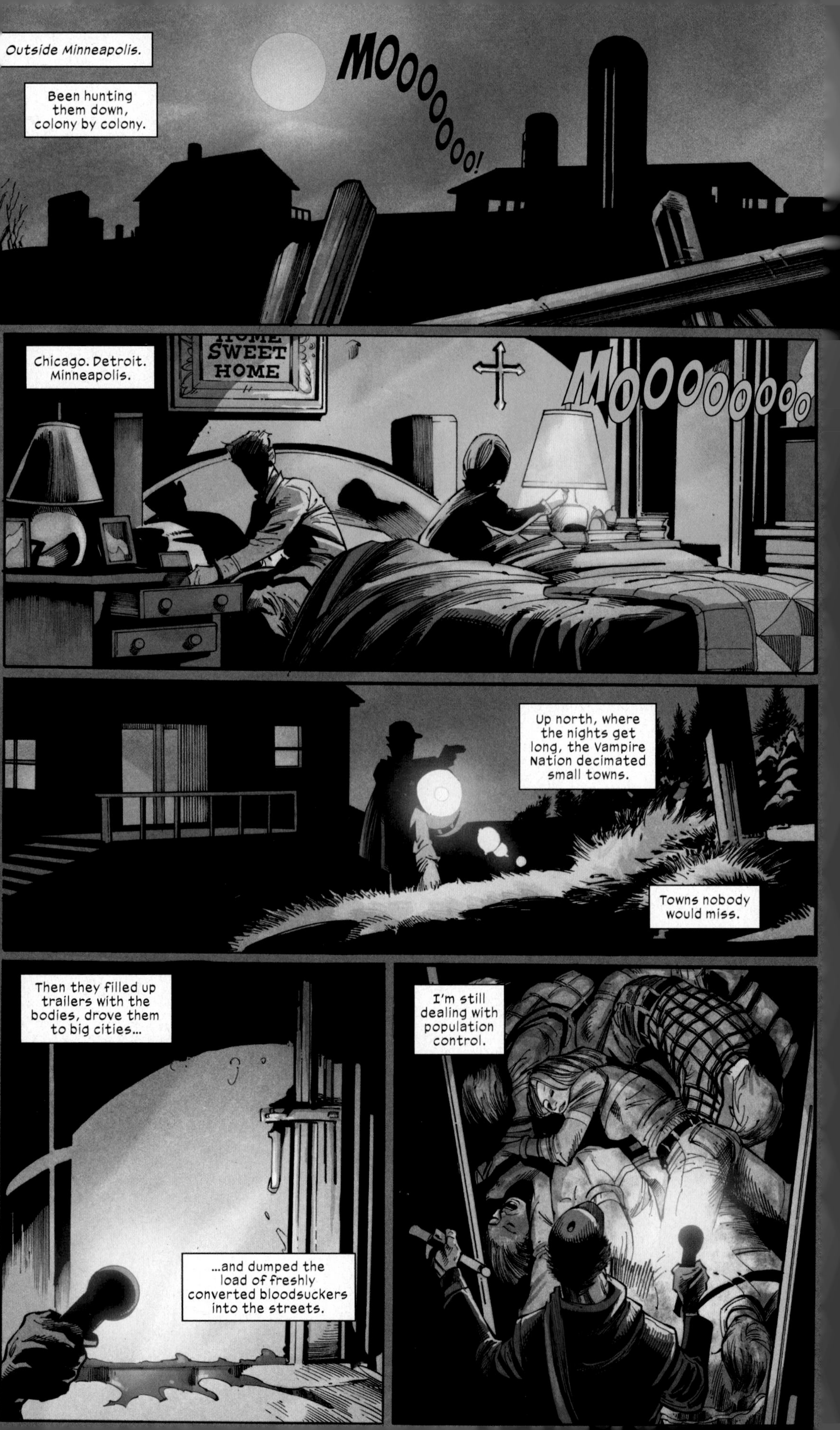
Outside Minneapolis.
Been hunting them down, colony by colony.
MOOOOOOOO!
Chicago. Detroit. Minneapolis.
HOME SWEET HOME
MOOOOOOOO
Up north, where the nights get long, the Vampire Nation decimated small towns.
Towns nobody would miss.
Then they filled up trailers with the bodies, drove them to big cities...
...and dumped the load of freshly converted bloodsuckers into the streets.
I'm still dealing with population control.

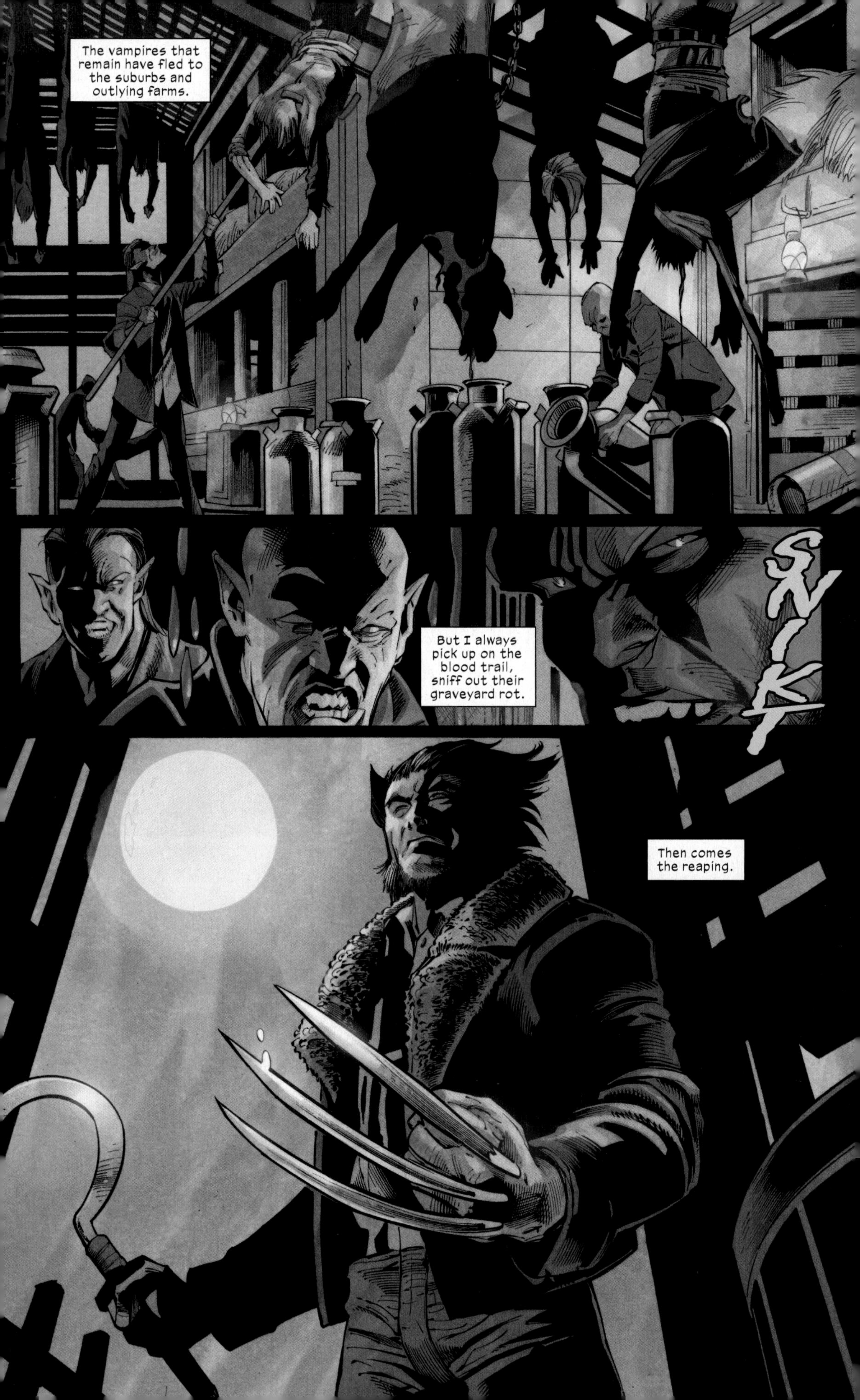
The vampires that remain have fled to the suburbs and outlying farms.
But I always pick up on the blood trail, sniff out their graveyard rot.
SNIKT
Then comes the reaping.

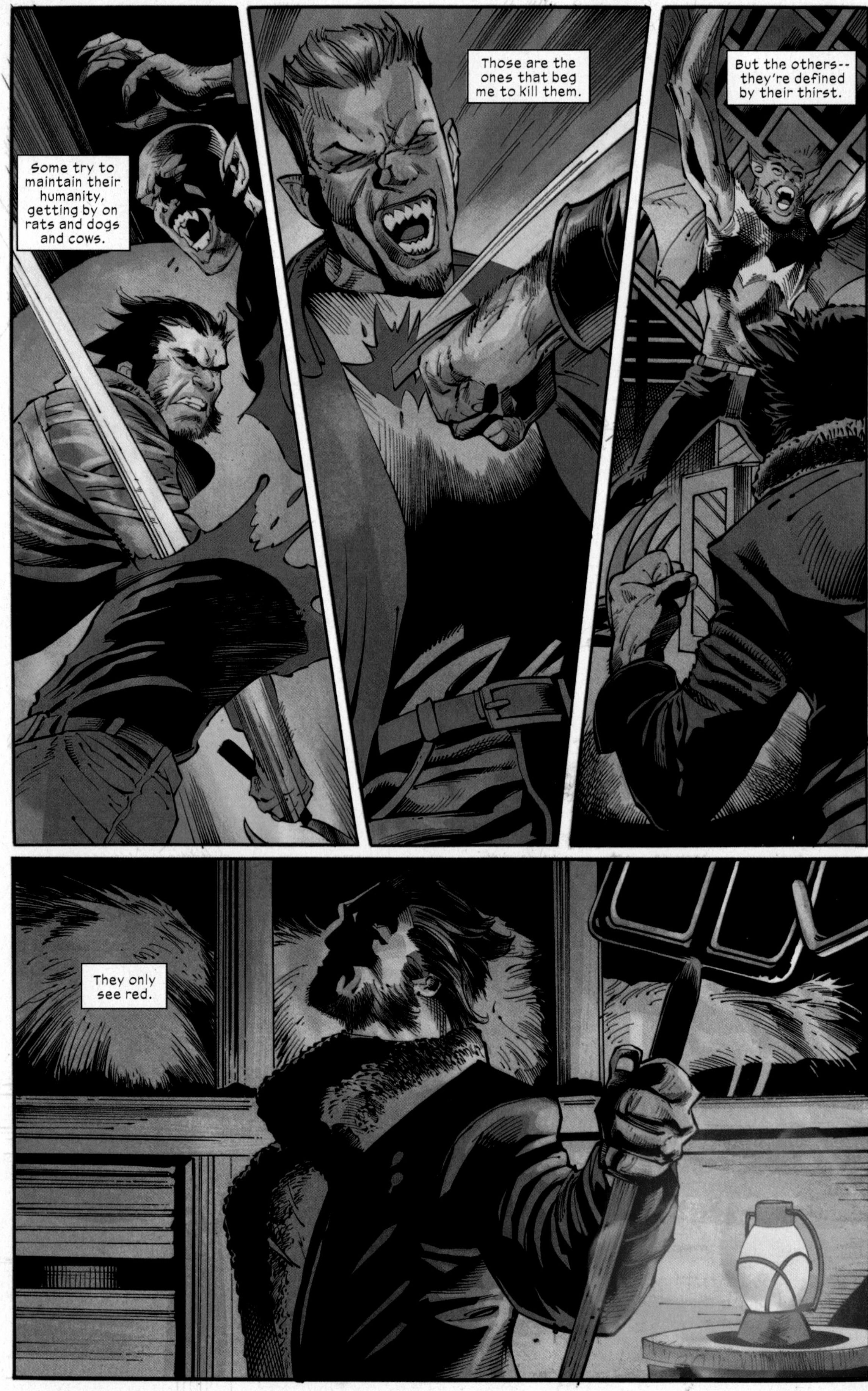
Some try to maintain their humanity, getting by on rats and dogs and cows.
Those are the ones that beg me to kill them.
But the others--they're defined by their thirst.
They only see red.

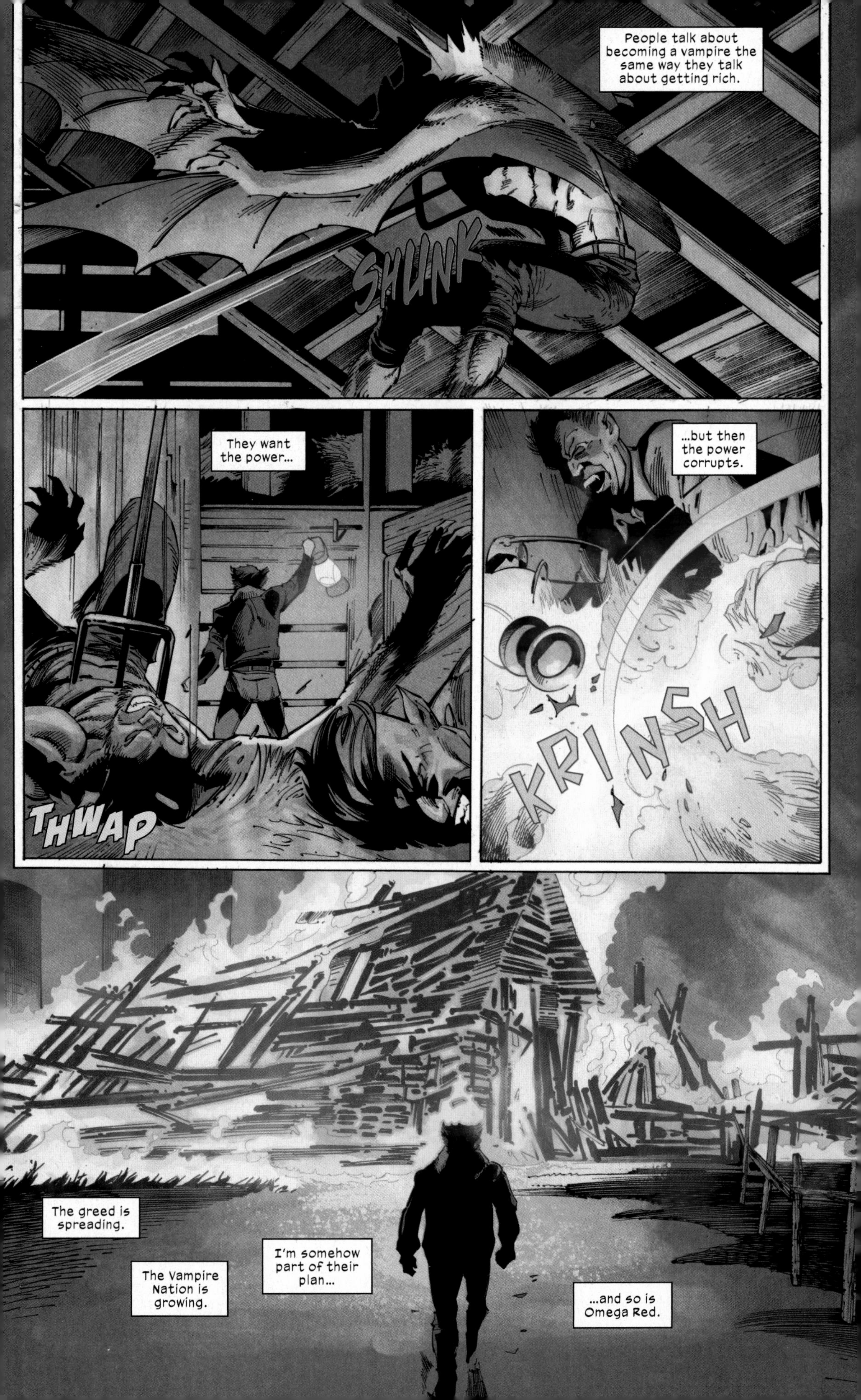
People talk about becoming a vampire the same way they talk about getting rich.
SHUNK
They want the power...
THWAP
...but then the power corrupts.
KRINSH
The greed is spreading.
The Vampire Nation is growing.
I'm somehow part of their plan...
...and so is Omega Red.

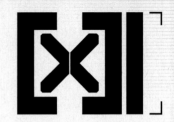

SAGE'S LOGBOOK: VAMPIRE COLONIES

Rolling Action Item

>> Wolverine requested a so-called vampire algorithm.

>> The program accounts for hospital admissions, police scanners, missing-person cases, missing-pet cases, livestock anomalies, blood bank supplies, and autopsy reports as primary variables.

<<<<ENTRIES>>>>

Detroit, MI. The Brightmoor section of the city -- including residential and commercial properties -- has suffered foreclosure and abandonment. Vampire blight took advantage of vacancy.

> **Wolverine's Report:** "Killed them good and dead."

Minneapolis, MN. Minneapolis was once the flour-milling capital of the world. The empty granaries banking the Mississippi River have been inhabited and now serve as giant roosts.

> **Wolverine's Report:** "Killed them too."

Chicago, IL. At the rail yards, hundreds of train cars rust on abandoned tracks and serve as coffins.

> **Wolverine's Report:** "Hacked off their heads and threw them in a pile and burned them and pissed on the fire to extinguish it."

Buffalo, NY. An abandoned church was hosting rave parties that swiftly decimated a portion of the population (ages 17-25).

> **Wolverine's Report:** "One #%&@ got away. Put down the rest. Then I got some wings."

<<<Surveillance: Ongoing>>>

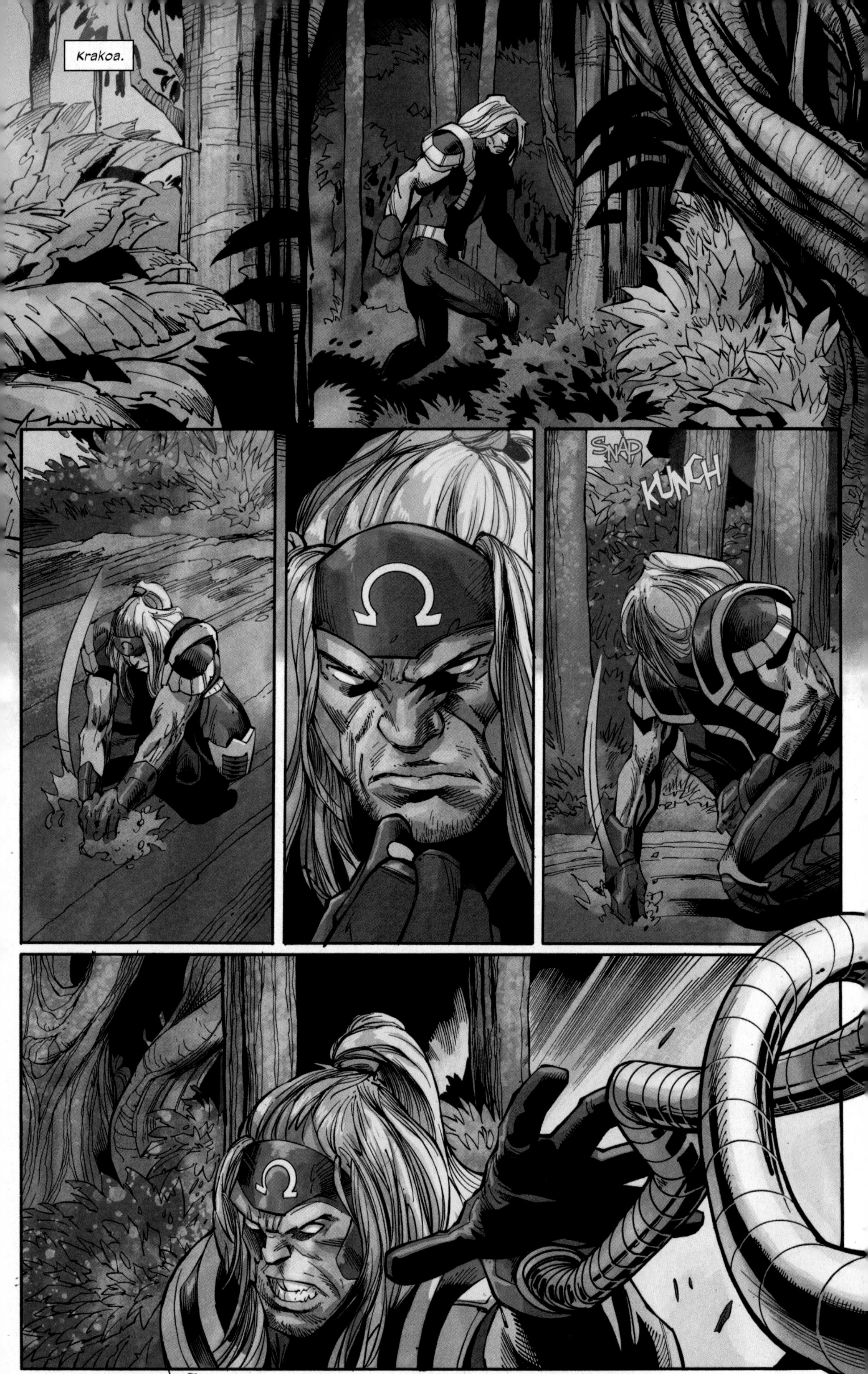
Krakoa.
SNAP
KUNCH

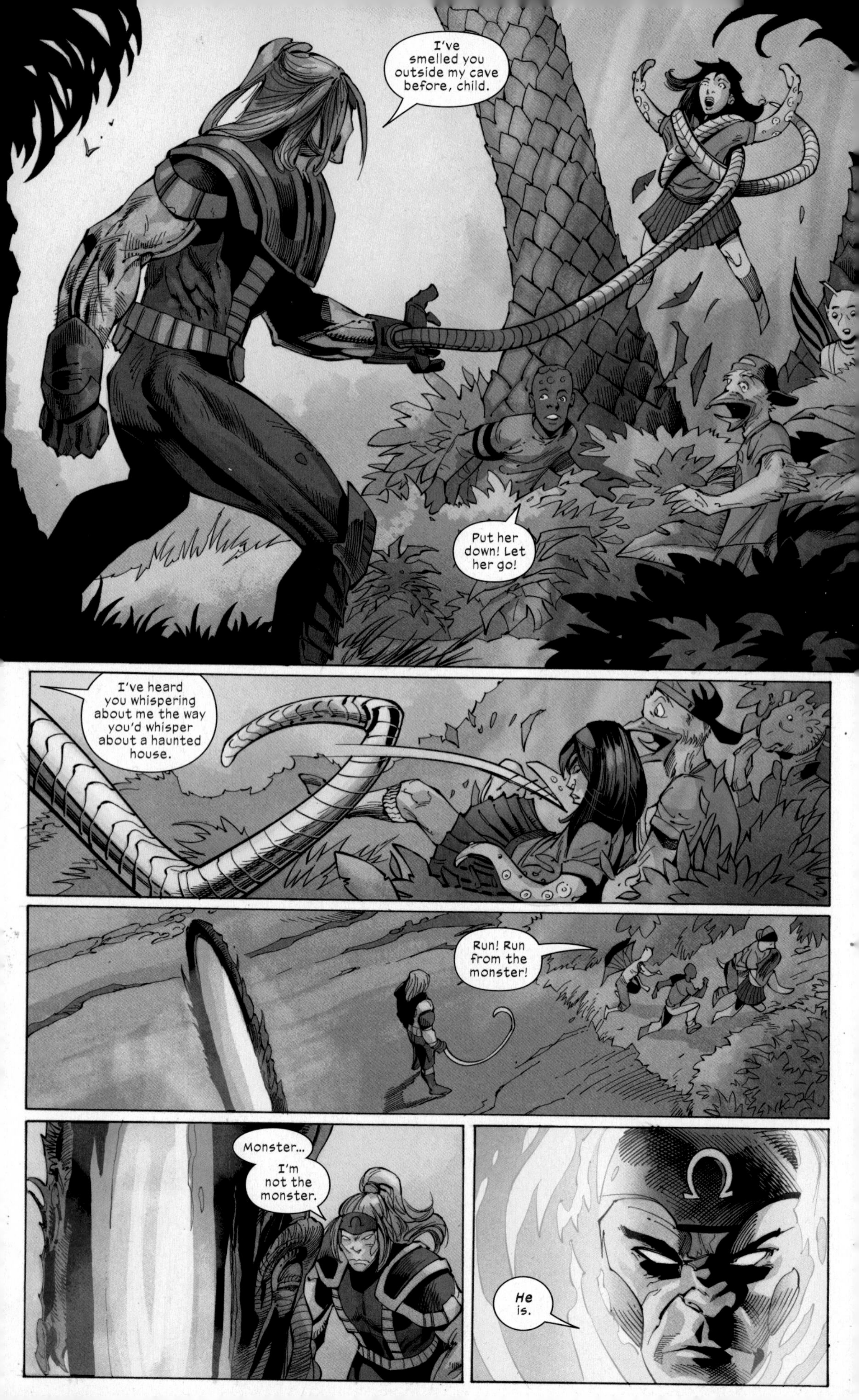
I've smelled you outside my cave before, child.
Put her down! Let her go!
I've heard you whispering about me the way you'd whisper about a haunted house.
Run! Run from the monster!
Monster...
I'm not the monster.
He is.

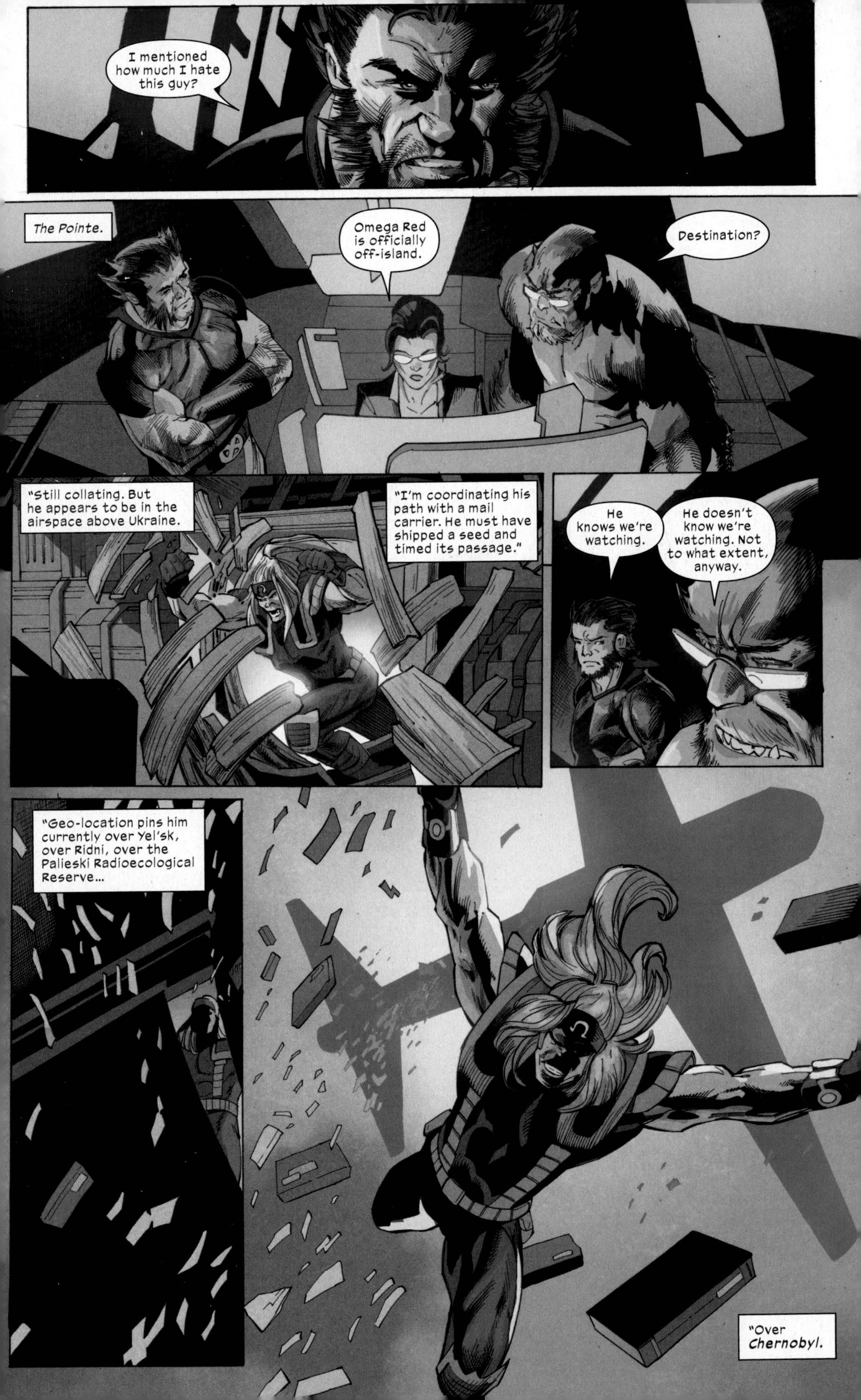
I mentioned how much I hate this guy?
The Pointe.
Omega Red is officially off-island.
Destination?
"Still collating. But he appears to be in the airspace above Ukraine.
"I'm coordinating his path with a mail carrier. He must have shipped a seed and timed its passage."
He knows we're watching.
He doesn't know we're watching. Not to what extent, anyway.
"Geo-location pins him currently over Yel'sk, over Ridni, over the Palieski Radioecological Reserve...
"Over Chernobyl.

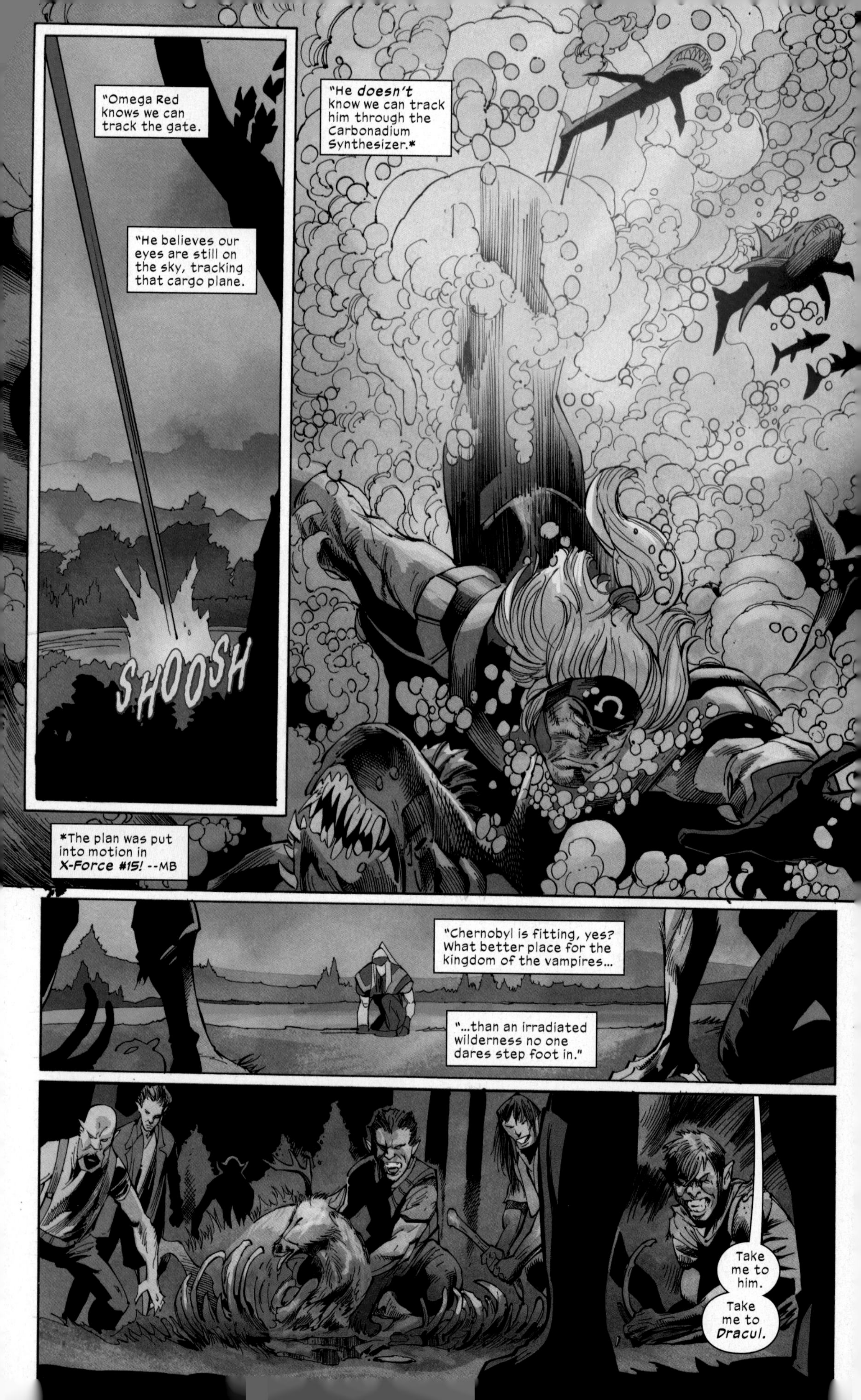
"Omega Red knows we can track the gate.
"He believes our eyes are still on the sky, tracking that cargo plane.
SHOOSH
"He *doesn't* know we can track him through the Carbonadium Synthesizer.*
*The plan was put into motion in *X-Force #15!* --MB
"Chernobyl is fitting, yes? What better place for the kingdom of the vampires...
"...than an irradiated wilderness no one dares step foot in."
Take me to him.
Take me to *Dracul.*

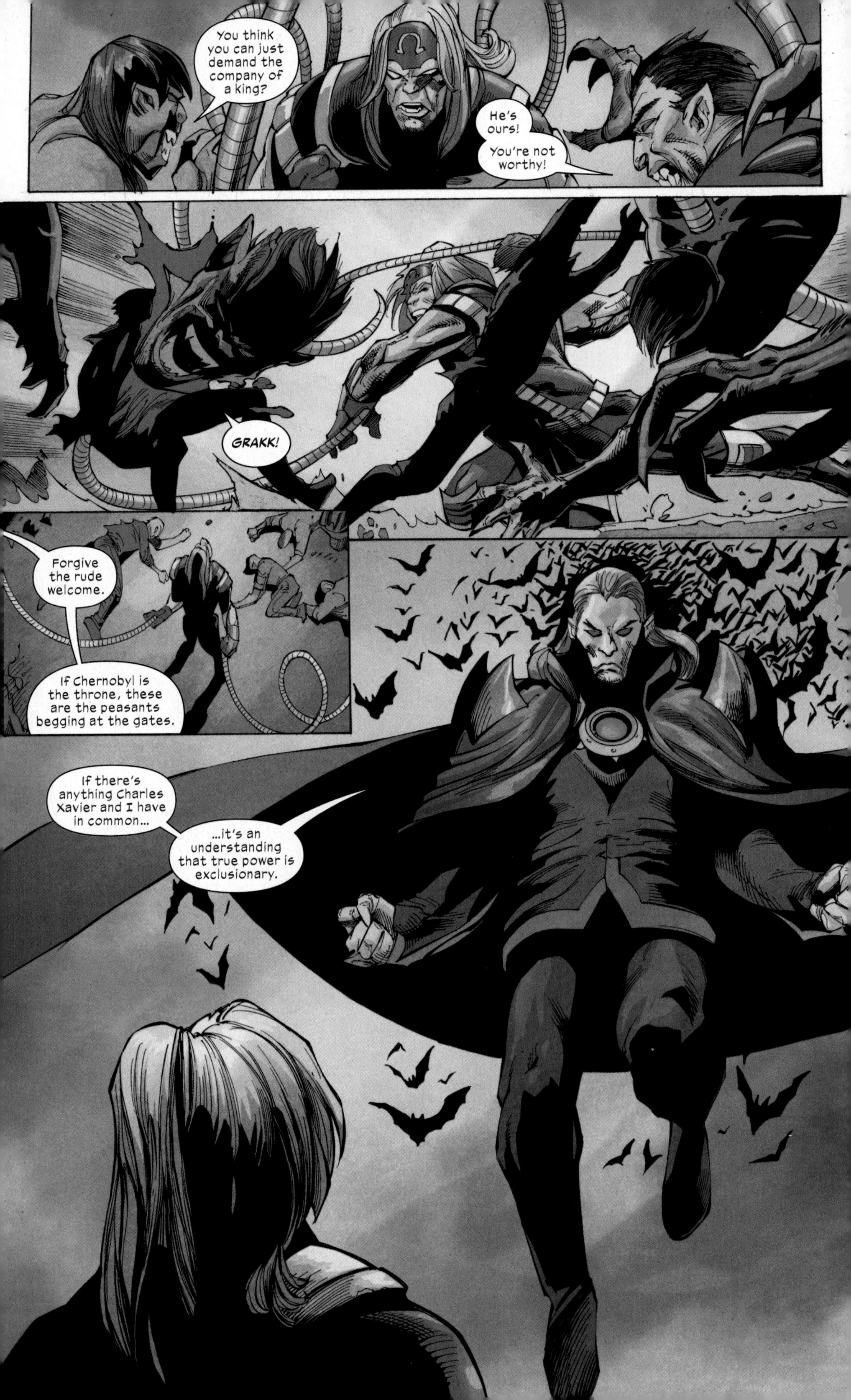
You think you can just demand the company of a king?
He's ours!
You're not worthy!
GRAKK!
Forgive the rude welcome.
If Chernobyl is the throne, these are the peasants begging at the gates.
If there's anything Charles Xavier and I have in common...
...it's an understanding that true power is exclusionary.

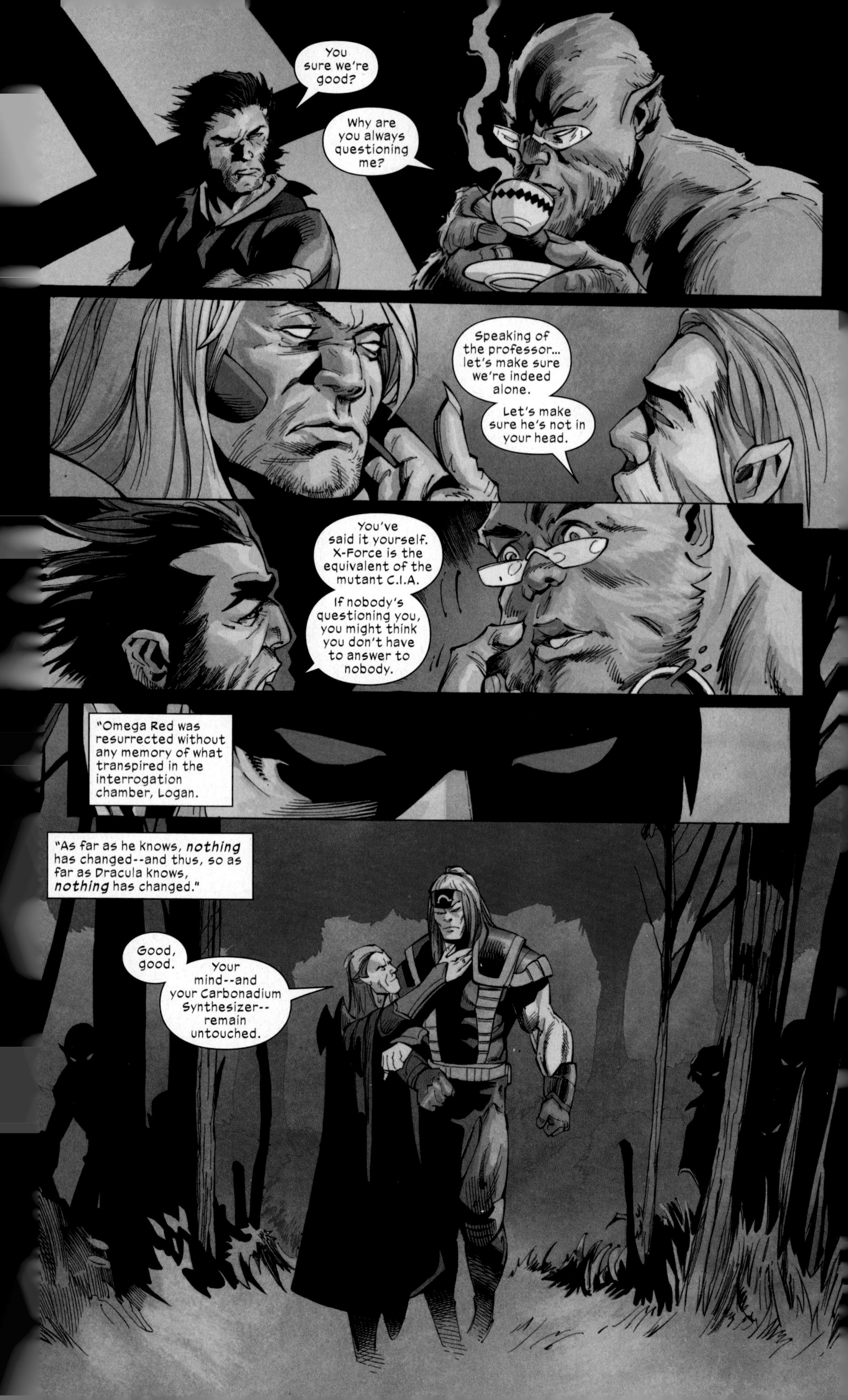

You sure we're good?
Why are you always questioning me?
Speaking of the professor... let's make sure we're indeed alone.
Let's make sure he's not in your head.
You've said it yourself. X-Force is the equivalent of the mutant C.I.A.
If nobody's questioning you, you might think you don't have to answer to nobody.
"Omega Red was resurrected without any memory of what transpired in the interrogation chamber, Logan.
"As far as he knows, *nothing* has changed--and thus, so as far as Dracula knows, *nothing* has changed."
Good, good.
Your mind--and your Carbonadium Synthesizer--remain untouched.

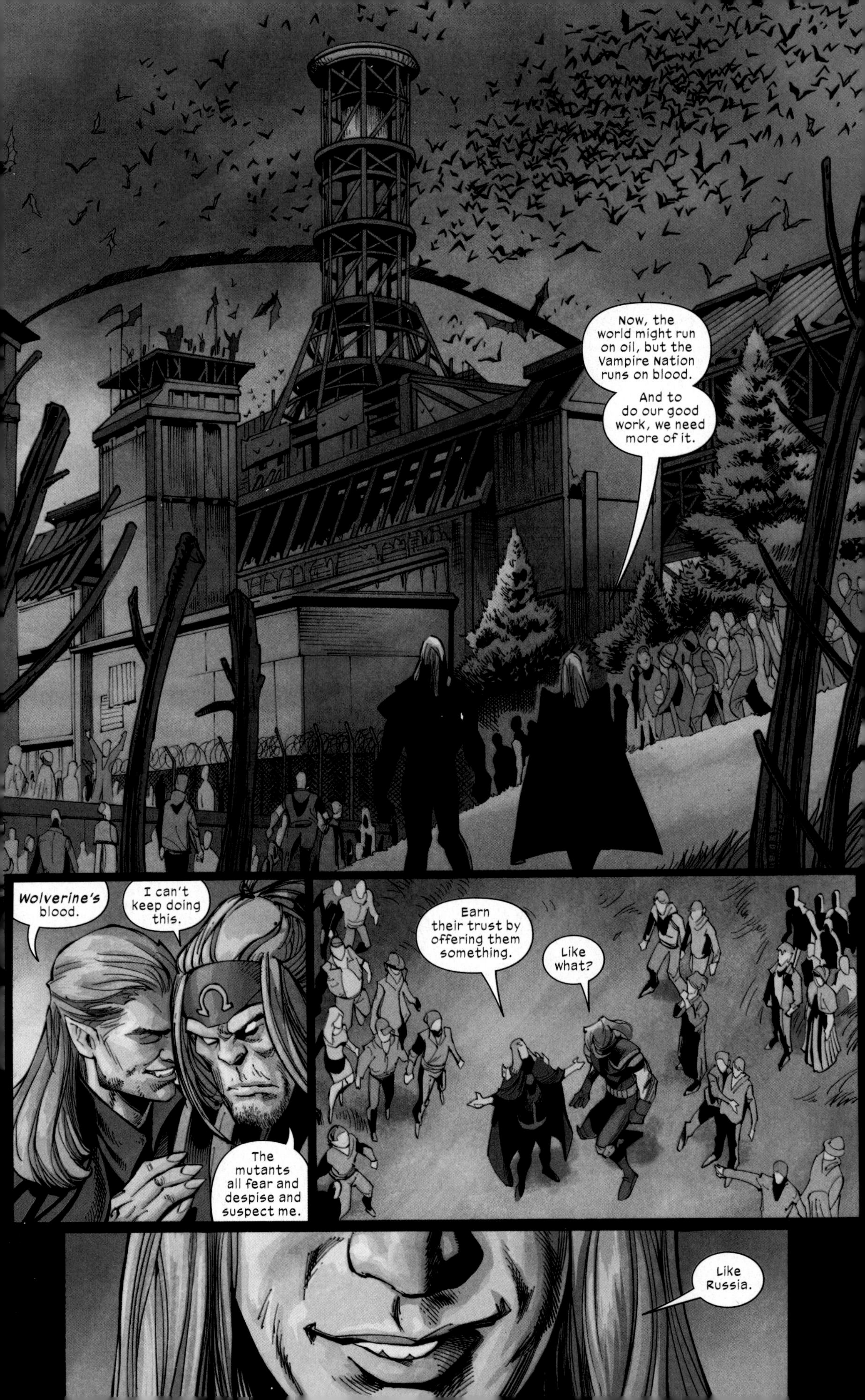
Now, the world might run on oil, but the Vampire Nation runs on blood.
And to do our good work, we need more of it.
Wolverine's blood.
I can't keep doing this.
The mutants all fear and despise and suspect me.
Earn their trust by offering them something.
Like what?
Like Russia.

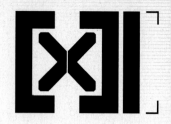

SAGE'S LOGBOOK:
THE HEAD AND THE FIST

Weekly Briefing between Intelligence and Field Operations
Subject: Vampire Nation
Transcript:

BEAST: I have a rather unorthodox idea.

> **WOLVERINE:** Sounds sketchy.

BEAST: Have you ever heard of KP4?

> **WOLVERINE:** Why do you even bother asking questions you're going to answer?

BEAST: It's a toxin. It's also a fungus that eats other fungi. Agricultural companies are constantly trying to come up with ways to prevent crop failure. And rather than taking a defensive route, which is their standard strategy, they recently made a brilliant offensive move. They wove a strain of KP4 into the genomic sequence of their corn.

> **WOLVERINE:** ...

BEAST: Don't you see? They fought infection with an infection of their own.

> **WOLVERINE:** ...

BEAST: We've made it into Chernobyl so far using deception. Let's continue on that same tack.

> **WOLVERINE:** ...

BEAST: They want you, yes? So I say let's offer you up on a platter. But what we'll do is --

> **WOLVERINE:** No.

BEAST: I don't think you're following me.

> **WOLVERINE:** I like my way better. Stabbing.

BEAST: Your way is slow, inefficient, and positively medieval.

> **WOLVERINE:** Stabbing. Hacking. Slashing.

BEAST: This can't possibly be the extent of your plan.

> **WOLVERINE:** Don't worry. There's another weapon I'm adding to the arsenal.

BEAST: And which weapon would that be?

> **WOLVERINE:** Name's Louise. Lives in Paris.

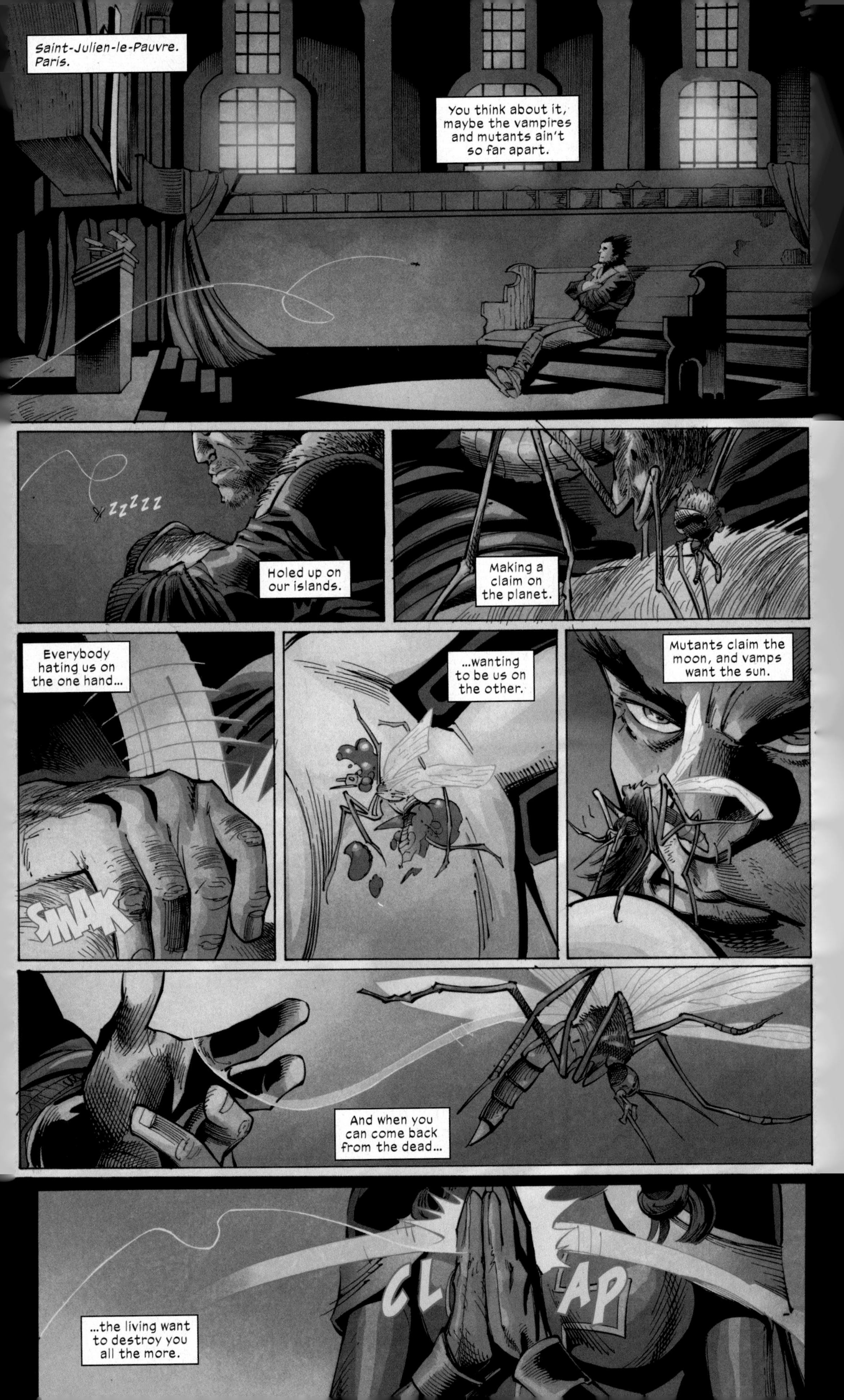
Saint-Julien-le-Pauvre. Paris.
You think about it, maybe the vampires and mutants ain't so far apart.
ZZZZZ
Holed up on our islands.
Making a claim on the planet.
Everybody hating us on the one hand...
SMAK
...wanting to be us on the other.
Mutants claim the moon, and vamps want the sun.
And when you can come back from the dead...
CLAP
...the living want to destroy you all the more.

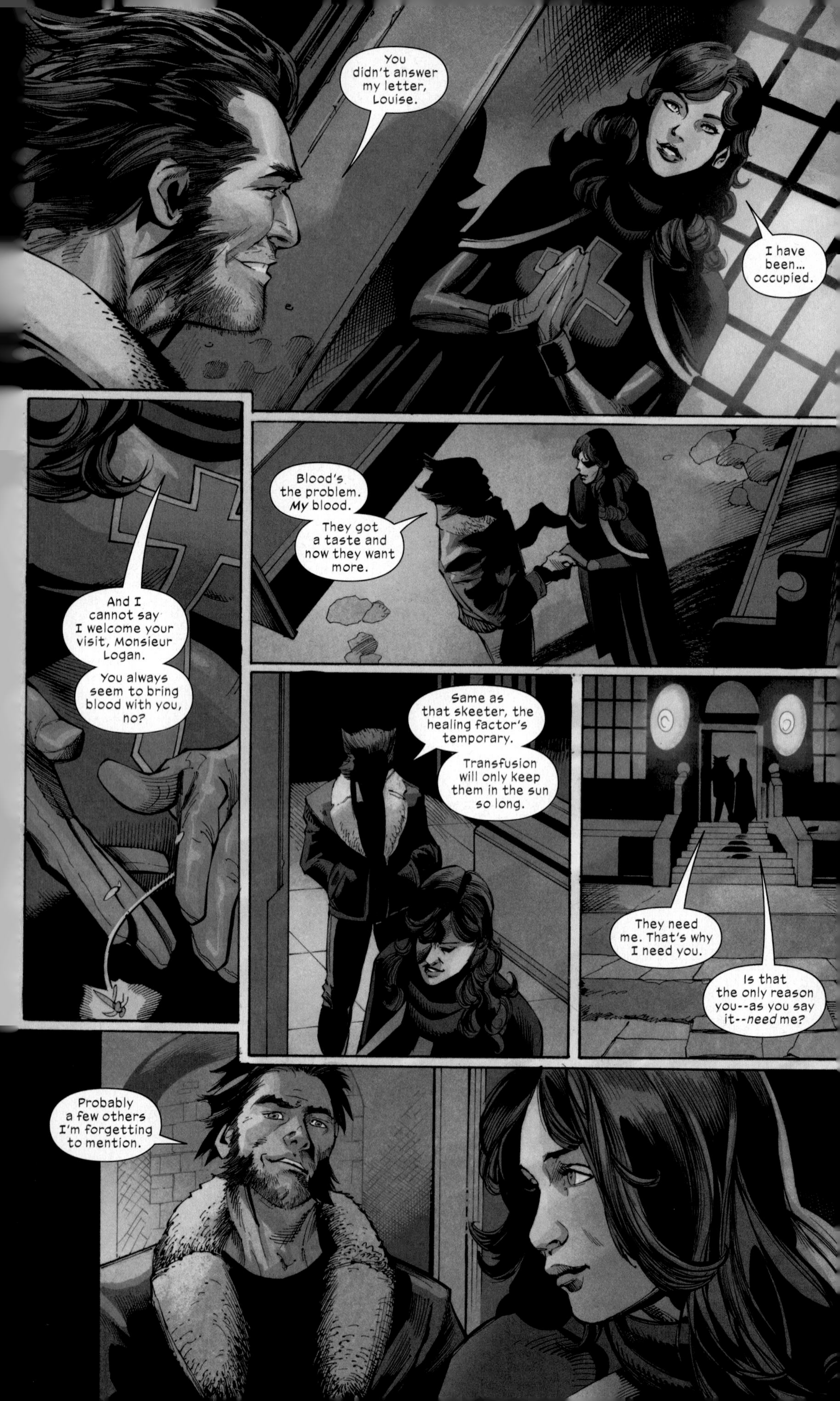
You didn't answer my letter, Louise.
I have been... occupied.
And I cannot say I welcome your visit, Monsieur Logan.
You always seem to bring blood with you, no?
Blood's the problem. *My* blood.
They got a taste and now they want more.
Same as that skeeter, the healing factor's temporary.
Transfusion will only keep them in the sun so long.
They need me. That's why I need you.
Is that the only reason you--as you say it--*need* me?
Probably a few others I'm forgetting to mention.

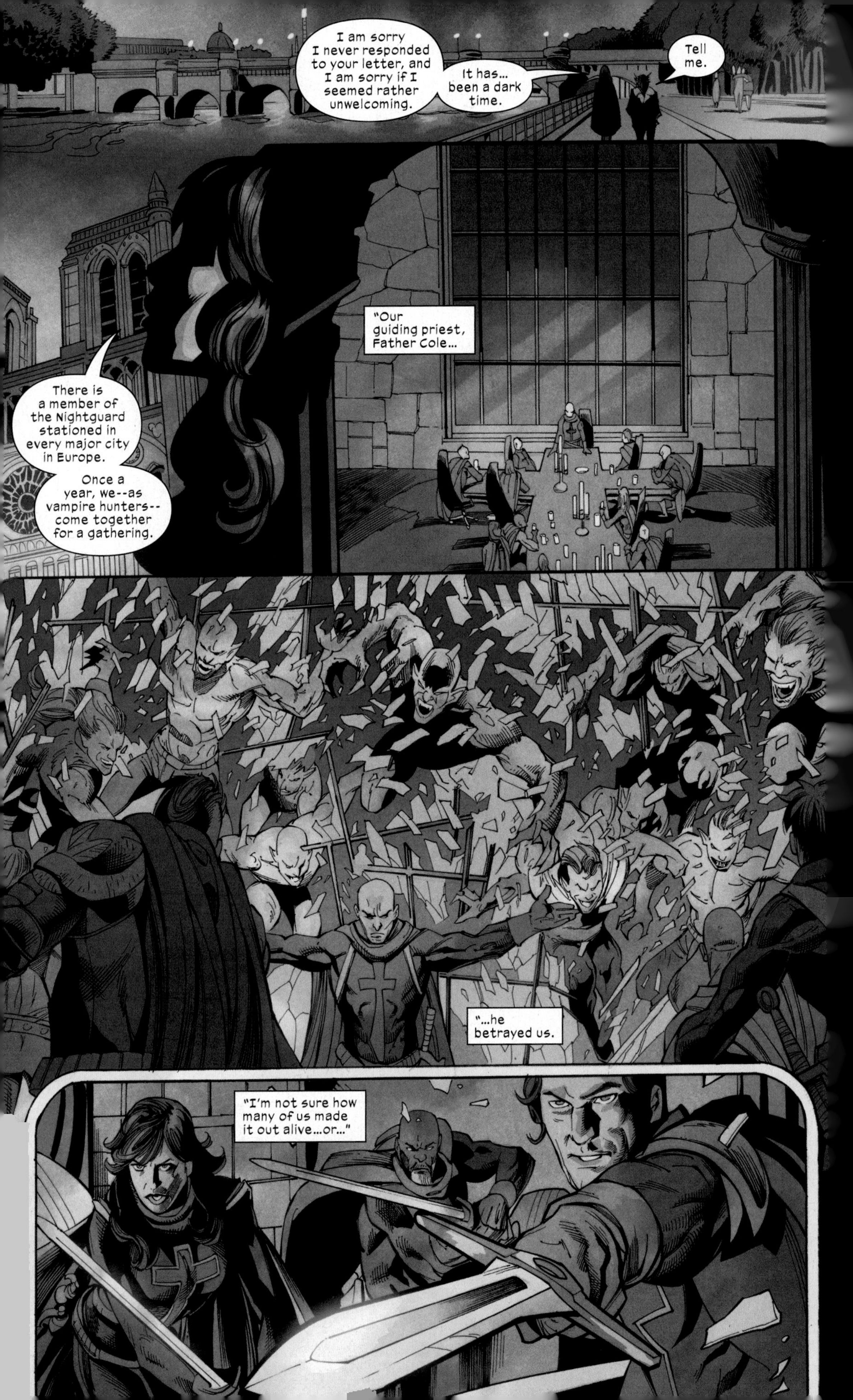
I am sorry I never responded to your letter, and I am sorry if I seemed rather unwelcoming.
It has... been a dark time.
Tell me.
There is a member of the Nightguard stationed in every major city in Europe.
Once a year, we--as vampire hunters--come together for a gathering.
"Our guiding priest, Father Cole...
"...he betrayed us.
"I'm not sure how many of us made it out alive...or..."

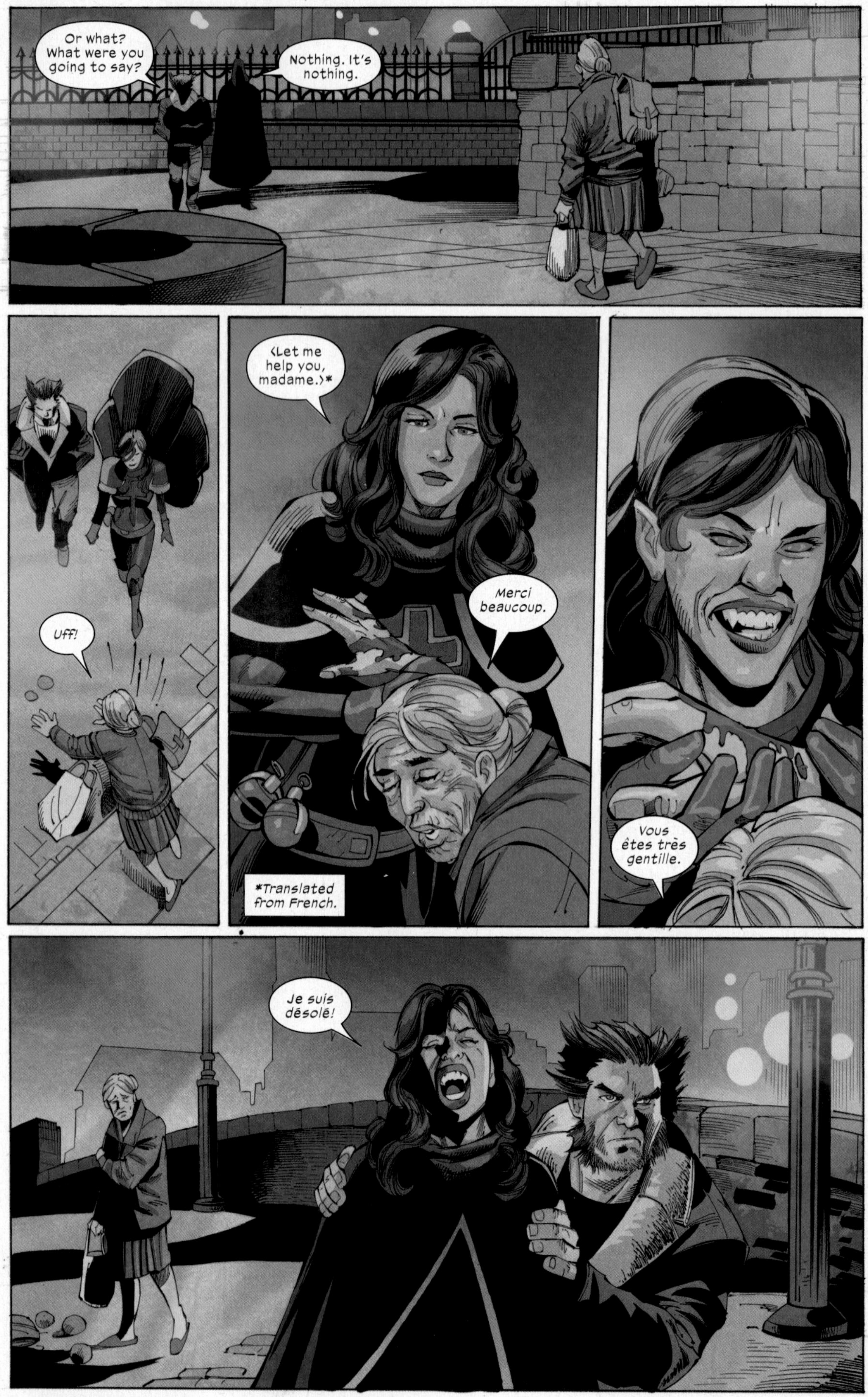
Or what? What were you going to say?
Nothing. It's nothing.
Uff!
‹Let me help you, madame.›*
Merci beaucoup.
*Translated from French.
Vous êtes très gentille.
Je suis désolé!

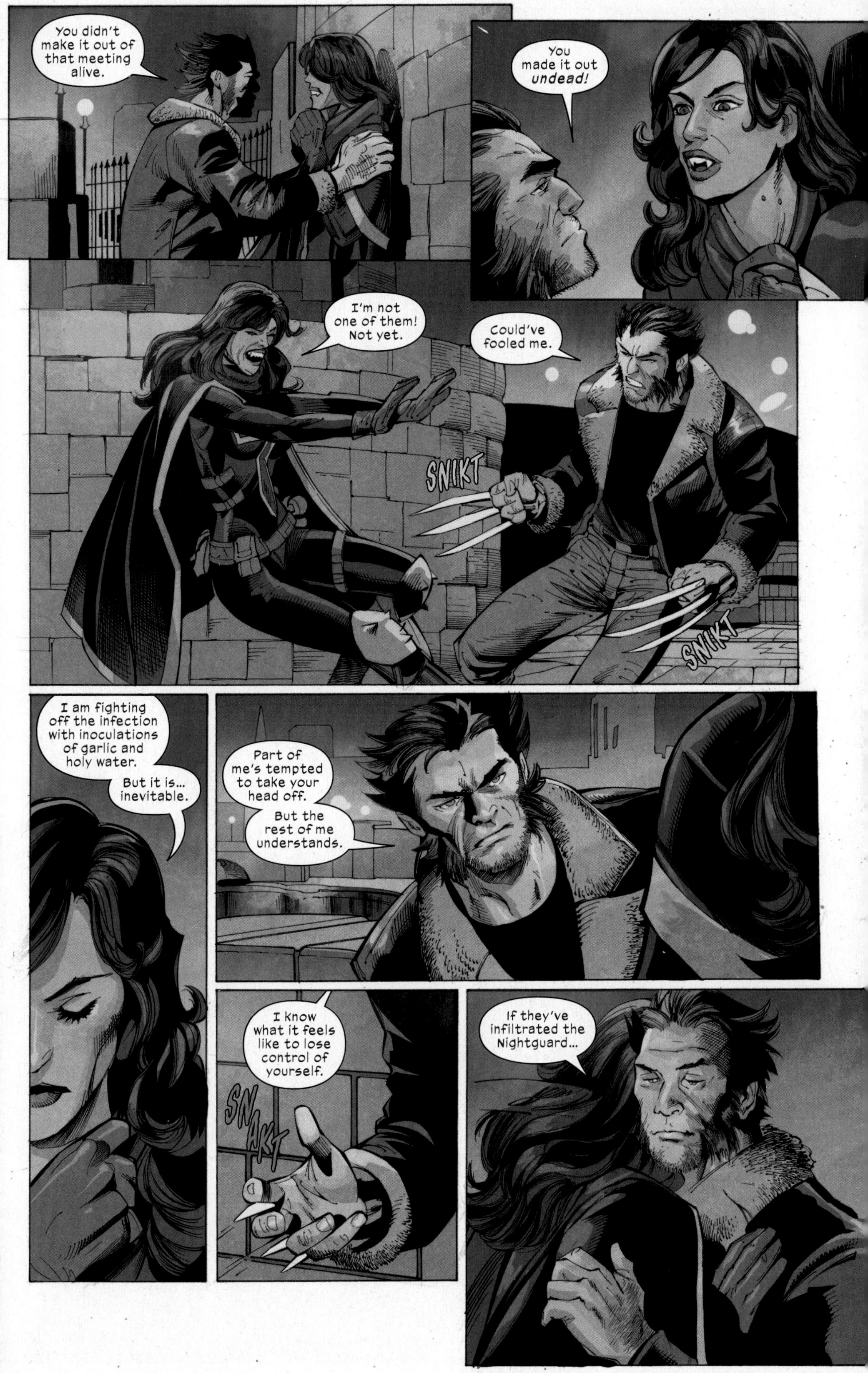

You didn't make it out of that meeting alive.
You made it out *undead!*
I'm not one of them! Not yet.
Could've fooled me.
SNIKT
SNIKT
I am fighting off the infection with inoculations of garlic and holy water.
But it is... inevitable.
Part of me's tempted to take your head off.
But the rest of me understands.
I know what it feels like to lose control of yourself.
SNAKT
If they've infiltrated the Nightguard...

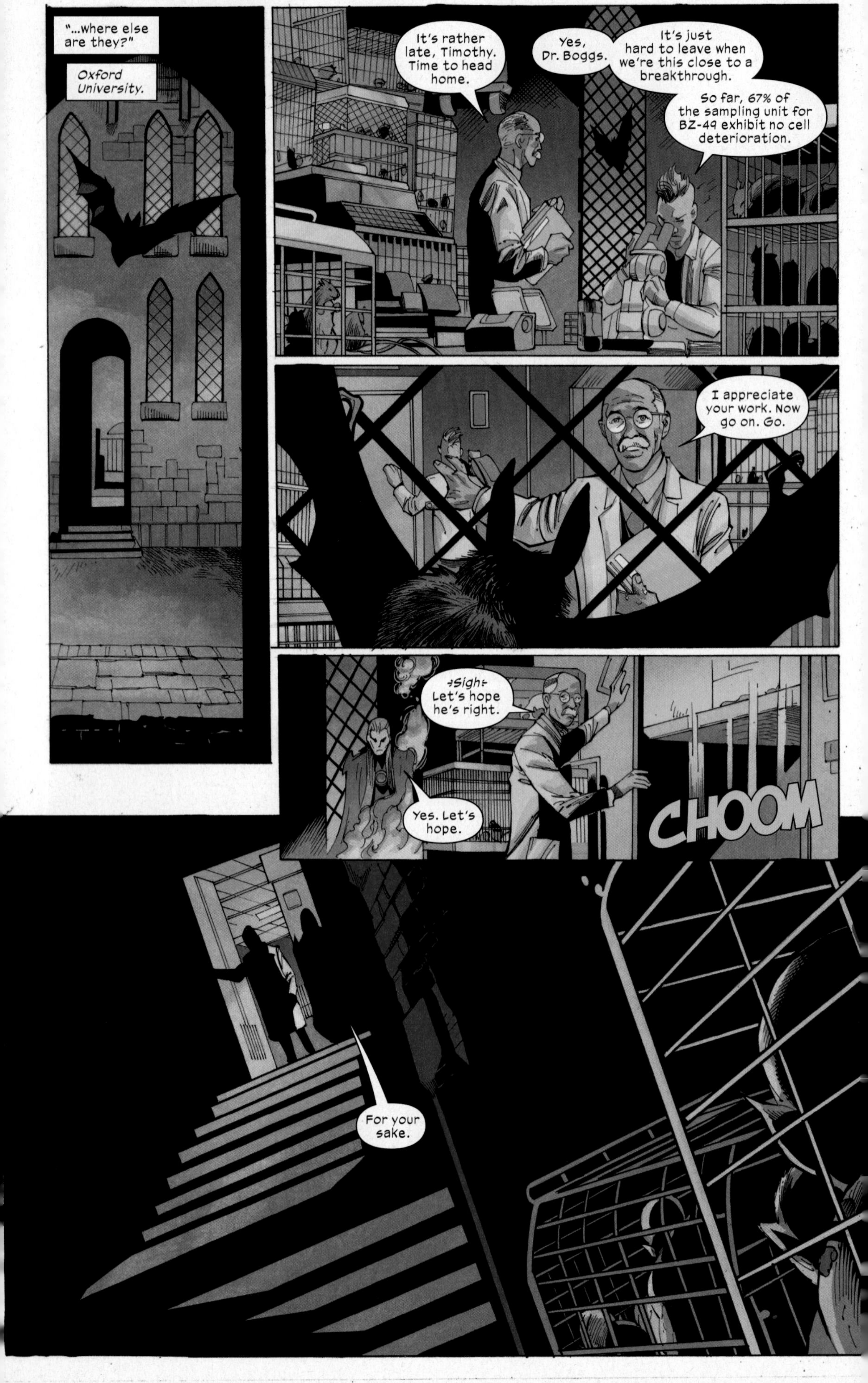
"...where else are they?"
Oxford University.
It's rather late, Timothy. Time to head home.
Yes, Dr. Boggs.
It's just hard to leave when we're this close to a breakthrough.
So far, 67% of the sampling unit for BZ-49 exhibit no cell deterioration.
I appreciate your work. Now go on. Go.
-Sigh- Let's hope he's right.
Yes. Let's hope.
CHOOM
For your sake.

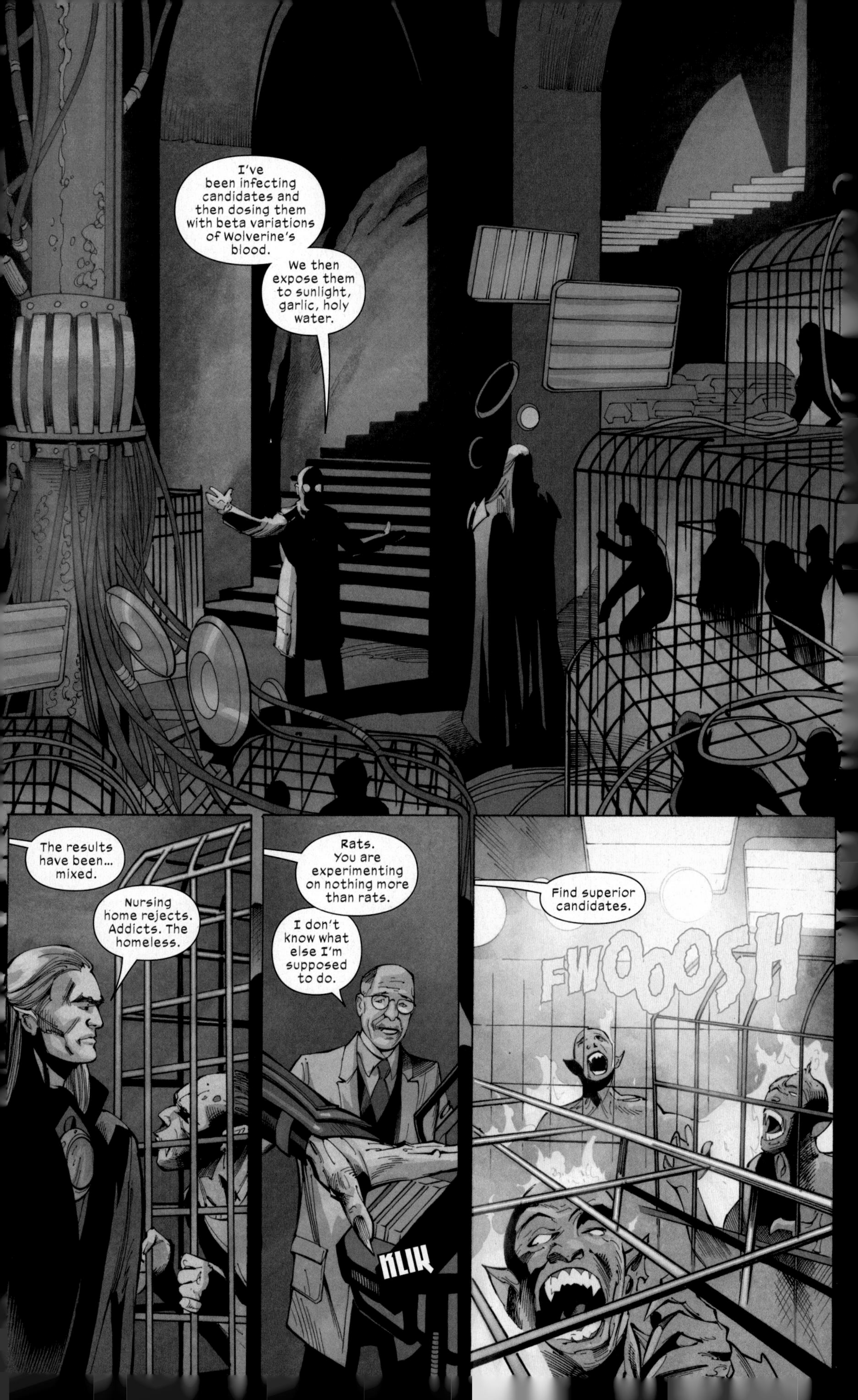
I've been infecting candidates and then dosing them with beta variations of Wolverine's blood.
We then expose them to sunlight, garlic, holy water.
The results have been... mixed.
Nursing home rejects. Addicts. The homeless.
Rats. You are experimenting on nothing more than rats.
I don't know what else I'm supposed to do.
KLIK
Find superior candidates.
FWOOOSH

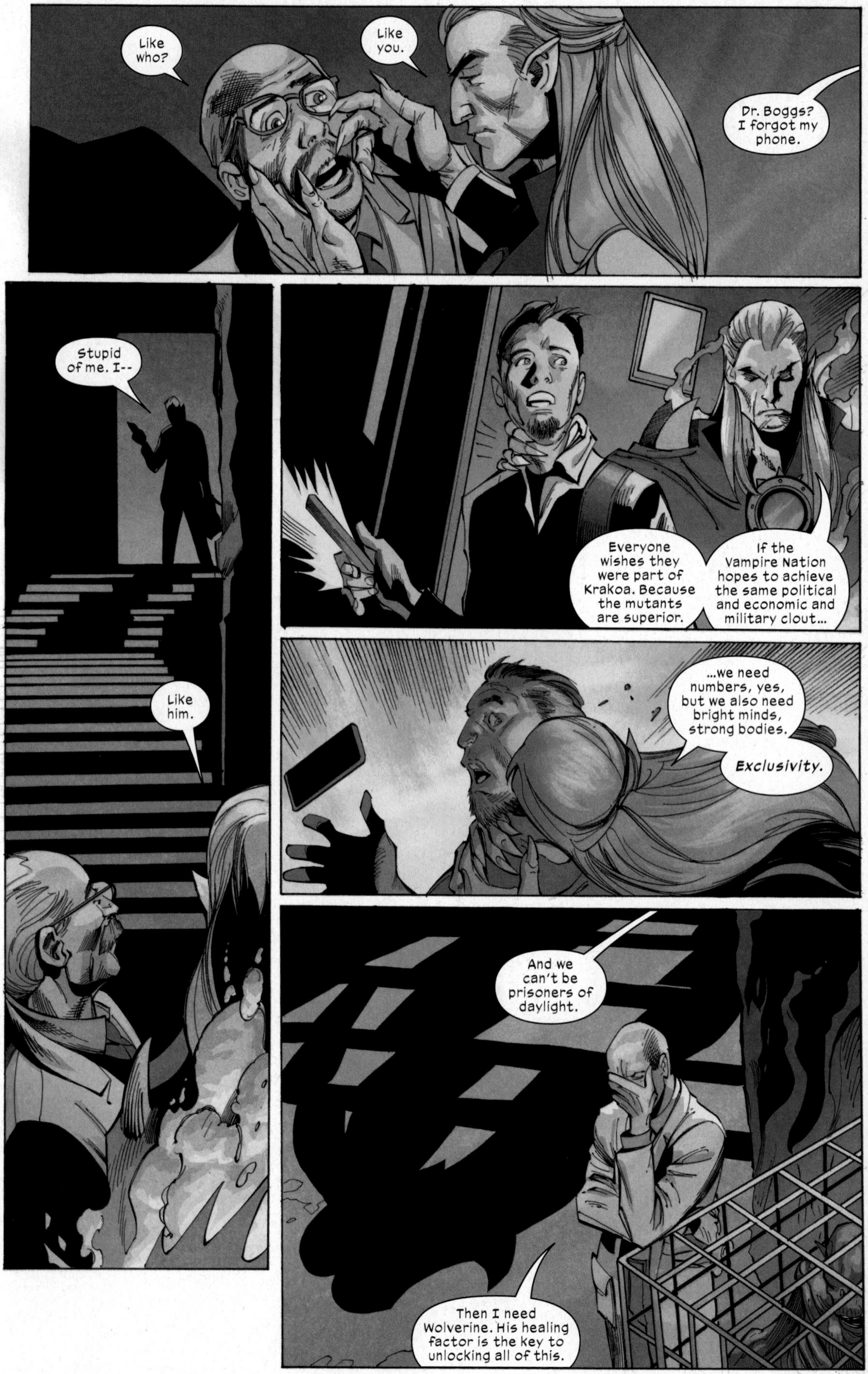
Like who?
Like you.
Dr. Boggs? I forgot my phone.
Stupid of me. I--
Like him.
Everyone wishes they were part of Krakoa. Because the mutants are superior.
If the Vampire Nation hopes to achieve the same political and economic and military clout...
...we need numbers, yes, but we also need bright minds, strong bodies.
Exclusivity.
And we can't be prisoners of daylight.
Then I need Wolverine. His healing factor is the key to unlocking all of this.

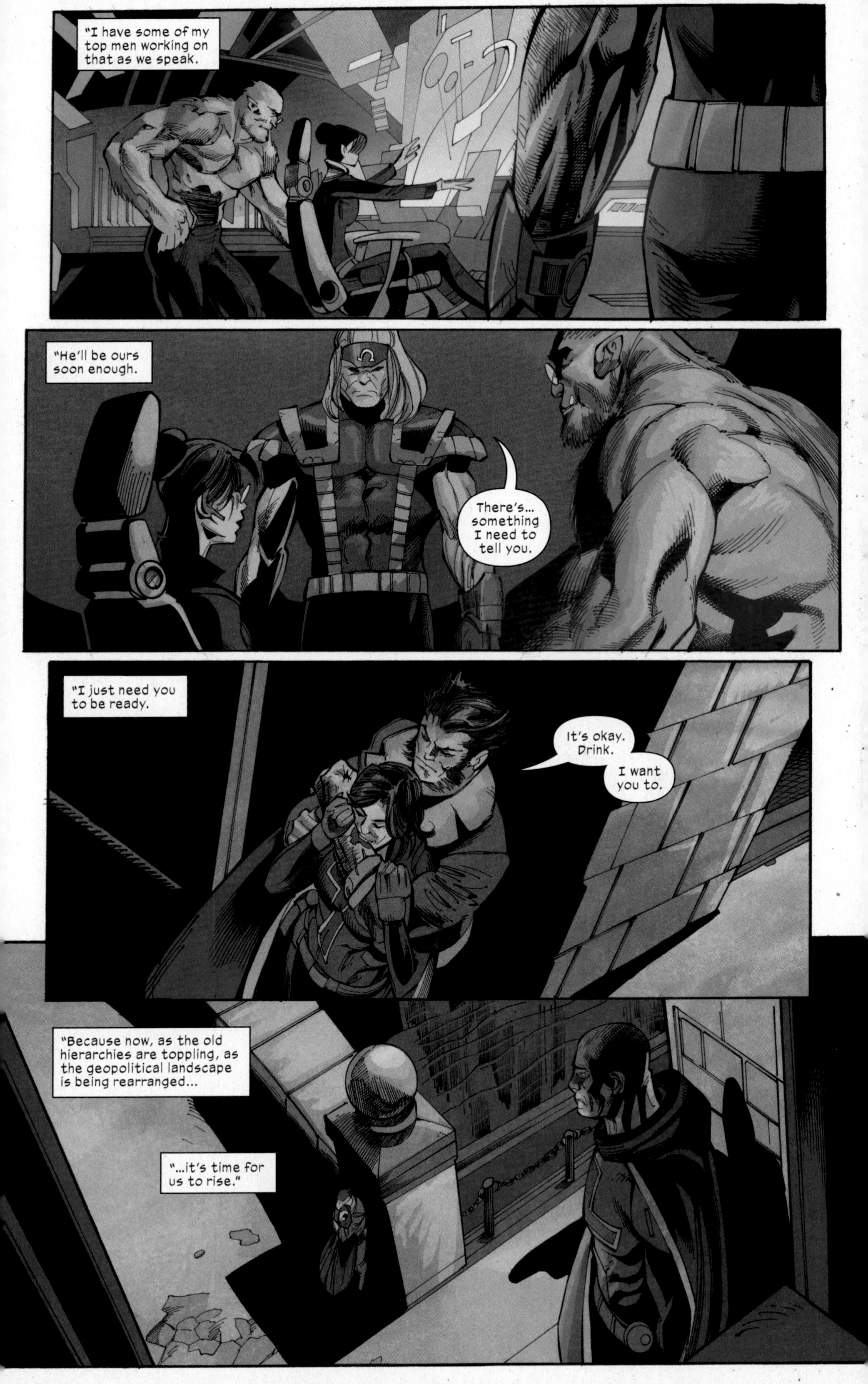
"I have some of my top men working on that as we speak.
"He'll be ours soon enough.
There's... something I need to tell you.
"I just need you to be ready.
It's okay. Drink.
I want you to.
"Because now, as the old hierarchies are toppling, as the geopolitical landscape is being rearranged...
"...it's time for us to rise."

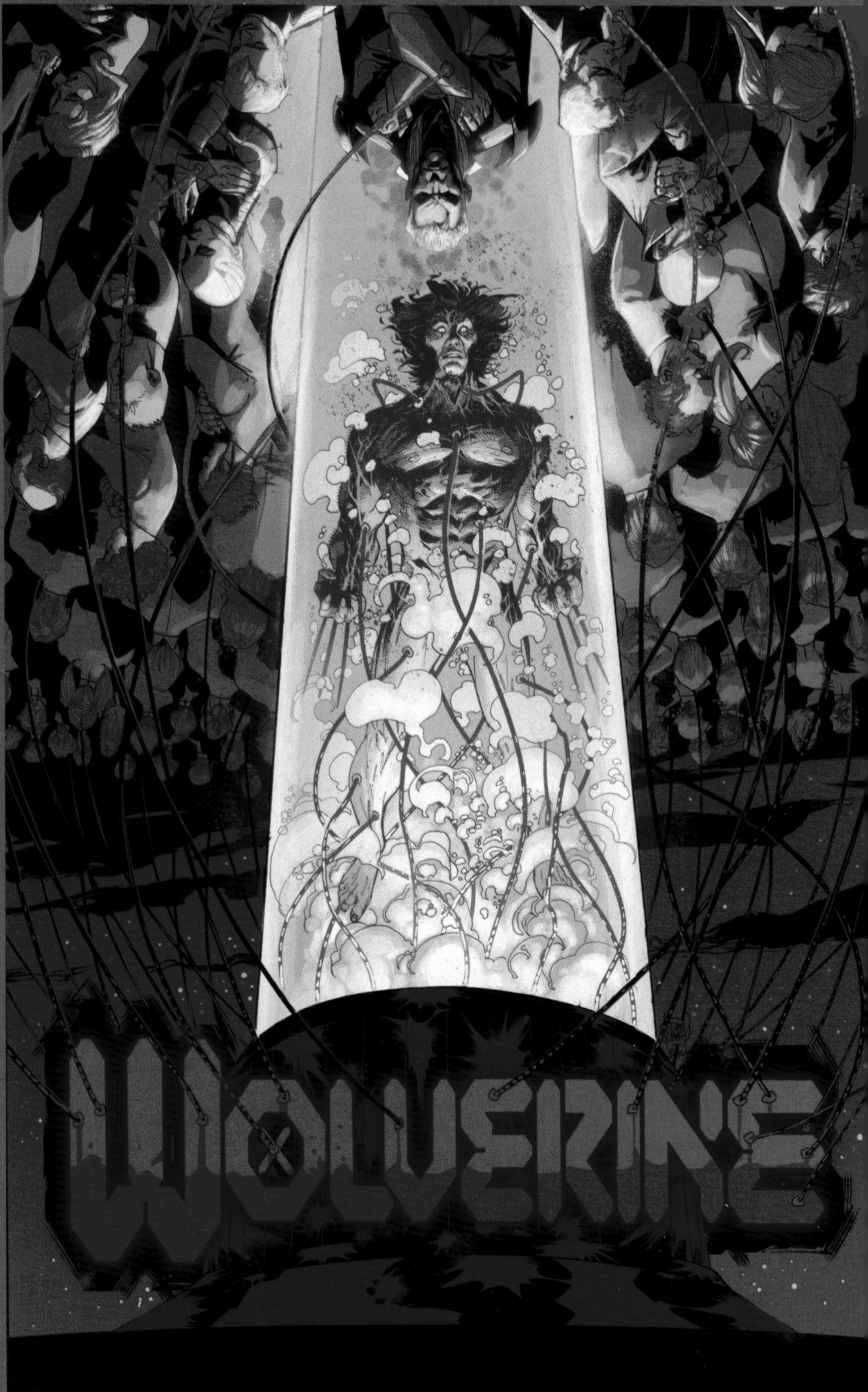
WOLVERINE

Penumbra

12

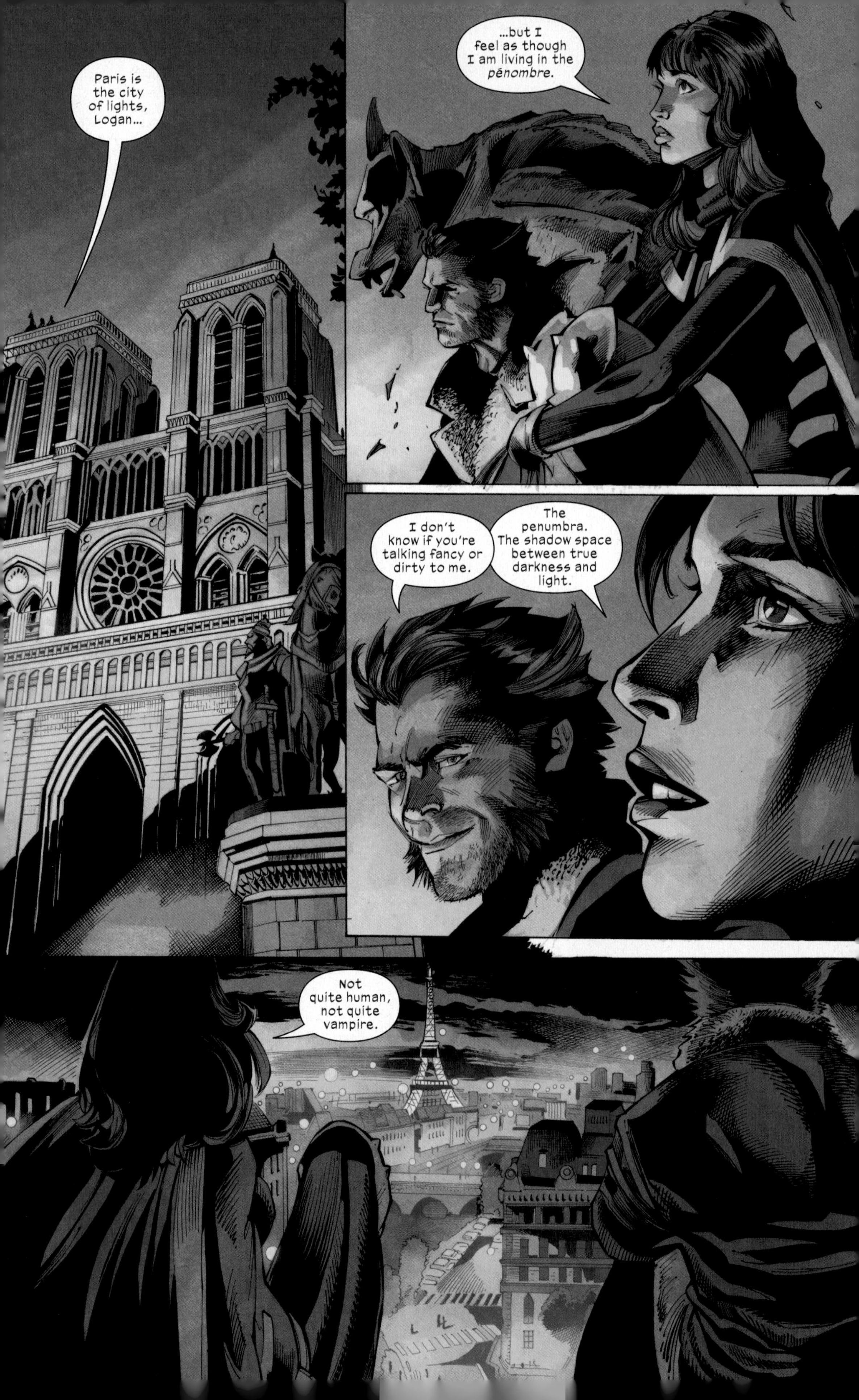
Paris is the city of lights, Logan...
...but I feel as though I am living in the pénombre.
I don't know if you're talking fancy or dirty to me.
The penumbra. The shadow space between true darkness and light.
Not quite human, not quite vampire.

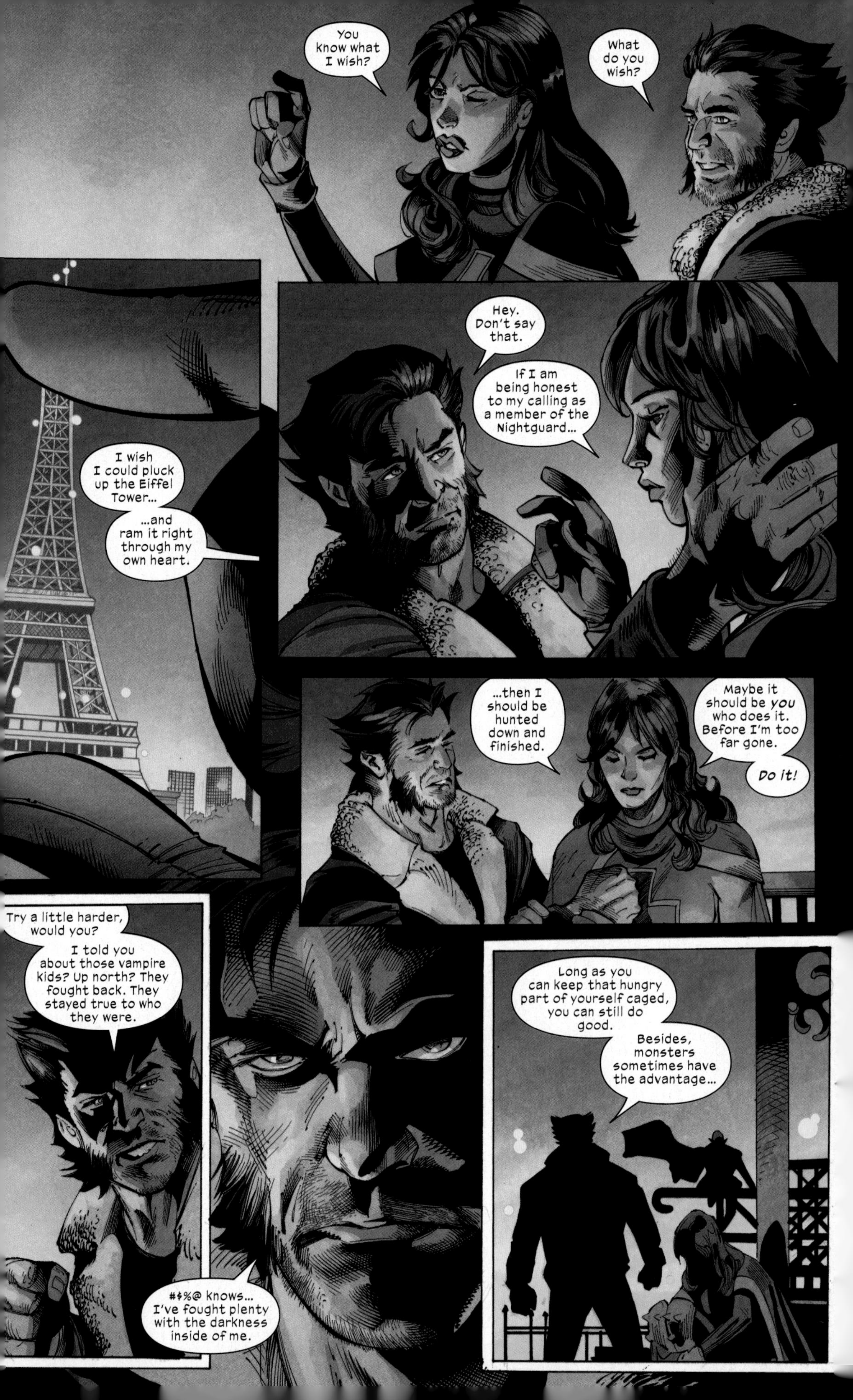
You know what I wish?
What do you wish?
I wish I could pluck up the Eiffel Tower...
...and ram it right through my own heart.
Hey. Don't say that.
If I am being honest to my calling as a member of the Nightguard...
...then I should be hunted down and finished.
Maybe it should be *you* who does it. Before I'm too far gone.
Do it!
Try a little harder, would you?
I told you about those vampire kids? Up north? They fought back. They stayed true to who they were.
#$%@ knows... I've fought plenty with the darkness inside of me.
Long as you can keep that hungry part of yourself caged, you can still do good.
Besides, monsters sometimes have the advantage...

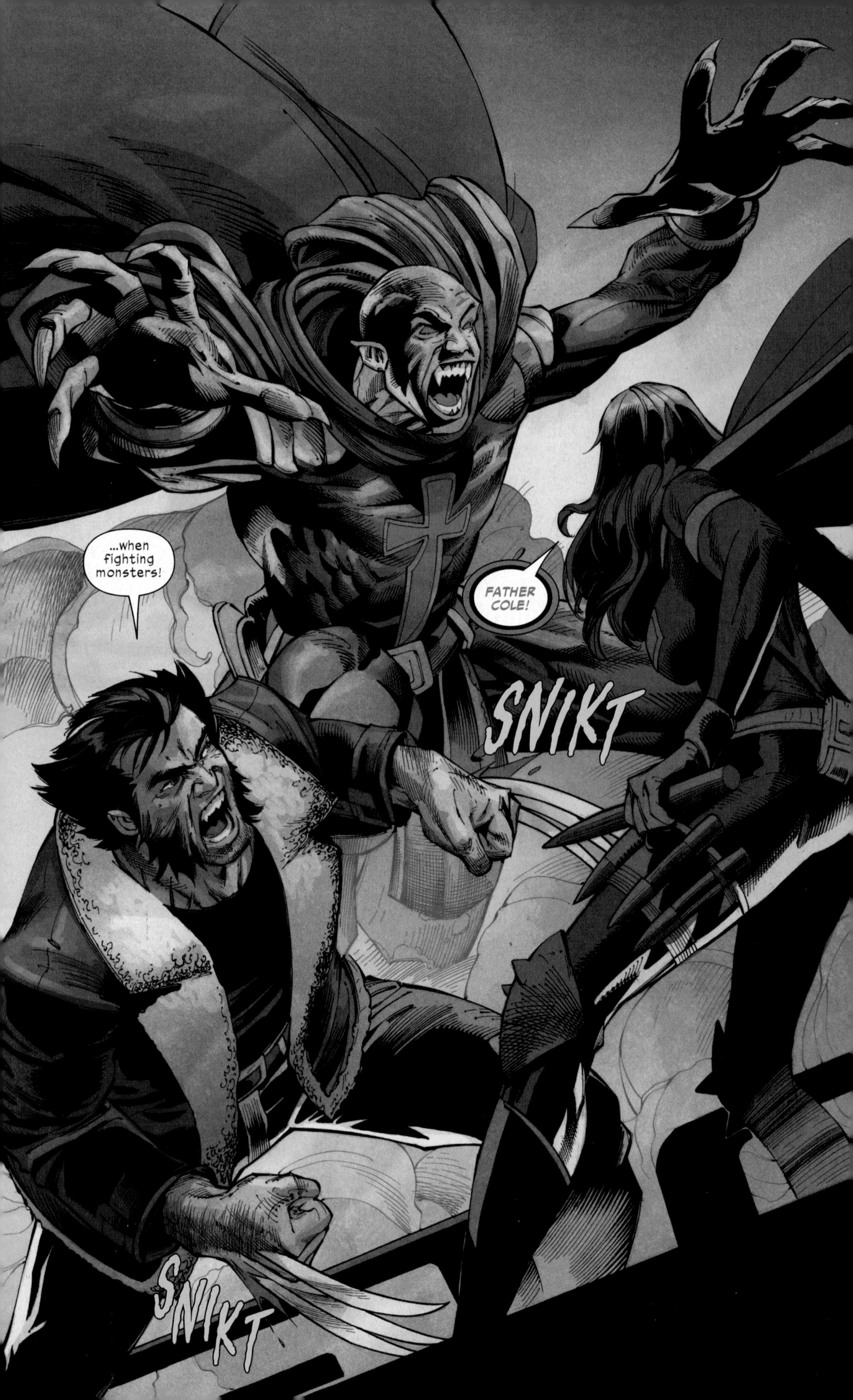
...when fighting monsters!
FATHER COLE!
SNIKT
SNIKT

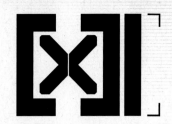

X-FORCE: EVIDENCE LOG

Notebook: Dr. James Boggs, Don of Microbiology, Oxford University

To say that the blood sample -- culled from the mutant known as Wolverine -- is abnormal would be an understatement. Its complexity is unguessable on a number of levels, and if I spent the next ten years studying it, I don't know that I would --

But what am I even saying? I don't have ten years. I don't know that I have ten days. And Timothy...poor Timothy... I daresay he might not last another ten hours.

Help me.

The antigen structure is unlike any other I've encountered. If a normal blood cell is a cardboard box -- simple, flexible, but sturdy in its structure -- Wolverine's is a brick house of many rooms and hallways with a fireplace roaring at its center.

I can hear him. Always. Whispering in my ear. Dracul.

Disease- and temperature-resistant, the muscular antibodies aggressively stand up to and wipe out any foreign intrusion. The exogenous polypeptides defy categorization. The hemoglobin count is an astonishing 30 grams per deciliter, so that one could say he is carrying around in his veins a nuclear arsenal of protein.

I see him in the mist oozing across the campus green, in the rat scurrying through the alley, in the bat clinging to an attic rafter. Dracul. His name is my command.

If only I could study the source himself, if only I could sample his bone marrow, things might be different. The answer -- to what some might call a veritable fountain of youth -- is in his stem cells.

Help me.

The lifespan of a standard red blood cell is 120 days. The lifespan of a vampire's is roughly one day. Whatever power comes with their virulence weakens the RBC membrane. The swift degradation of hemoglobin requires constant transfusion. A kind of daily dialysis. Thus their permanent thirst. They have to refresh their systems or they will collapse.

I saw a fly on a windowsill earlier today. I snatched it and shoved it in my mouth before I knew what I was doing.

An infusion of Wolverine's blood controls the standard antagonistic effects of phosphatidylserine, CD47, infrared, visible, and ultraviolet light. And the bloodclocks manage to replicate -- poorly but serviceably enough -- the liver and spleen, creating a sustainable environment, prolonging the healing factor's potential.

He's going to kill me soon. Please, God, forgive me for helping him.

—

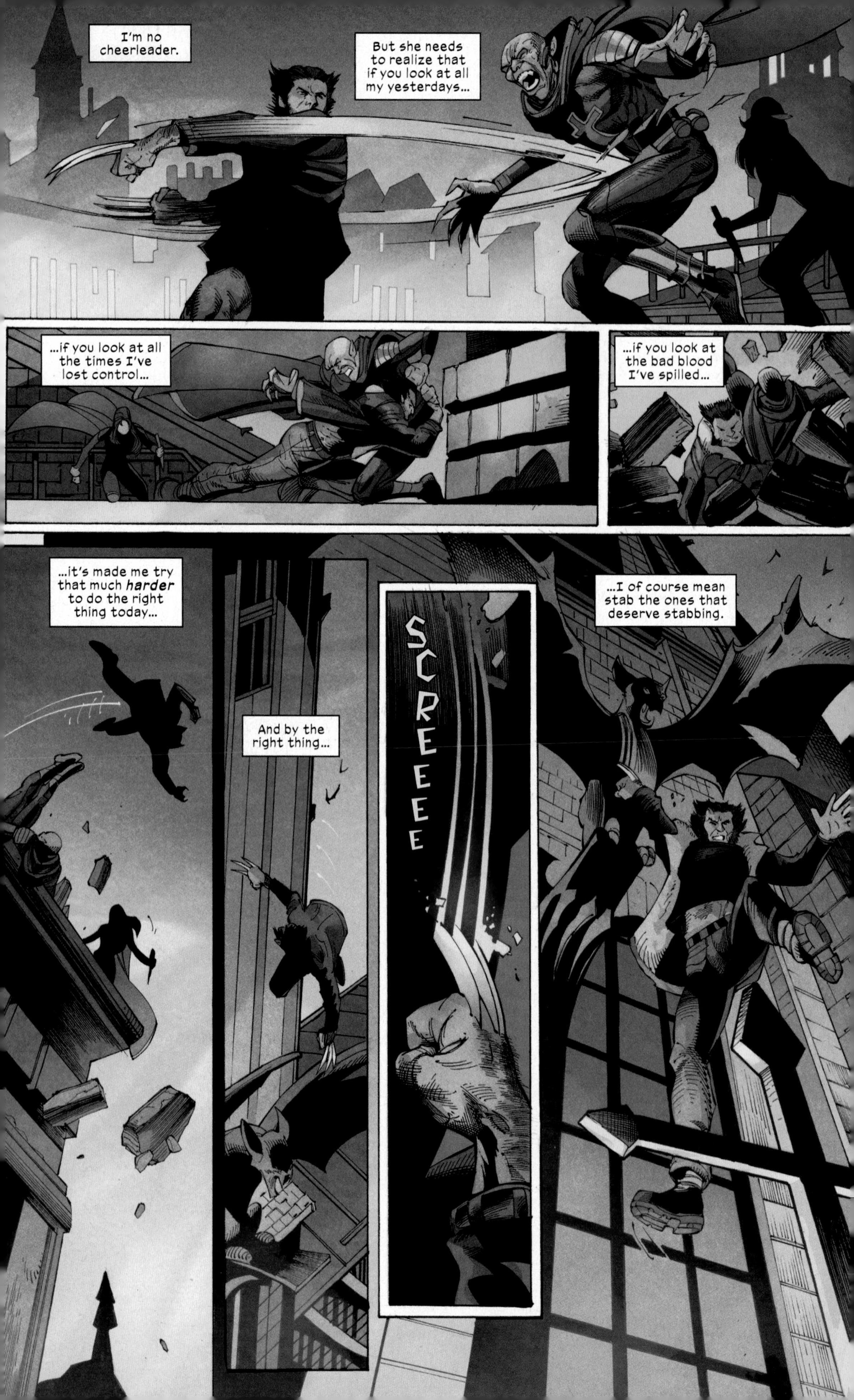
I'm no cheerleader.
But she needs to realize that if you look at all my yesterdays...
...if you look at all the times I've lost control...
...if you look at the bad blood I've spilled...
...it's made me try that much *harder* to do the right thing today...
And by the right thing...
SCREEEE
...I of course mean stab the ones that deserve stabbing.

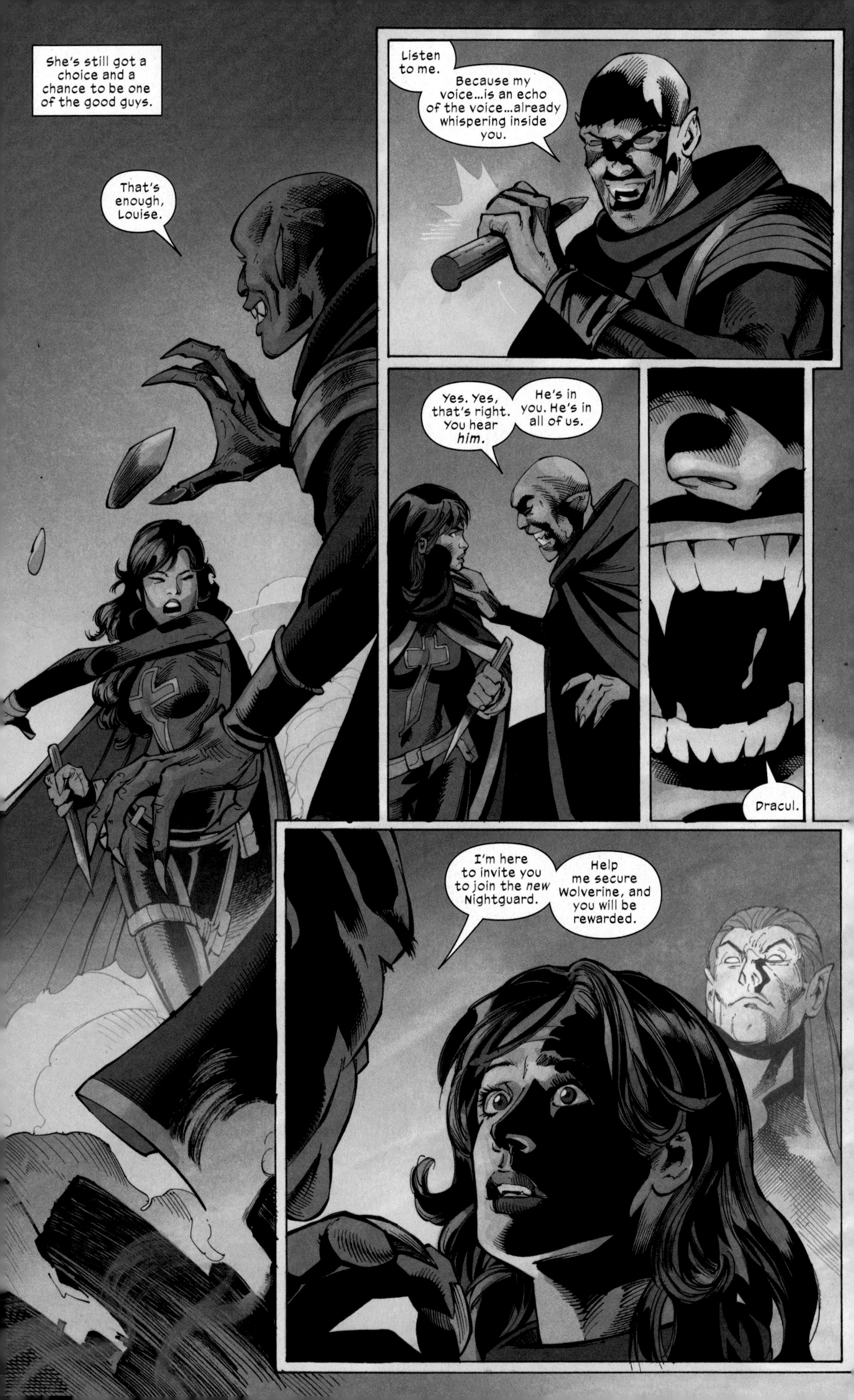
She's still got a choice and a chance to be one of the good guys.
That's enough, Louise.
Listen to me.
Because my voice...is an echo of the voice...already whispering inside you.
Yes. Yes, that's right. You hear *him.*
He's in you. He's in all of us.
Dracul.
I'm here to invite you to join the *new* Nightguard.
Help me secure Wolverine, and you will be rewarded.

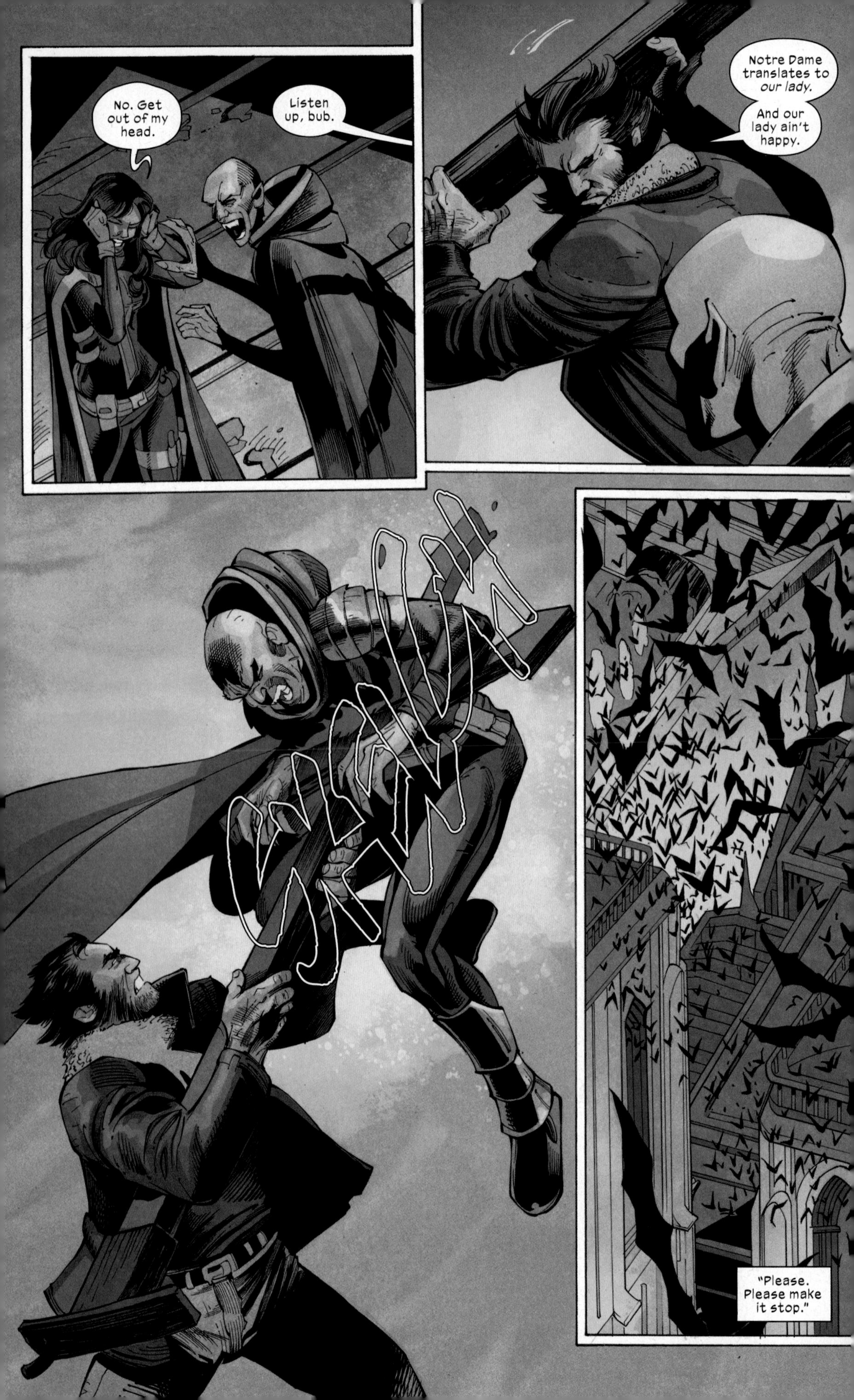
No. Get out of my head.
Listen up, bub.
Notre Dame translates to *our lady.*
And our lady ain't happy.
"Please. Please make it stop."

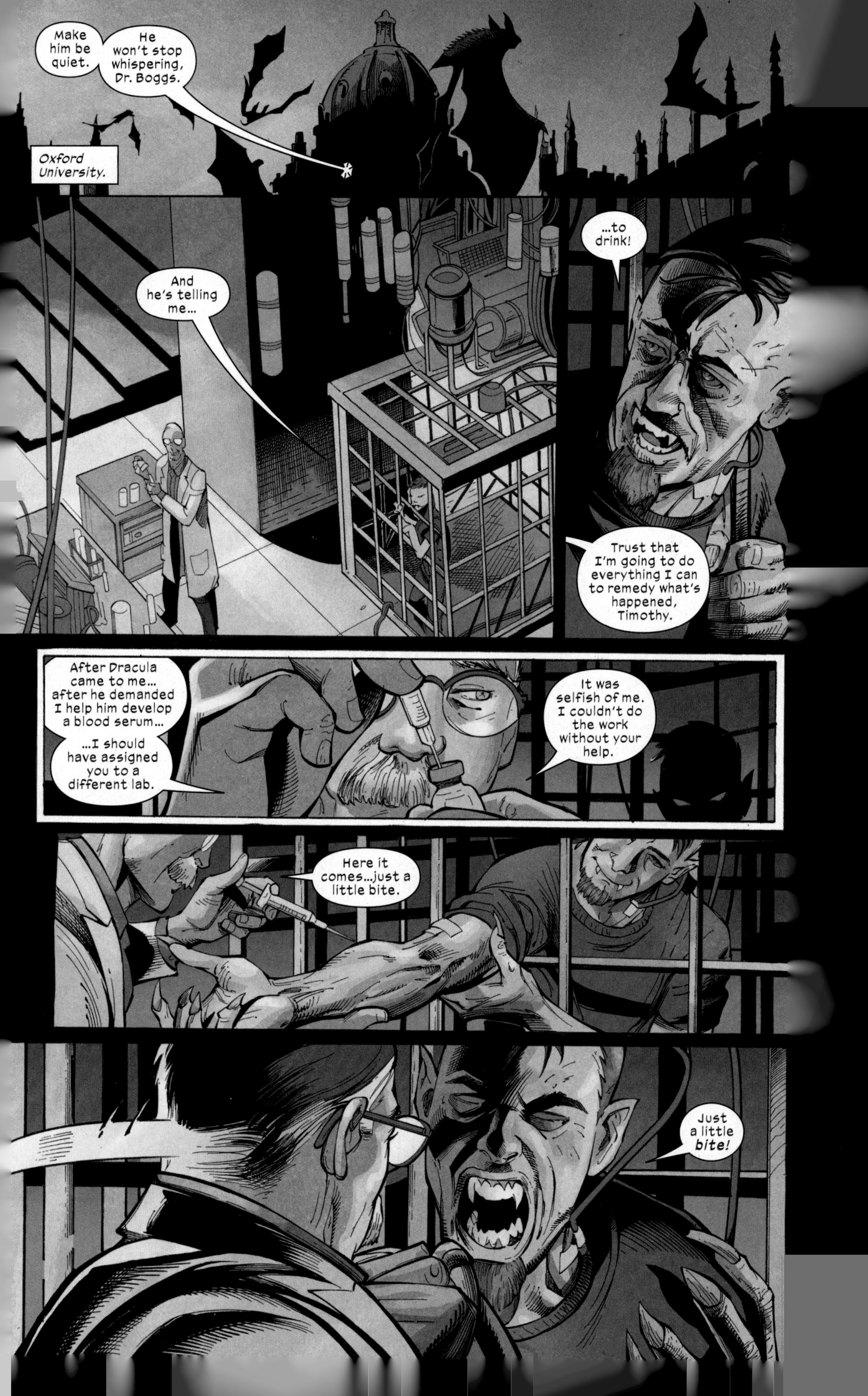
Make him be quiet.
He won't stop whispering, Dr. Boggs.
Oxford University.
And he's telling me...
...to drink!
Trust that I'm going to do everything I can to remedy what's happened, Timothy.
After Dracula came to me... after he demanded I help him develop a blood serum...
...I should have assigned you to a different lab.
It was selfish of me. I couldn't do the work without your help.
Here it comes...just a little bite.
Just a little *bite!*

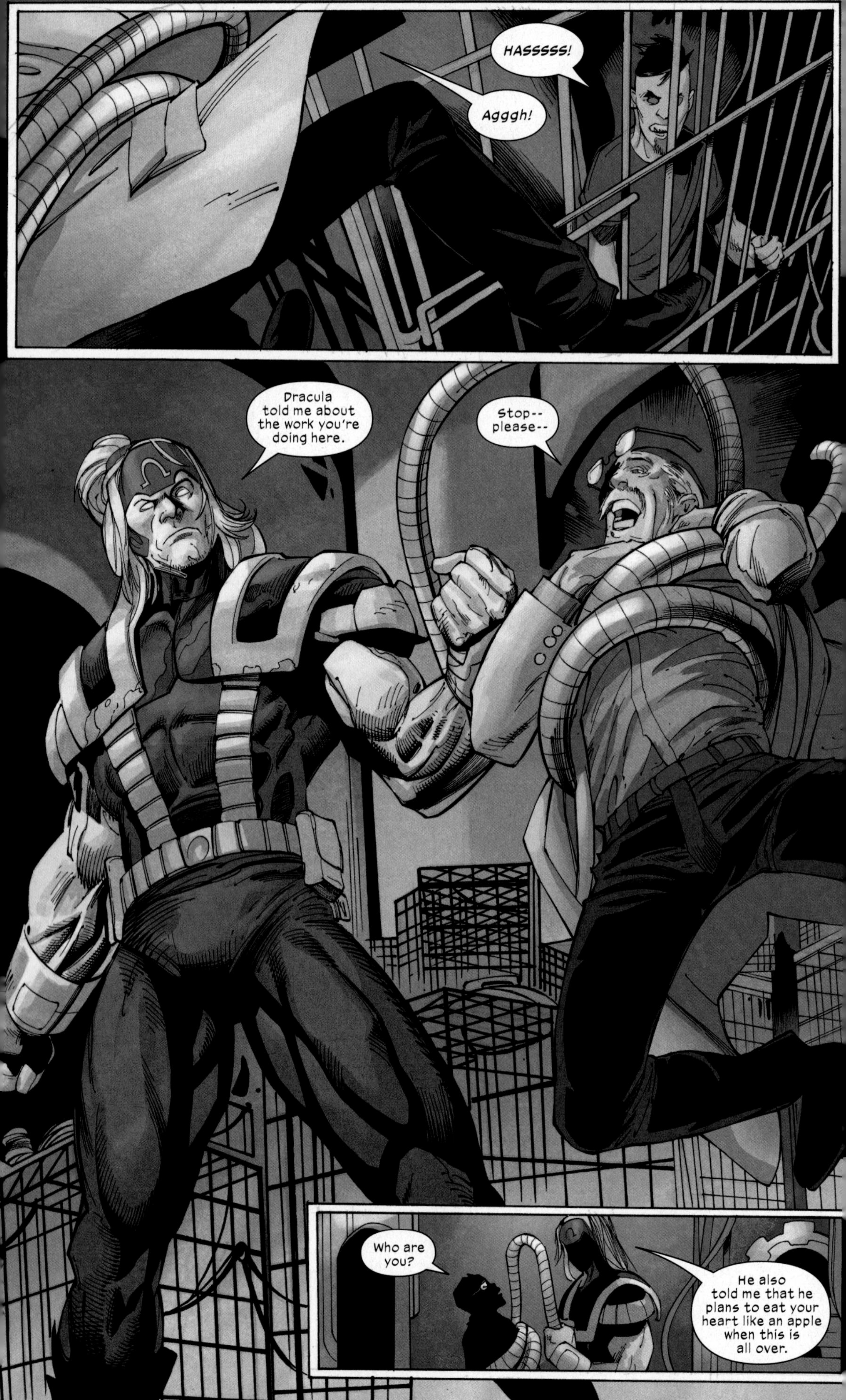
HASSSSS!
Agggh!
Dracula told me about the work you're doing here.
Stop-- please--
Who are you?
He also told me that he plans to eat your heart like an apple when this is all over.

I can't pretend to be surprised.

Then why are you doing this? Why help Dracula if you know you're as good as dead?

I first agreed to help... because I'm a coward.

But now... I have to save him, even if I can't save myself.

What if I told you... ...you could do both?

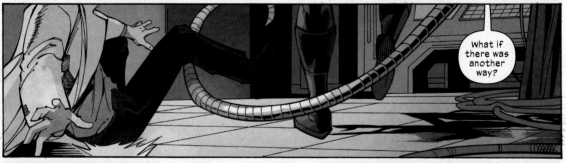

What if there was another way?

A way we could help each other?

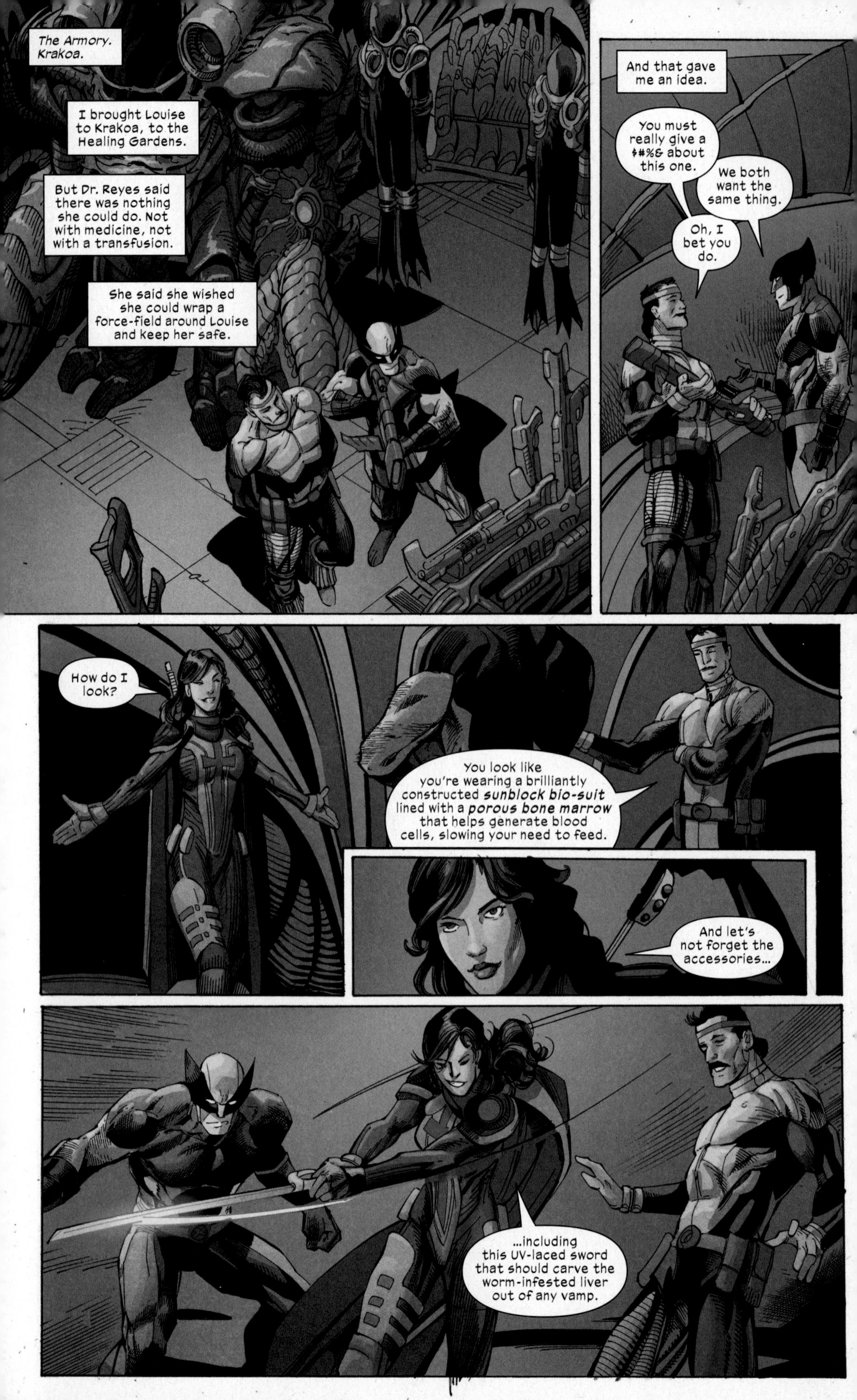
The Armory.
Krakoa.
I brought Louise to Krakoa, to the Healing Gardens.
But Dr. Reyes said there was nothing she could do. Not with medicine, not with a transfusion.
She said she wished she could wrap a force-field around Louise and keep her safe.
And that gave me an idea.
You must really give a $#%& about this one.
We both want the same thing.
Oh, I bet you do.
How do I look?
You look like you're wearing a brilliantly constructed *sunblock bio-suit* lined with a *porous bone marrow* that helps generate blood cells, slowing your need to feed.
And let's not forget the accessories...
...including this UV-laced sword that should carve the worm-infested liver out of any vamp.

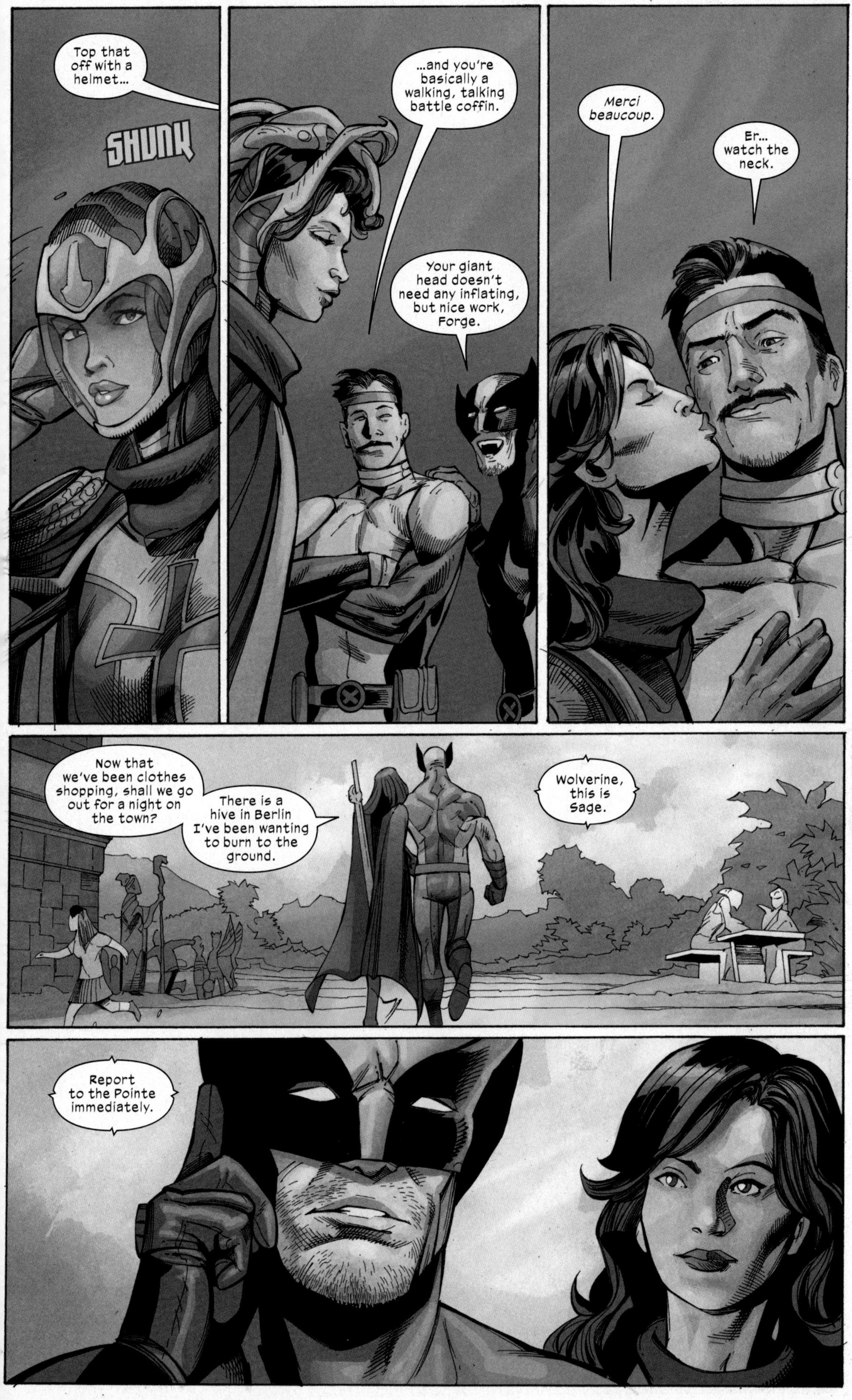
Top that off with a helmet...
SHUNK
...and you're basically a walking, talking battle coffin.
Your giant head doesn't need any inflating, but nice work, Forge.
Merci beaucoup.
Er... watch the neck.
Now that we've been clothes shopping, shall we go out for a night on the town?
There is a hive in Berlin I've been wanting to burn to the ground.
Wolverine, this is Sage.
Report to the Pointe immediately.

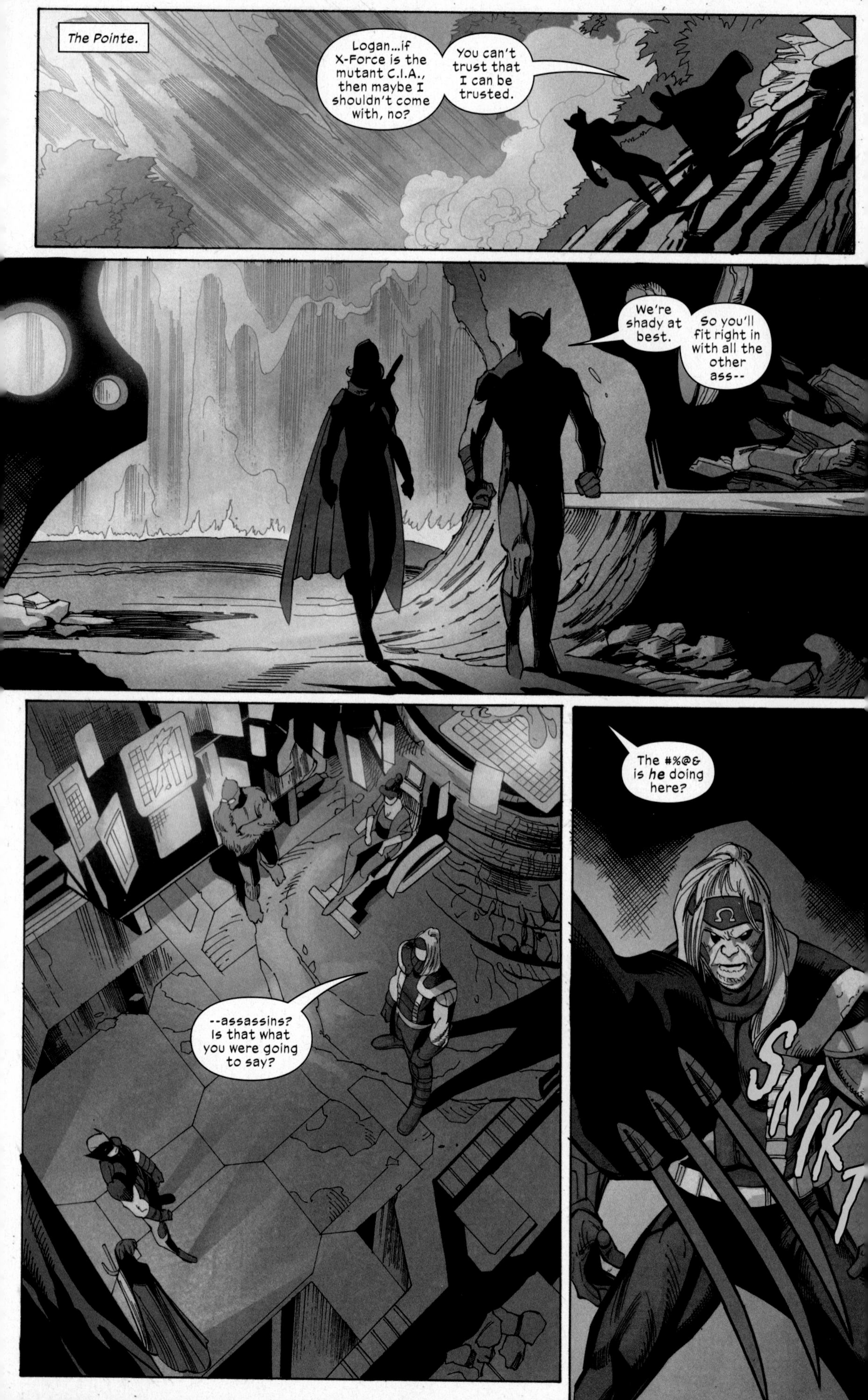
The Pointe.
Logan...if X-Force is the mutant C.I.A., then maybe I shouldn't come with, no?
You can't trust that I can be trusted.
We're shady at best.
So you'll fit right in with all the other ass--
--assassins? Is that what you were going to say?
The #%@& is *he* doing here?
SNIKT

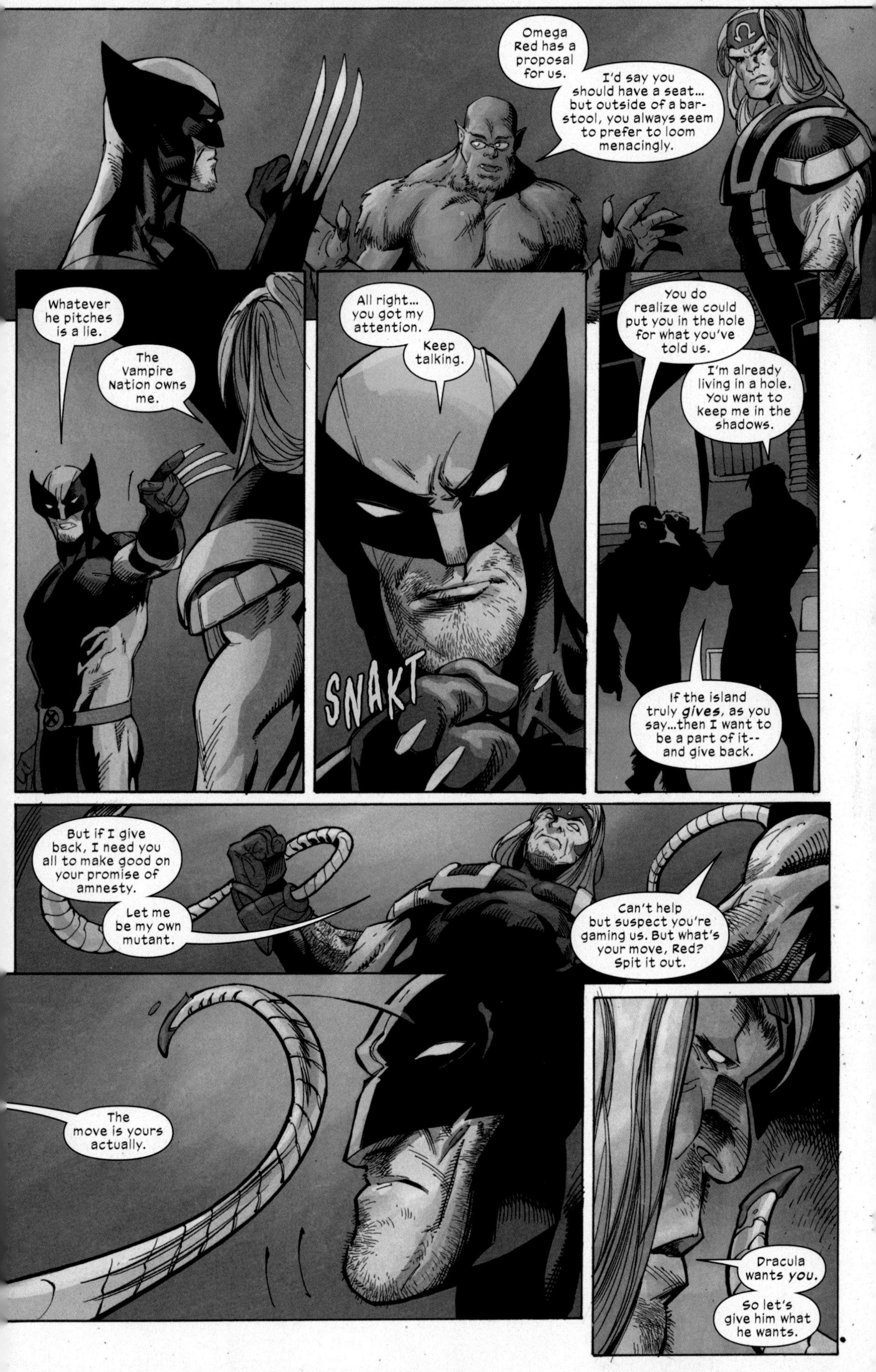
Omega Red has a proposal for us.
I'd say you should have a seat... but outside of a bar-stool, you always seem to prefer to loom menacingly.
Whatever he pitches is a lie.
The Vampire Nation owns me.
All right... you got my attention.
Keep talking.
SNAKT
You do realize we could put you in the hole for what you've told us.
I'm already living in a hole. You want to keep me in the shadows.
If the island truly *gives*, as you say...then I want to be a part of it-- and give back.
But if I give back, I need you all to make good on your promise of amnesty.
Let me be my own mutant.
Can't help but suspect you're gaming us. But what's your move, Red? Spit it out.
The move is yours actually.
Dracula wants *you*.
So let's give him what he wants.

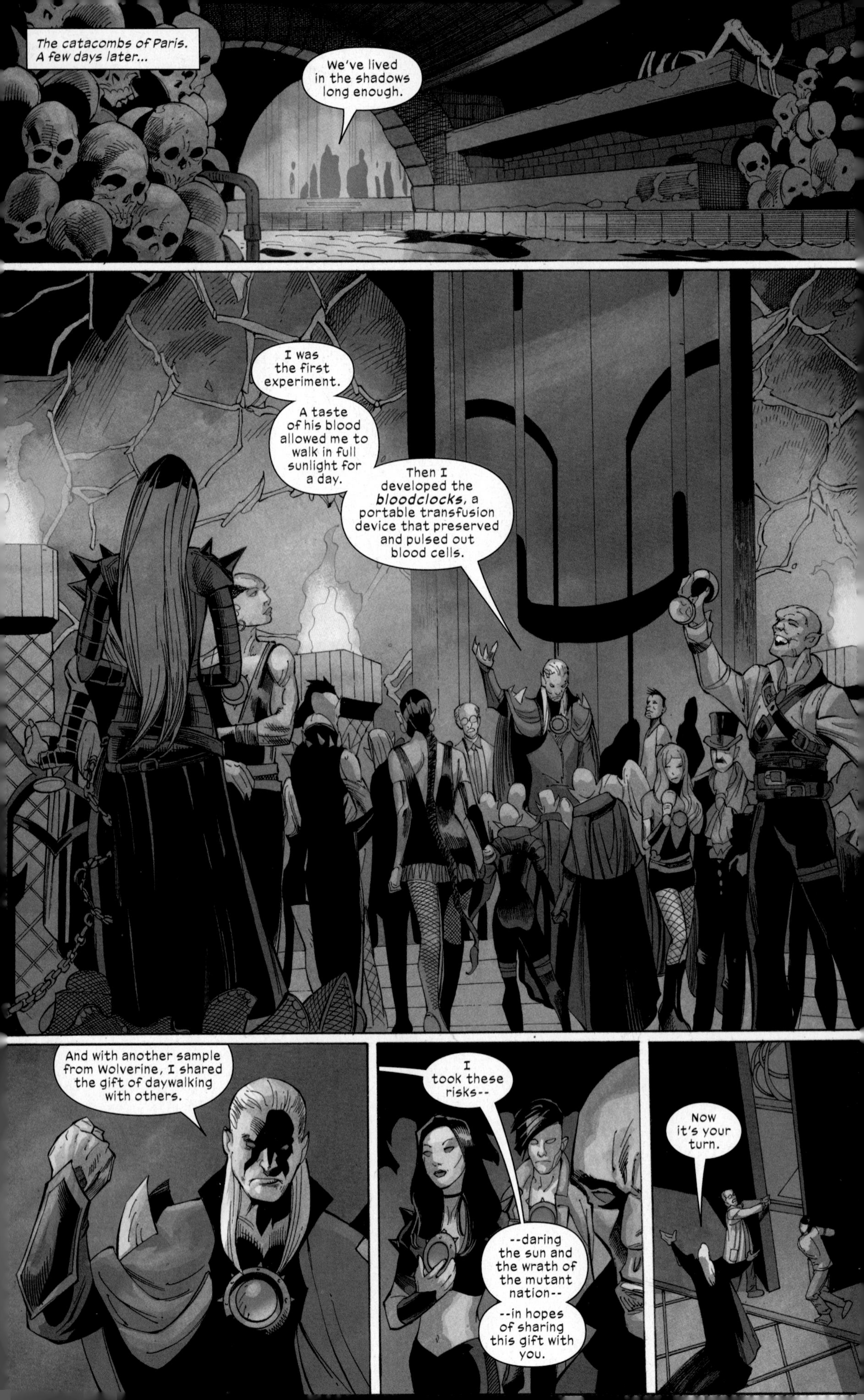
The catacombs of Paris. A few days later...
We've lived in the shadows long enough.
I was the first experiment.
A taste of his blood allowed me to walk in full sunlight for a day.
Then I developed the bloodclocks, a portable transfusion device that preserved and pulsed out blood cells.
And with another sample from Wolverine, I shared the gift of daywalking with others.
I took these risks--
--daring the sun and the wrath of the mutant nation--
--in hopes of sharing this gift with you.
Now it's your turn.

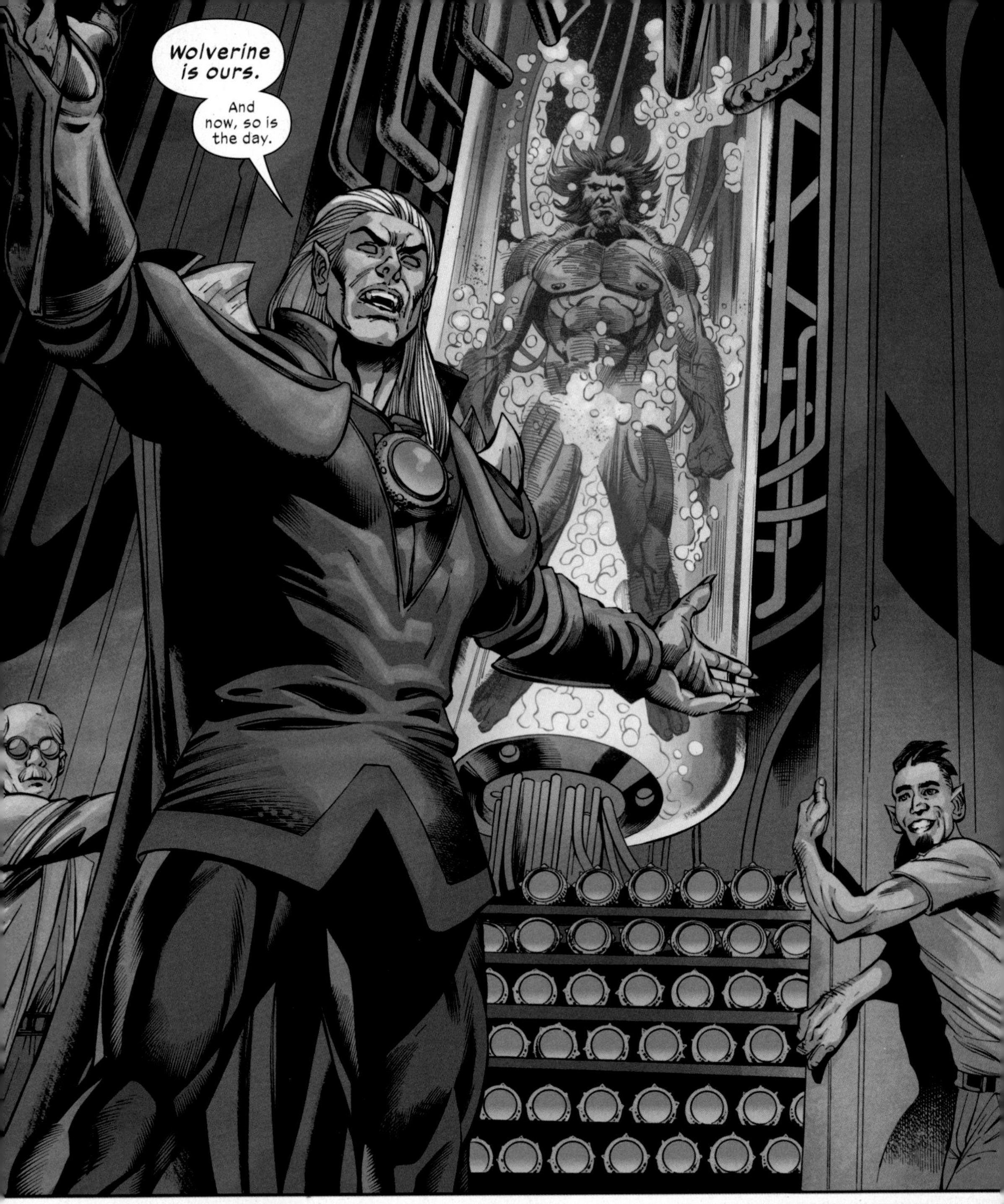
Wolverine is ours.
And now, so is the day.

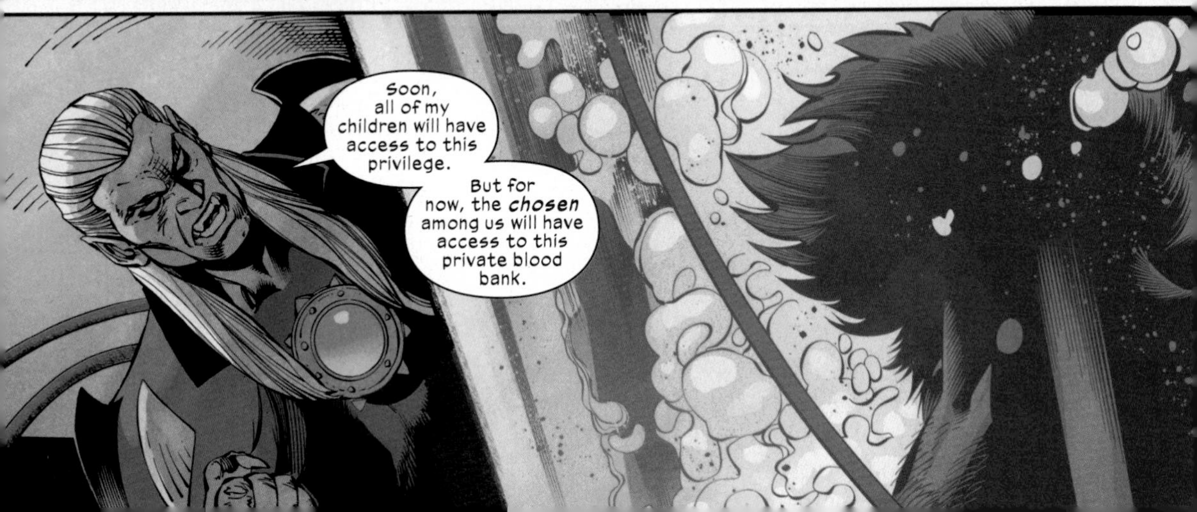
Soon, all of my children will have access to this privilege.
But for now, the chosen among us will have access to this private blood bank.

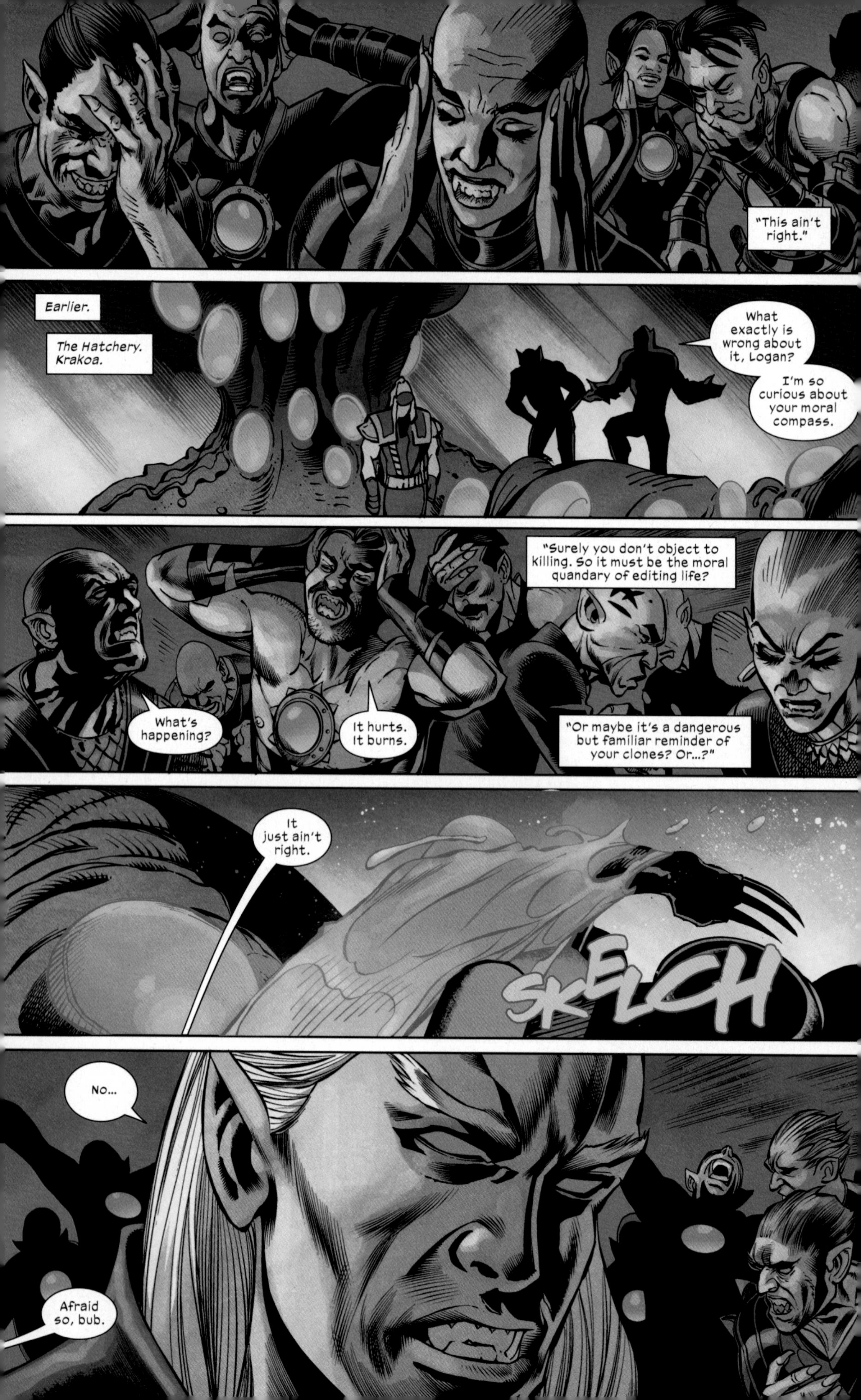

"This ain't right."
Earlier.
The Hatchery. Krakoa.
What exactly is wrong about it, Logan?
I'm so curious about your moral compass.
"Surely you don't object to killing. So it must be the moral quandary of editing life?
What's happening?
It hurts. It burns.
"Or maybe it's a dangerous but familiar reminder of your clones? Or...?"
It just ain't right.
SKELCH
No...
Afraid so, bub.

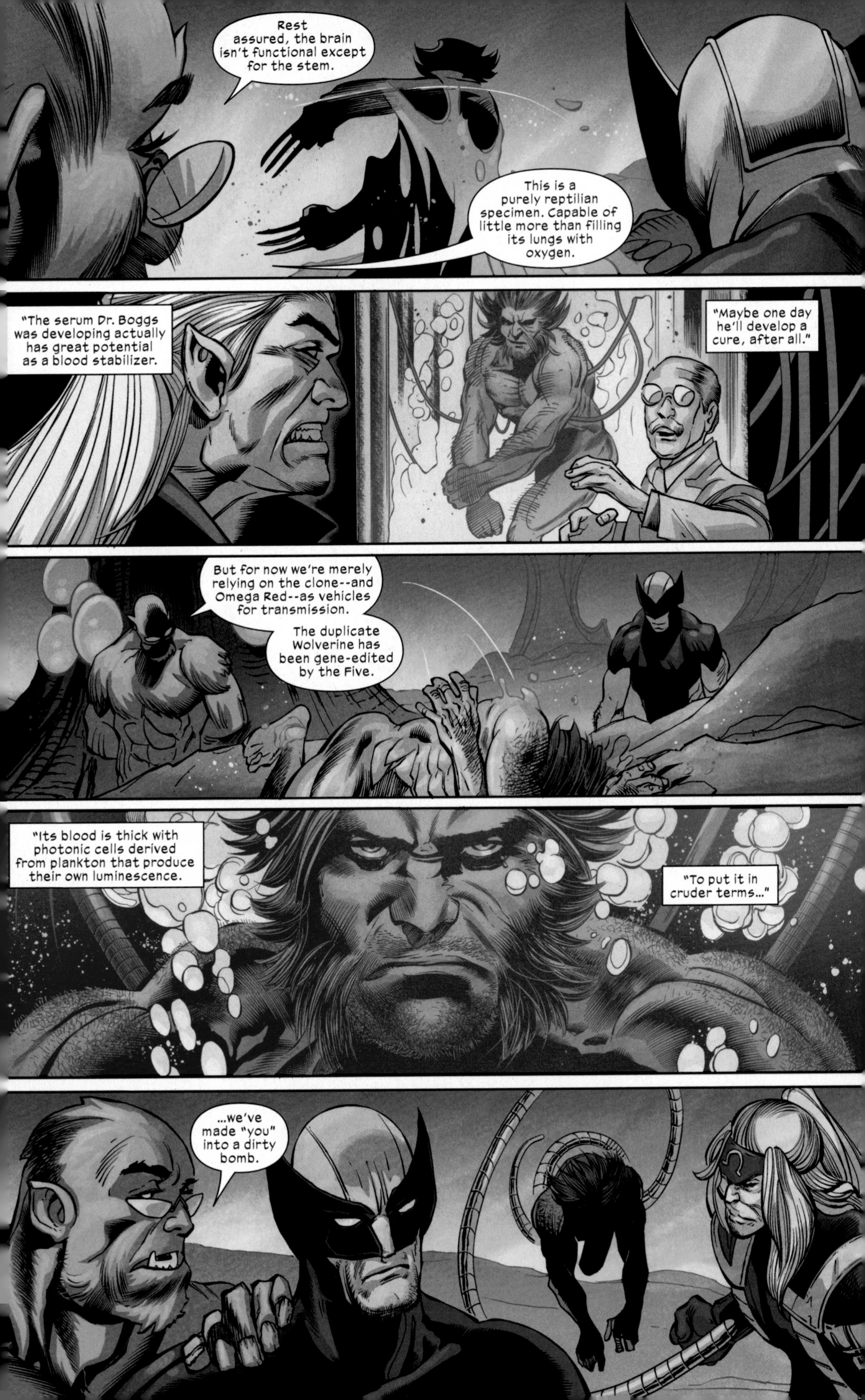
Rest assured, the brain isn't functional except for the stem.
This is a purely reptilian specimen. Capable of little more than filling its lungs with oxygen.
"The serum Dr. Boggs was developing actually has great potential as a blood stabilizer.
"Maybe one day he'll develop a cure, after all."
But for now we're merely relying on the clone--and Omega Red--as vehicles for transmission.
The duplicate Wolverine has been gene-edited by the Five.
"Its blood is thick with photonic cells derived from plankton that produce their own luminescence.
"To put it in cruder terms..."
...we've made "you" into a dirty bomb.

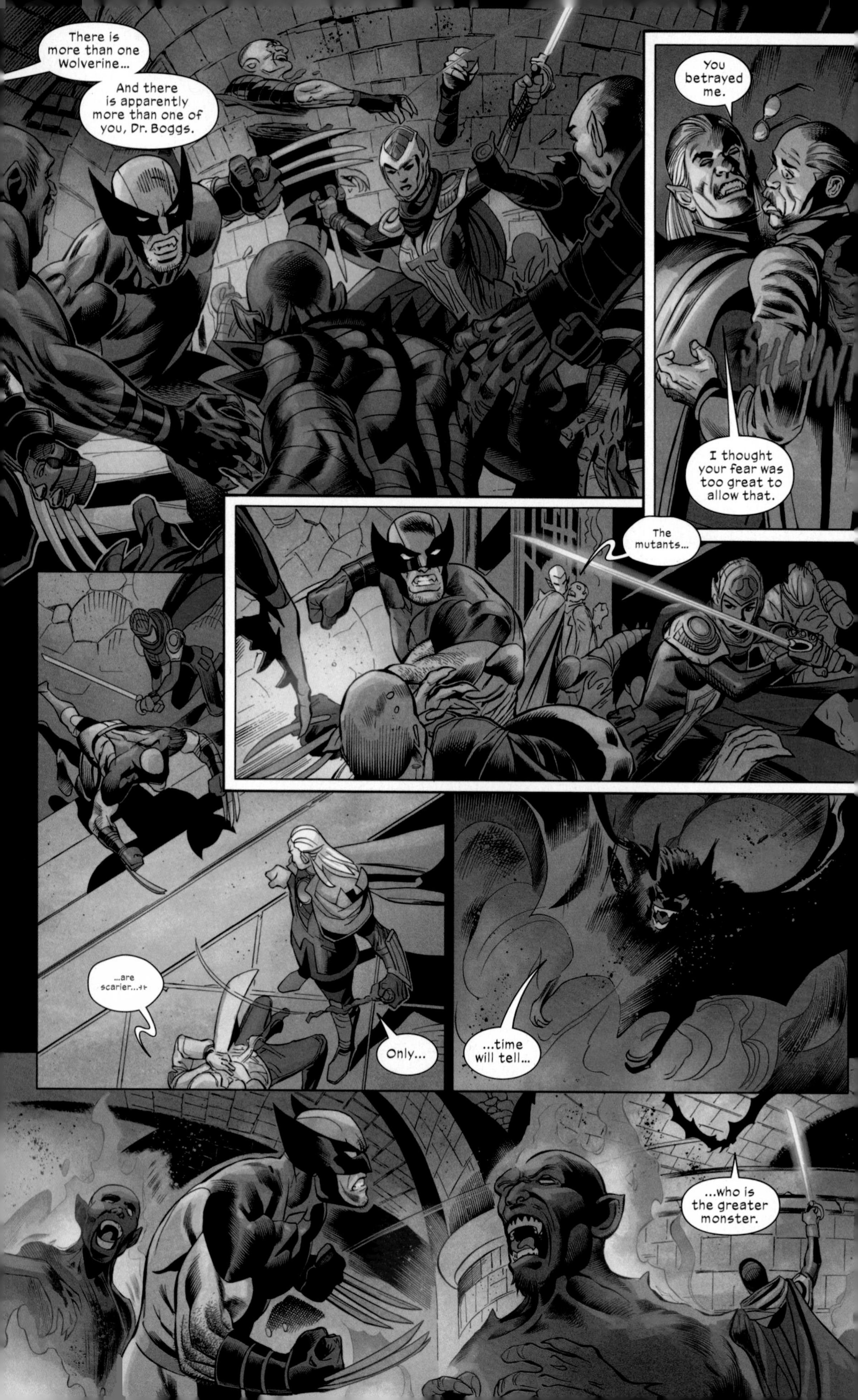
There is more than one Wolverine...
And there is apparently more than one of you, Dr. Boggs.
You betrayed me.
SHLUN
I thought your fear was too great to allow that.
The mutants...
...are scarier...
Only...
...time will tell...
...who is the greater monster.

Not sure what I hate more: vegetables, whiners, or #@$% vampires.

-- WOLVERINE

```
 ┌ [wolv__[0.12]
   [erine_[0.12]
```

```
 ┌ [wolv__[0.XX]
   [erine_[0.XX]
```

```
[wolv__[0.12].....]
[erine_[0.12].....]

[Wolverine_alpha.]
```

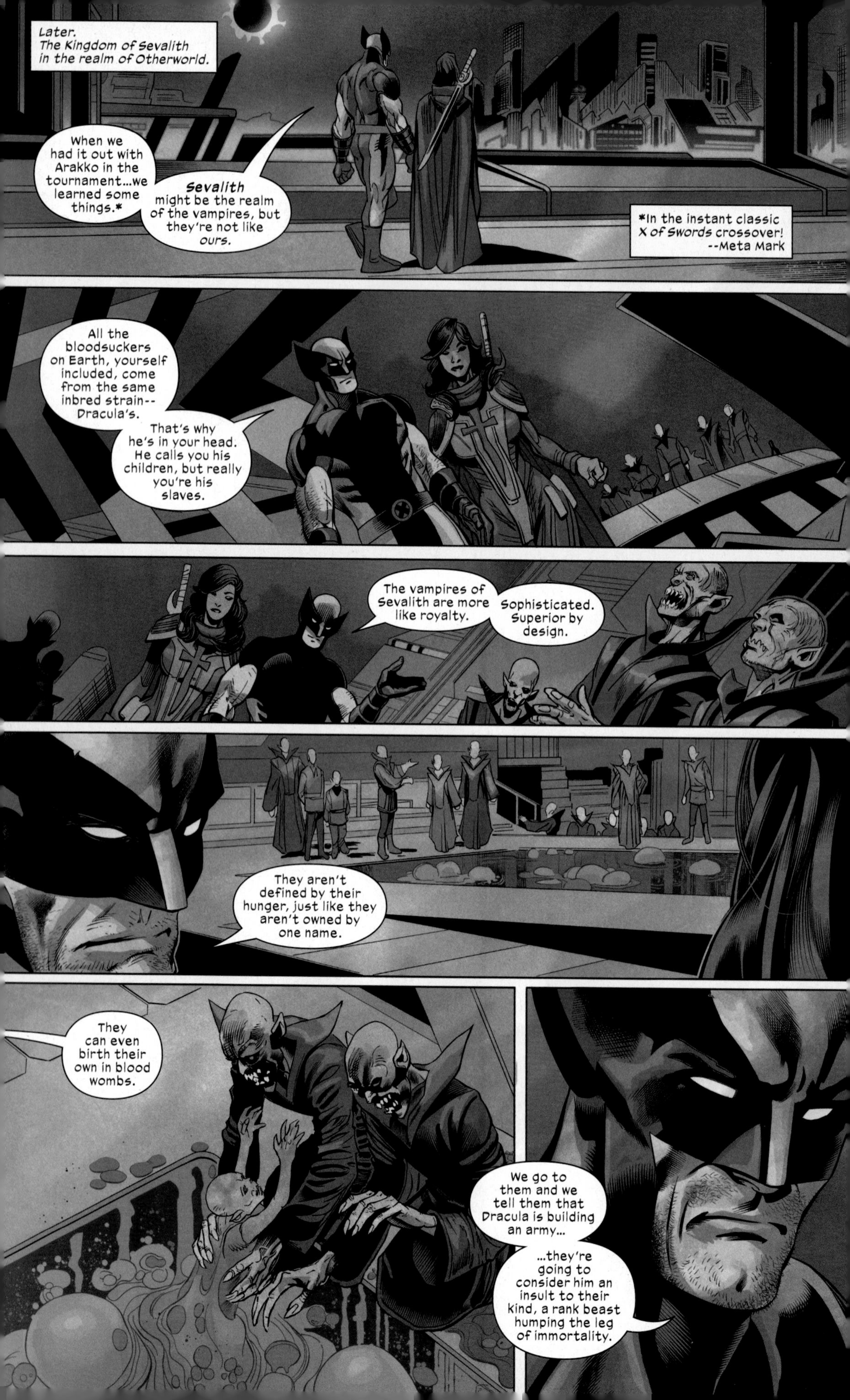
Later.
The Kingdom of Sevalith in the realm of Otherworld.
When we had it out with Arakko in the tournament...we learned some things.*
Sevalith might be the realm of the vampires, but they're not like ours.
*In the instant classic X of Swords crossover! --Meta Mark
All the bloodsuckers on Earth, yourself included, come from the same inbred strain--Dracula's.
That's why he's in your head. He calls you his children, but really you're his slaves.
The vampires of Sevalith are more like royalty.
Sophisticated. Superior by design.
They aren't defined by their hunger, just like they aren't owned by one name.
They can even birth their own in blood wombs.
We go to them and we tell them that Dracula is building an army...
...they're going to consider him an insult to their kind, a rank beast humping the leg of immortality.

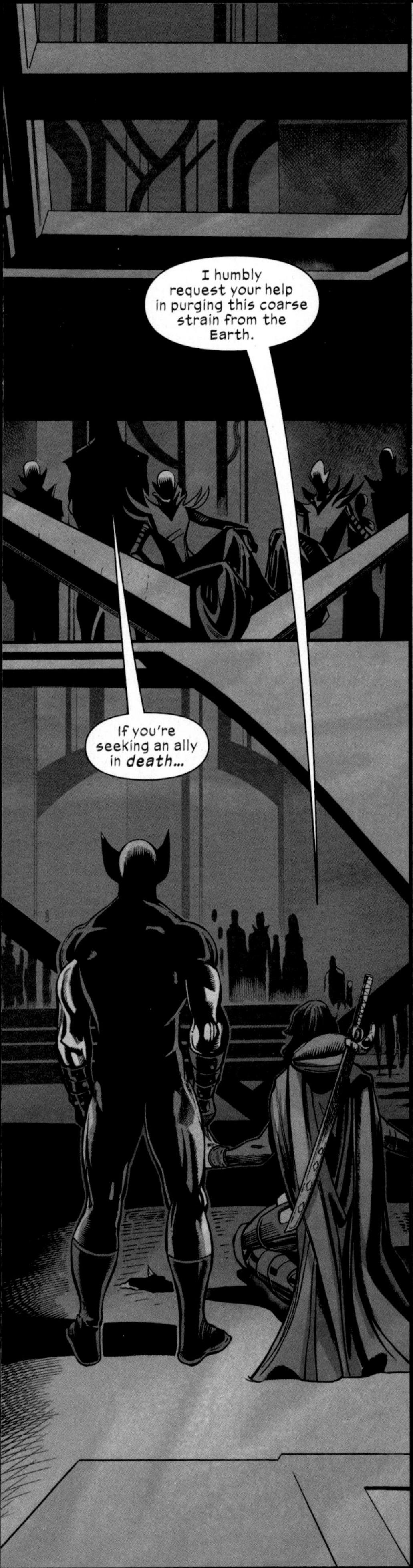
I humbly request your help in purging this coarse strain from the Earth.
If you're seeking an ally in *death*...
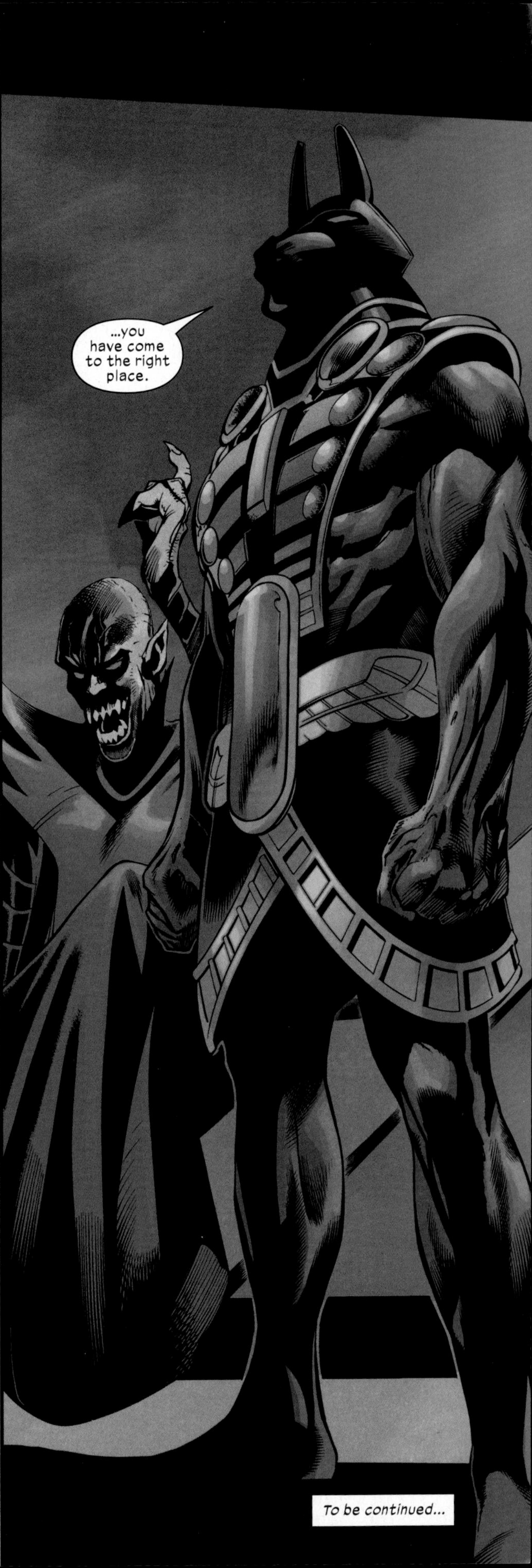
...you have come to the right place.
To be continued...

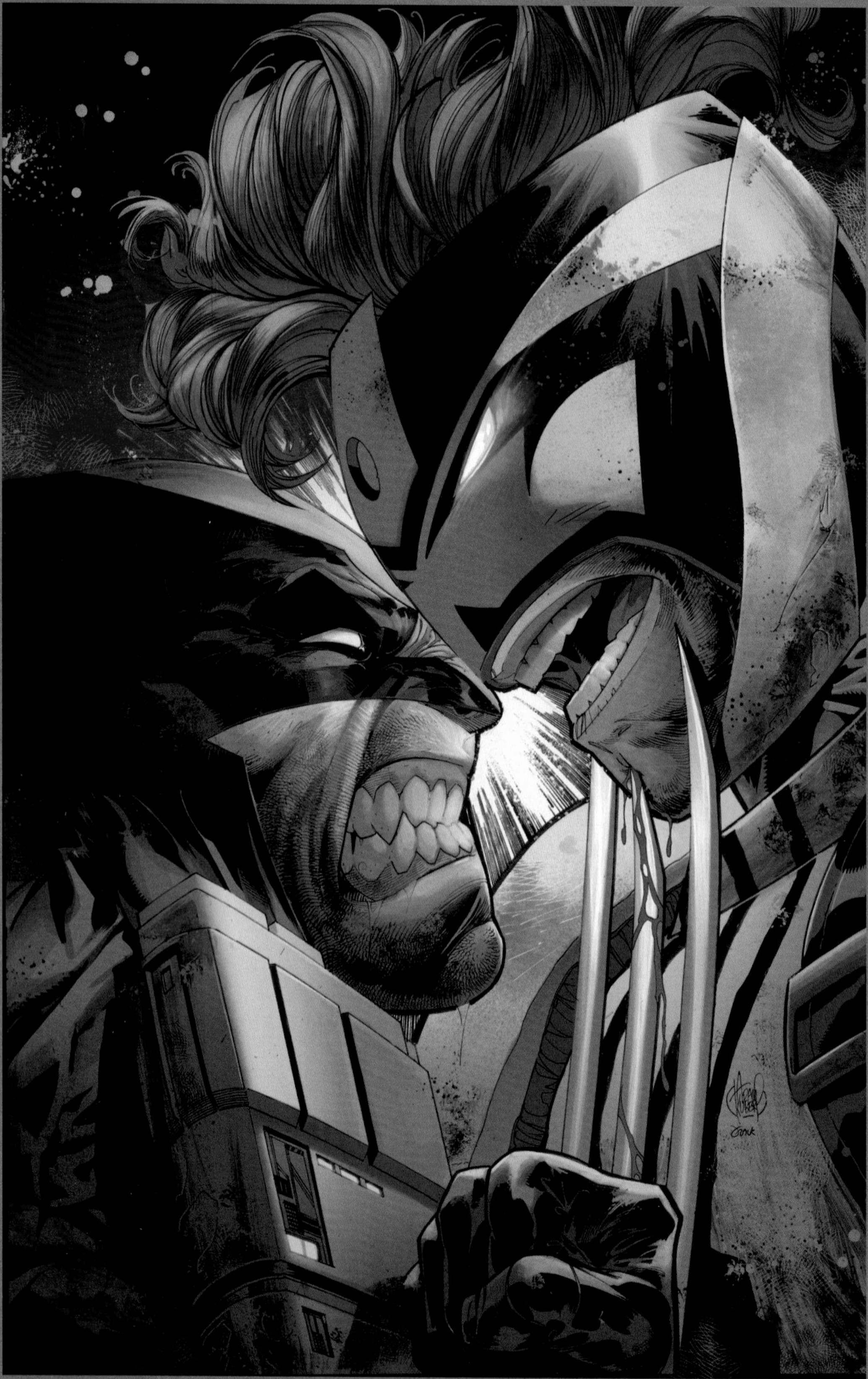

Wolverine #8

by Adam Kubert
& Frank Martin

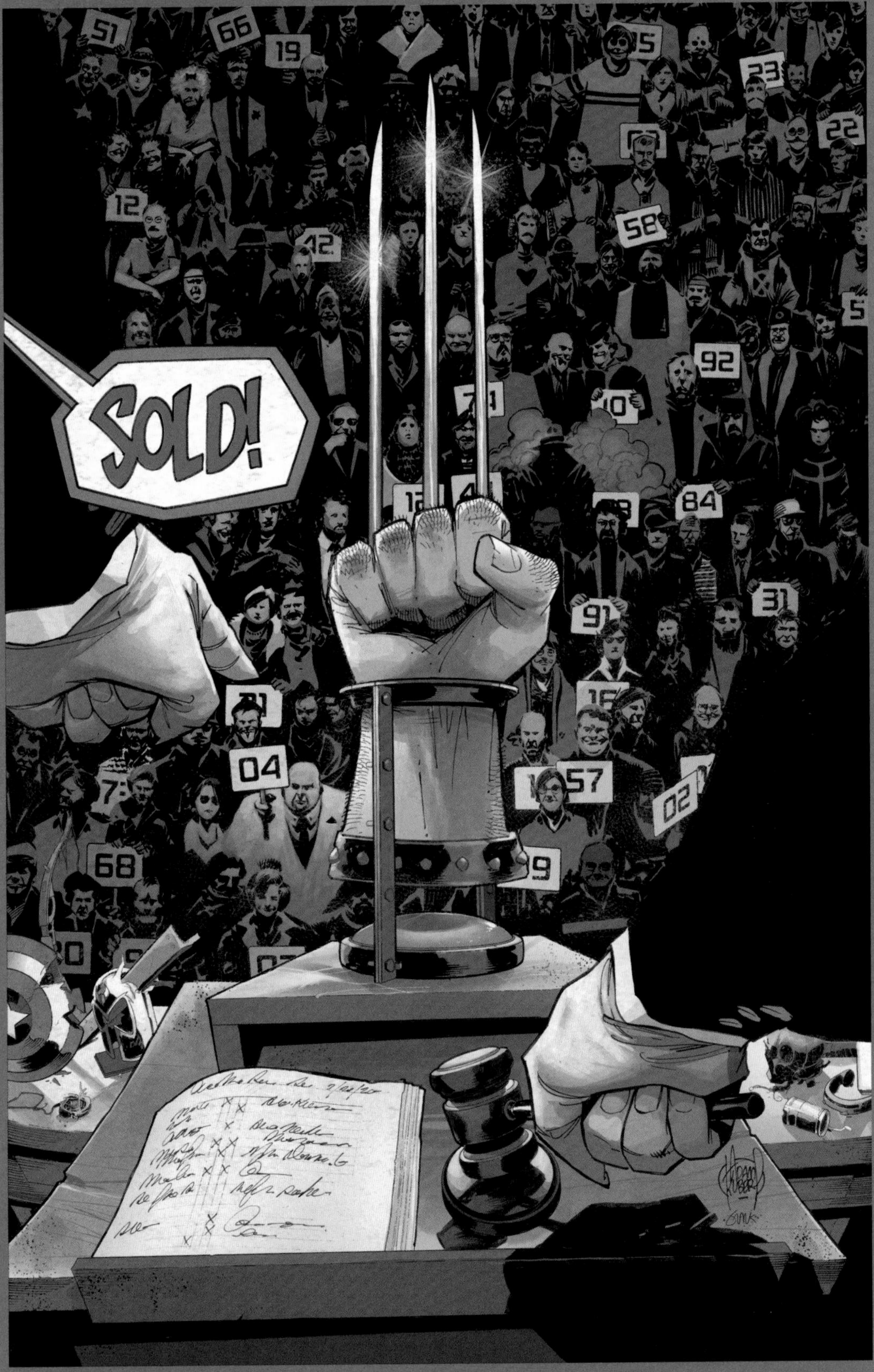
SOLD!

Wolverine #9

by Adam Kubert
& Frank Martin

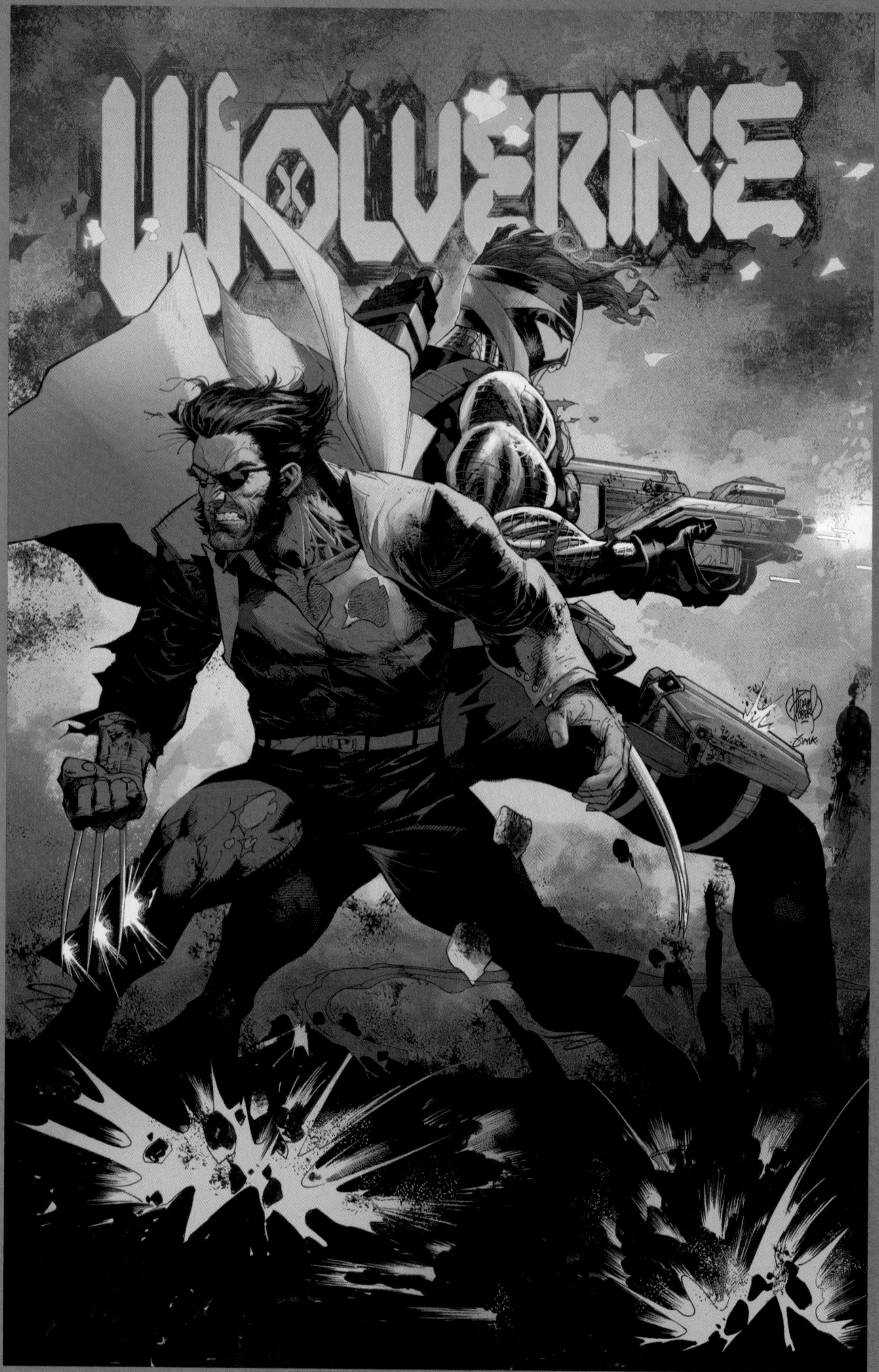
WOLVERINE

Wolverine #10

by Adam Kubert
& Frank Martin

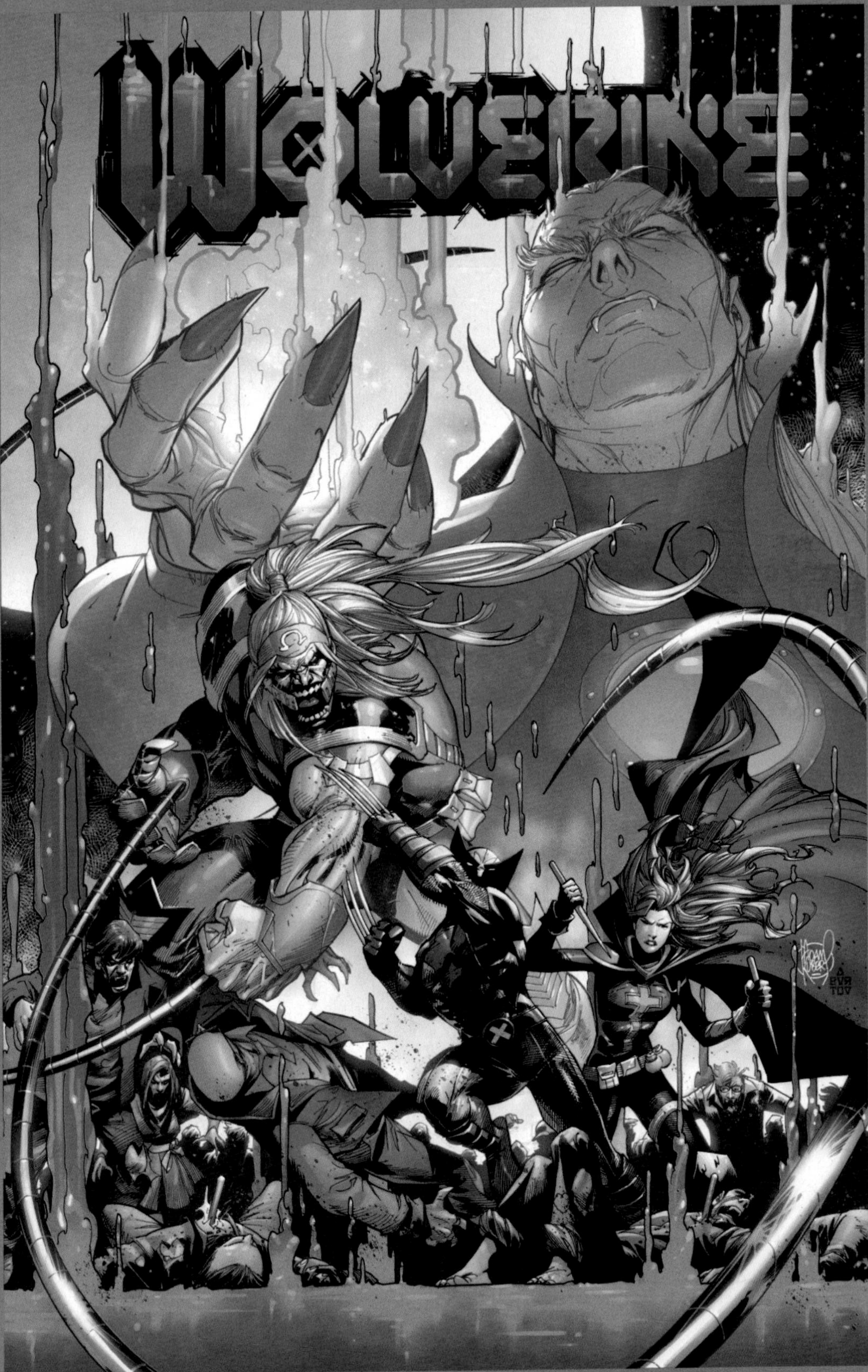
WOLVERINE

Wolverine #11

by Adam Kubert
& Frank Martin

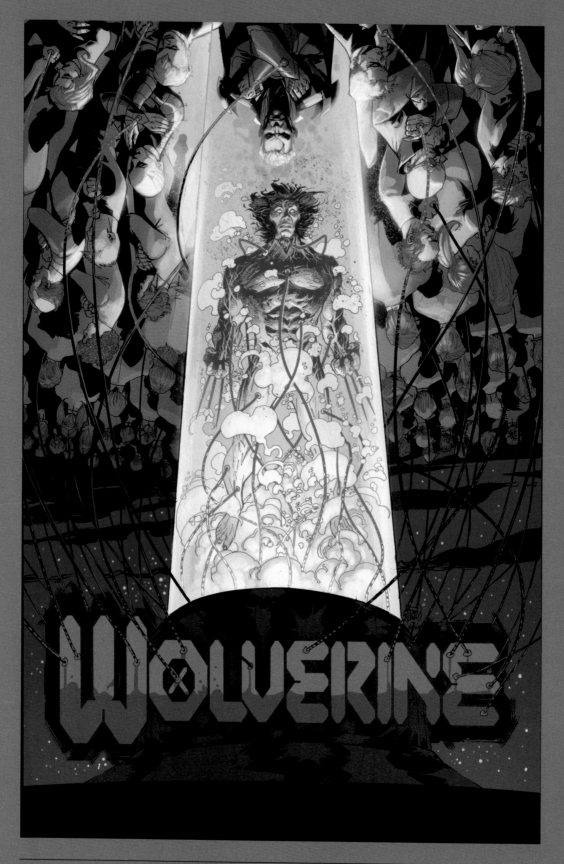

Wolverine #12

by Adam Kubert
& Frank Martin

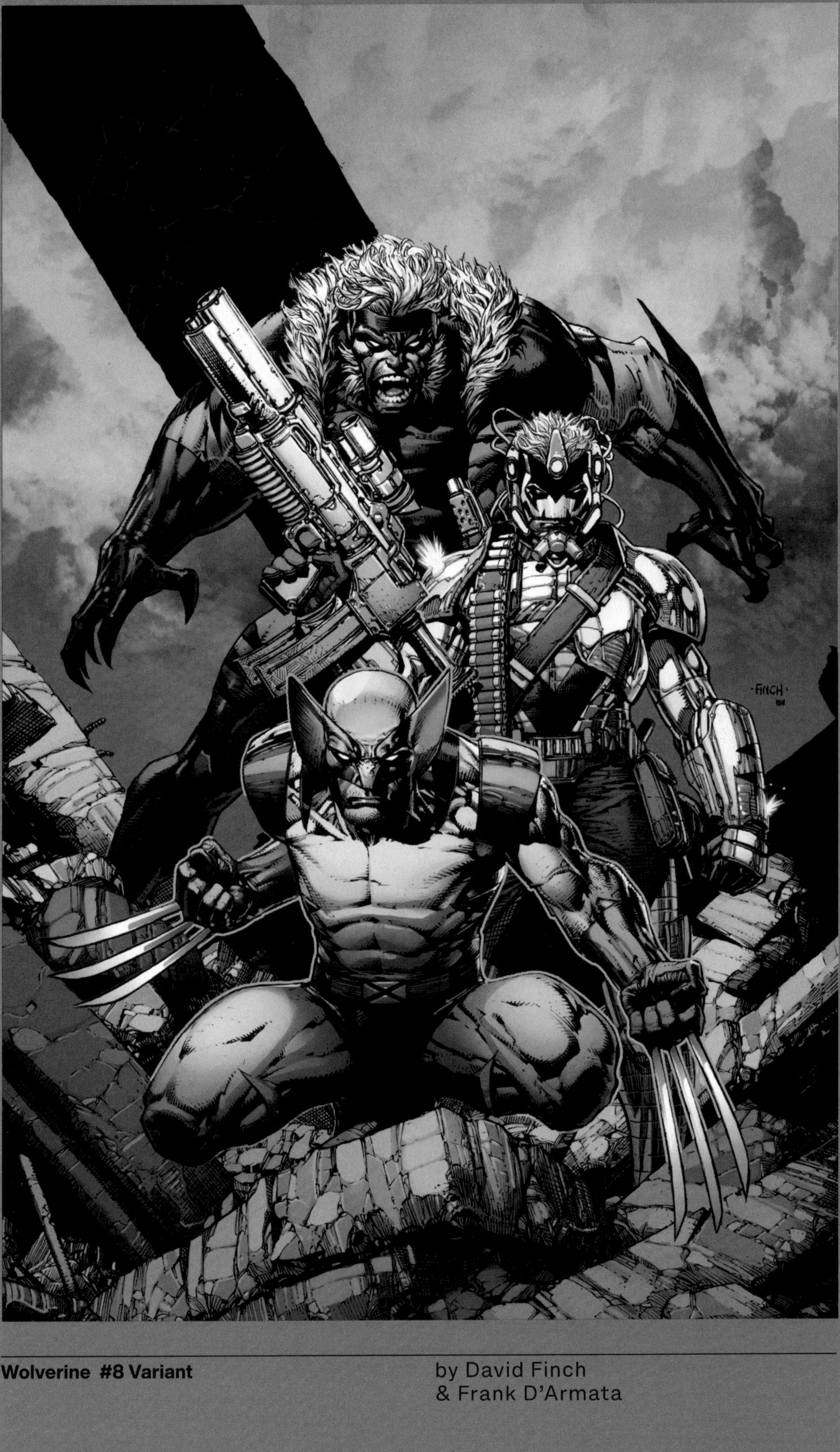
FINCH

Wolverine #8 Variant

by David Finch
& Frank D'Armata

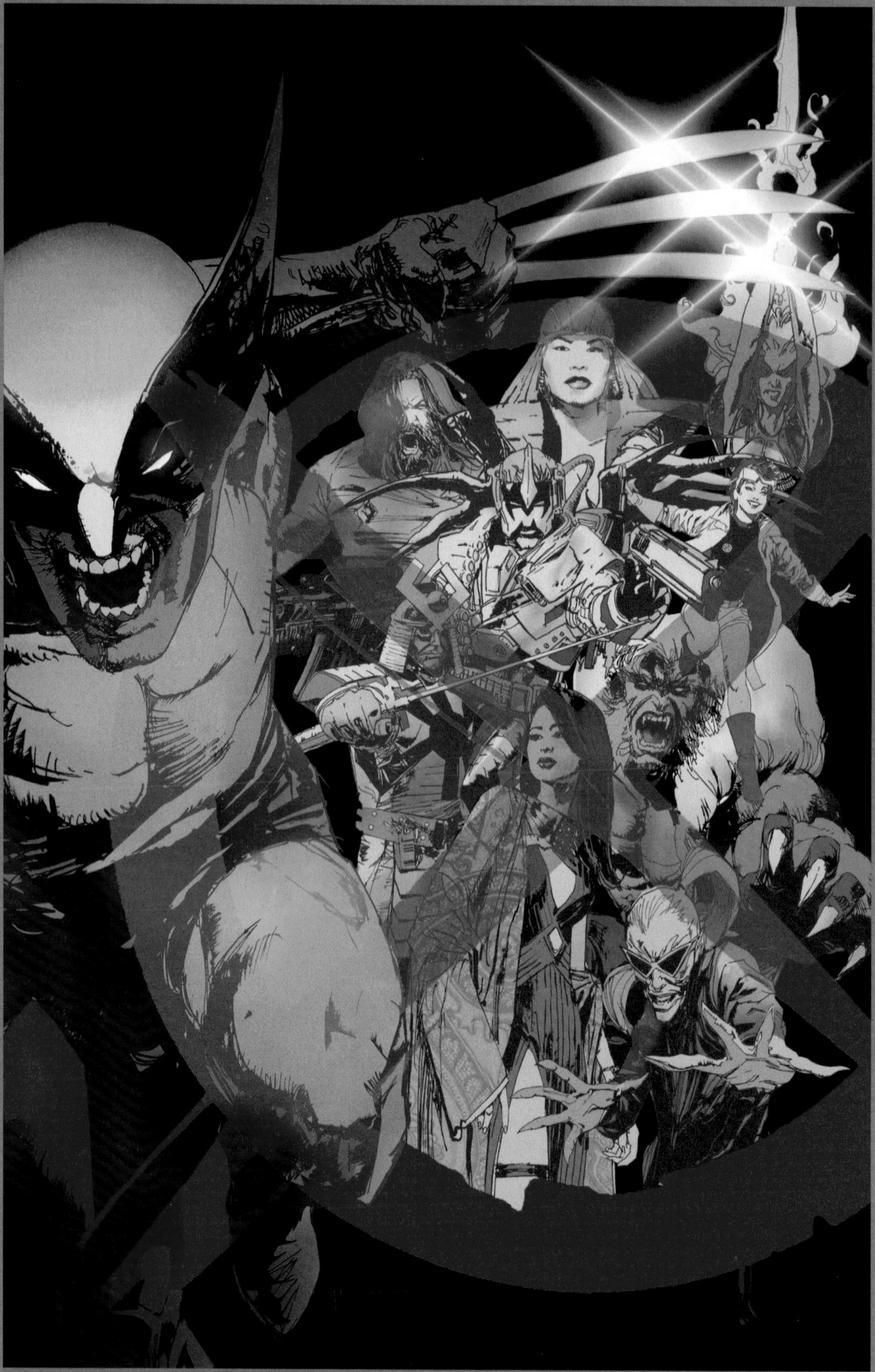

Wolverine #8 Variant by Bill Sienkiewicz

©ARTHUR ADAMS ©
11-10-99
AFTER A. ADAMS
1986
mounts

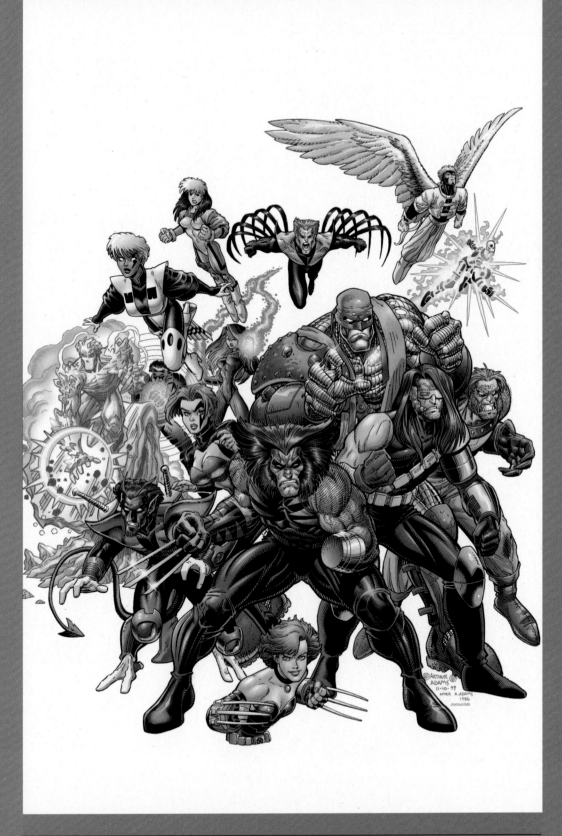

Wolverine #8 Hidden Gem Variant

by Arthur Adams
& Paul Mounts

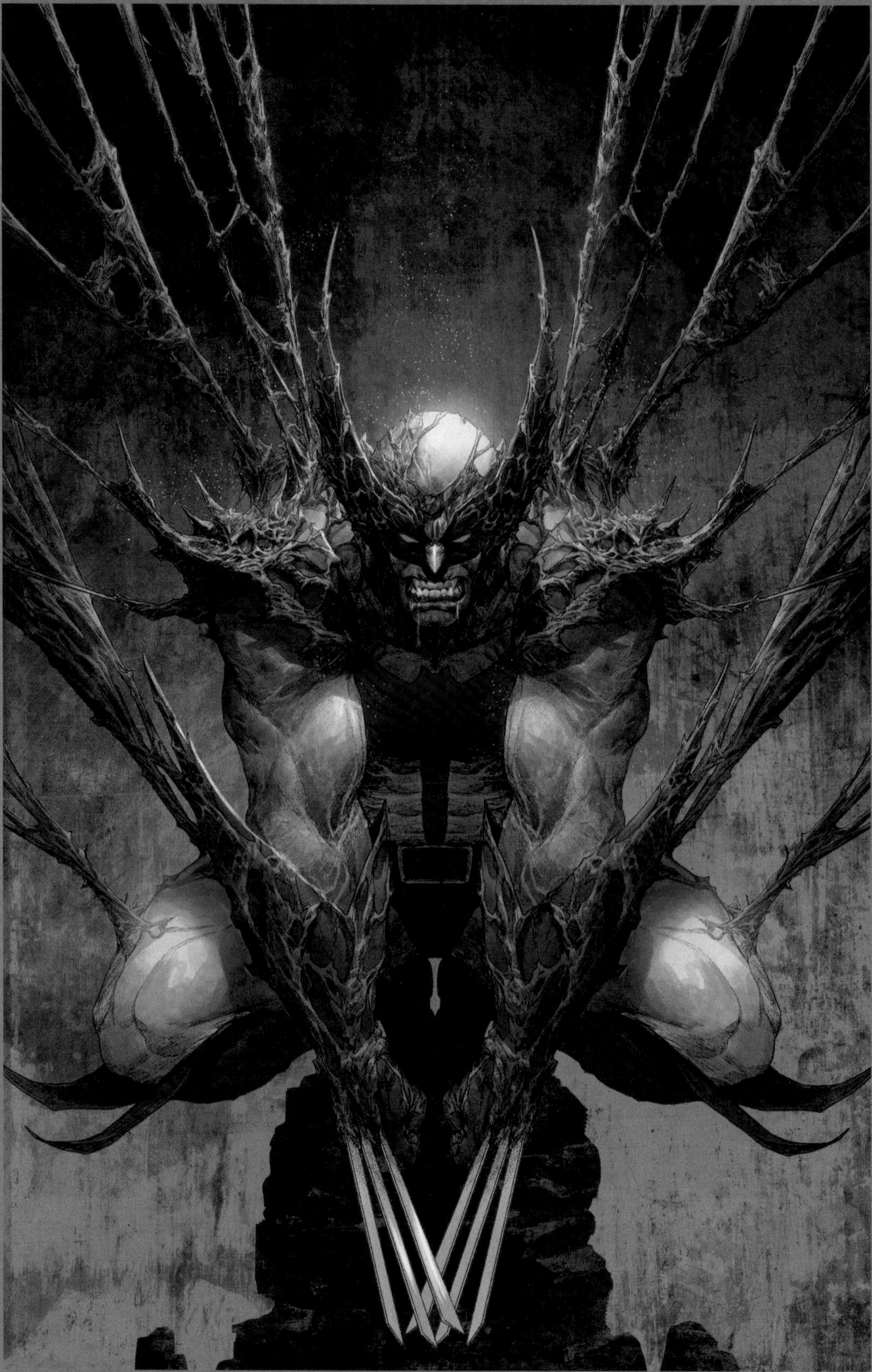

Wolverine #9 Knullified Variant by Dave Rapoza

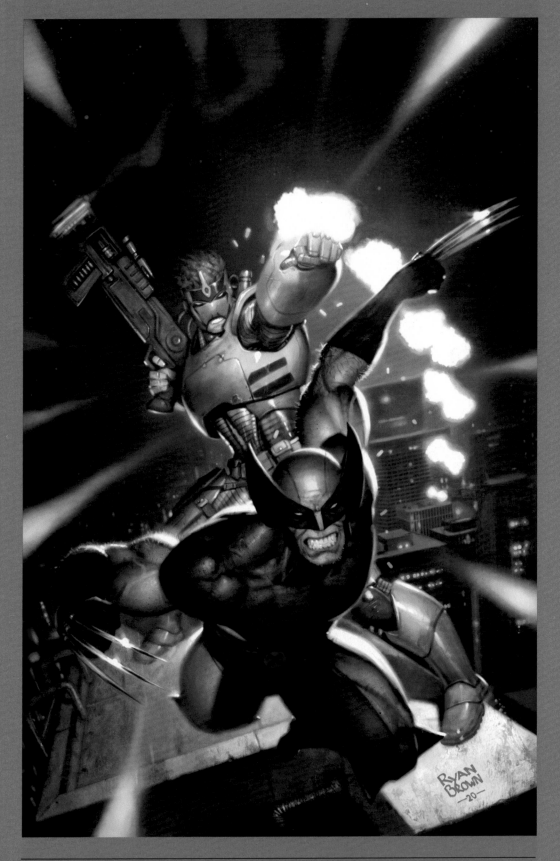

Wolverine #9 Variant   by Ryan Brown

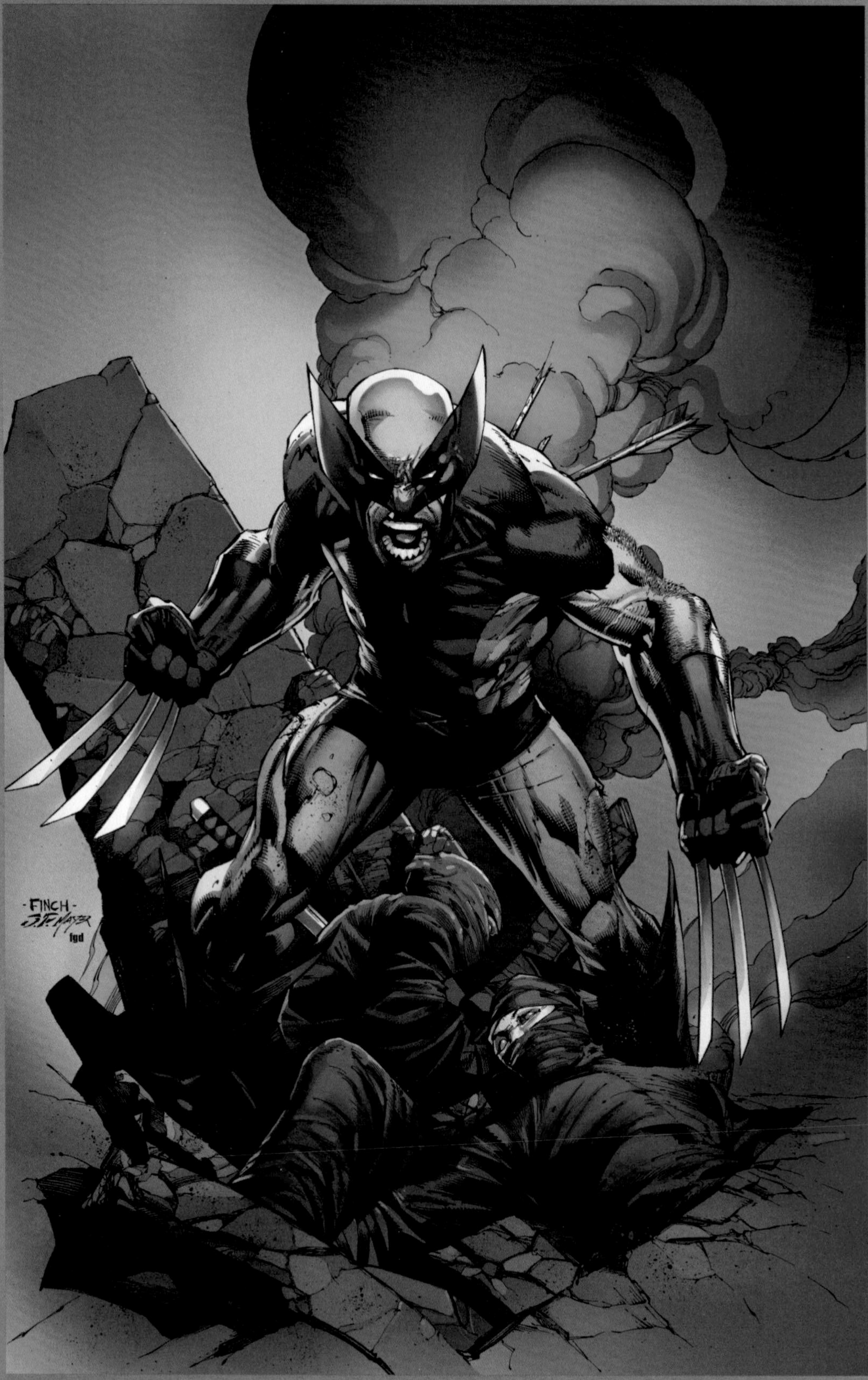
-FINCH-
fgd

Wolverine #10 Variant

by David Finch, JP Mayer
& Frank D'Armata

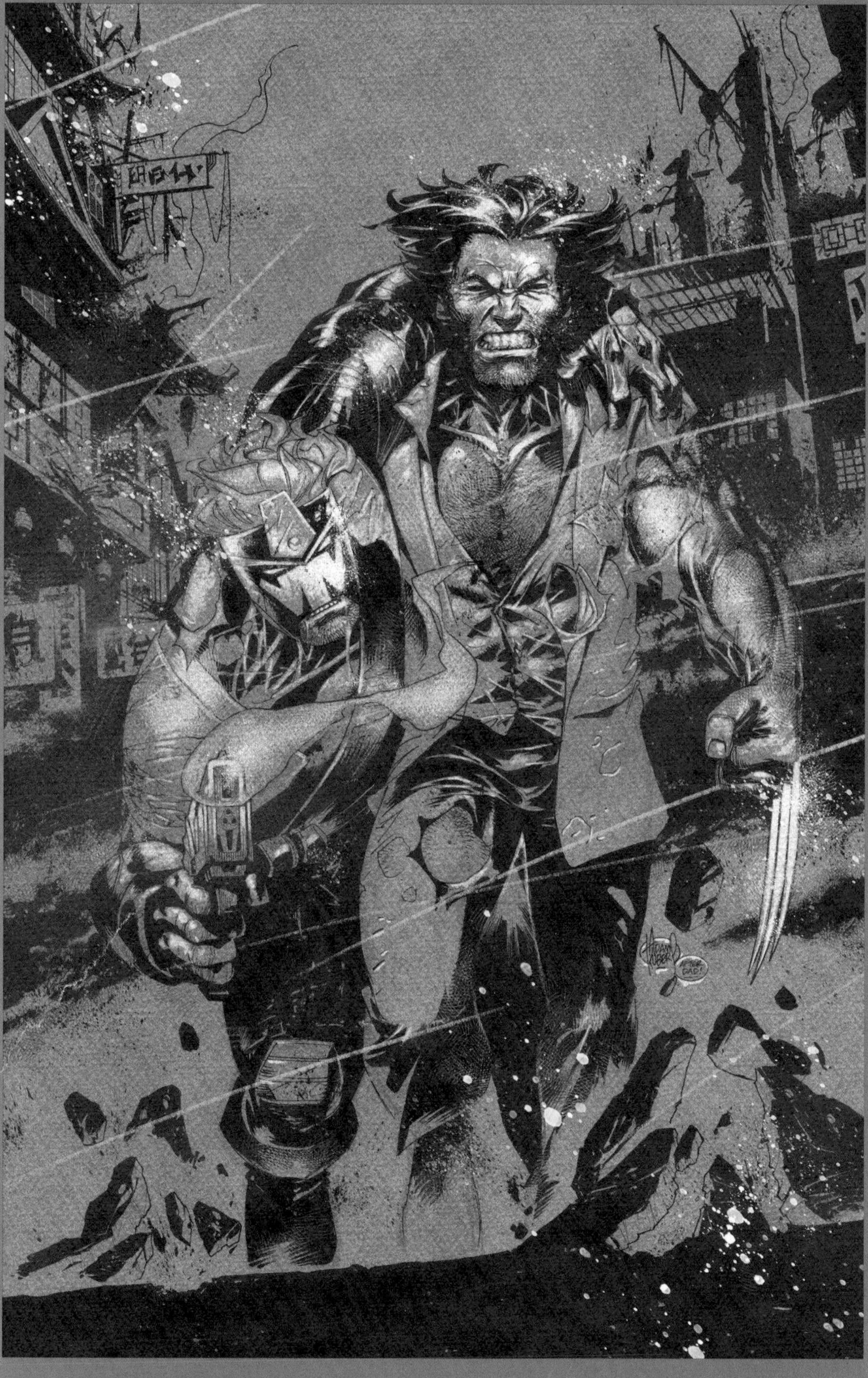

Wolverine #10 Variant by Adam Kubert

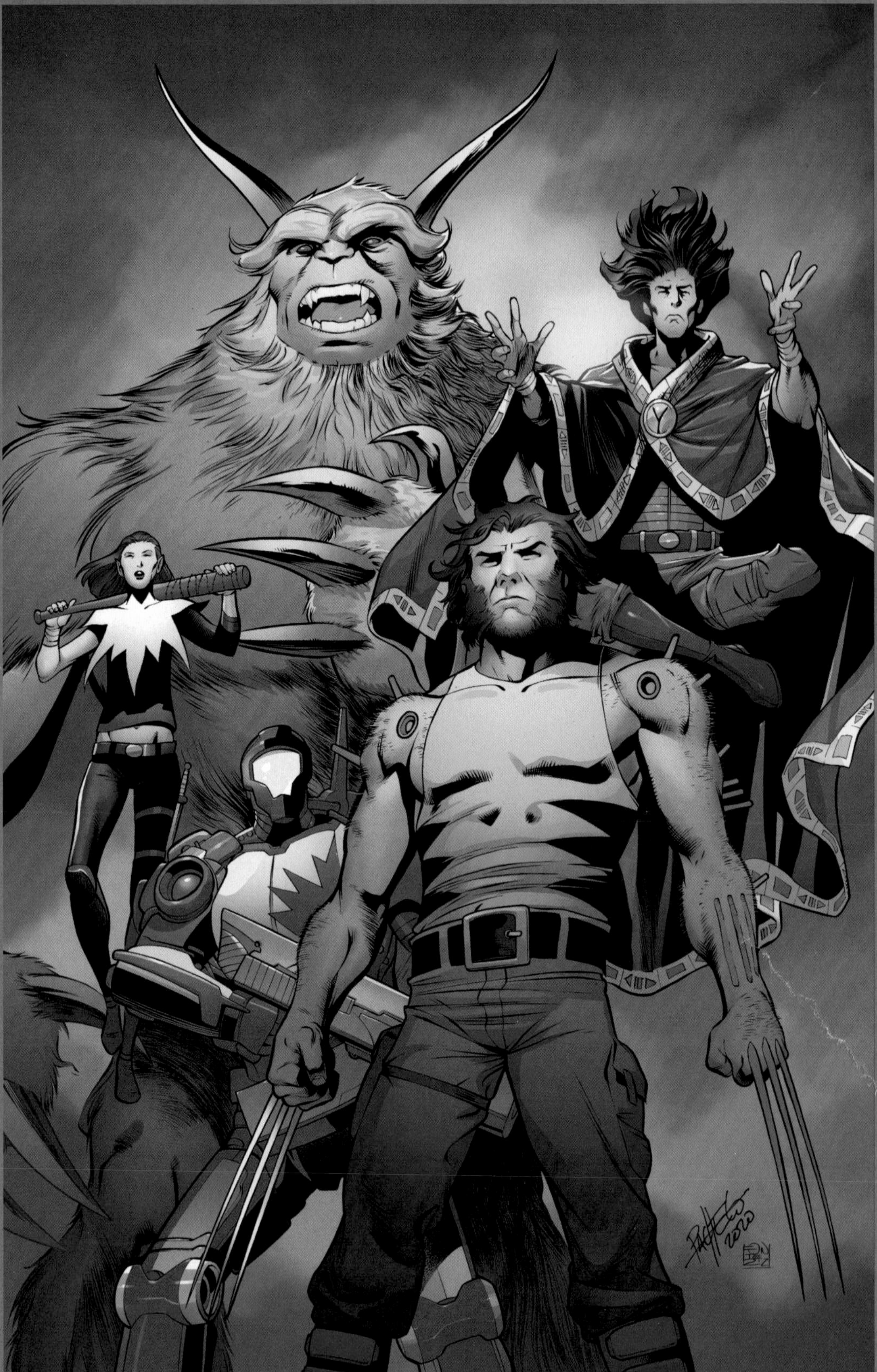

Wolverine #11 Heroes Reborn Variant by Carlos Pacheco, Rafael Fonteriz & Matt Milla